IMAGES
of America
MONTCLAIR

IMAGES
of America

MONTCLAIR

City of Montclair

ARCADIA
PUBLISHING

ISBN 978-0-7385-3038-3

Published by Arcadia Publishing
Charleston, South Carolina

Printed in the United States of America

Library of Congress Catalog Card Number: 2005929116

For all general information contact Arcadia Publishing at:
Telephone 843-853-2070
Fax 843-853-0044
E-mail sales@arcadiapublishing.com
For customer service and orders:
Toll-Free 1-888-313-2665

Visit us on the Internet at www.arcadiapublishing.com

Contents

ACKNOWLEDGMENTS

Researching and compiling the history and photographs for this book was not a one-person job; it required the knowledge, memories, personal treasures, and involvement of many to accomplish. Employees and residents of Montclair came forward to share their stories and entrust us with their precious family photographs. Without their gracious contributions, this book would be a shadow of its current breadth. We regret that all memories and photographs contributed to our effort cannot be shared. It would take a Herculean effort and much larger volume to contain the many fascinating facts and stories about this young community—that effort will be reserved, we hope, for a future book.

We were daunted, if not simply surprised, by the effort it takes to publish a pictorial history. Collecting photographs is, perhaps, the easiest part of the task. Identifying people, places, and things in photographs is far more arduous—memories fade, people pass from the scene, buildings are removed from the landscape, and time has a way of distorting all things. There are, however, a few employees of the City of Montclair whose efforts we wish to recognize. Technical assistance in preserving photographic images was provided by the city's GIS specialist, Steve Dague. Administrative analyst April Mitts was the "heart and soul" of the project. Only through her tireless efforts did this pictorial history become a reality. Personnel aide Lisa Shannon, benefits coordinator Leslie Phillips, departmental secretary Yvonne Smith, and secretary to the city manager Sharon Agajanian were invaluable in critiquing the book's content. Finally, administrative services director Edward C. Starr refused to let the book move forward until it satisfied impeccable standards.

We also wish to provide our special thanks to the following individuals and organizations who contributed their time and photographs for the successful completion of this project:

Mr. Steve Alba
Mrs. Theresa DeNolfo
Mr. Neal Froese
Mrs. Meredith Guinn
Mr. Mike Hance
Mrs. Charlotte Hayes
Mrs. Sylvia Martens
Montclair Chamber of Commerce
Monte Vista Water District
Mr. Wes Reeder
Mrs. Marcia Richter
San Bernardino County Museum
Mrs. Janet Taylor
Mrs. Vivian Warren
Mrs. Doris Yehnert
Mr. Doug Zoccoli
Montclair City Council
Lee C. McDougal, city manager
Montclair Redevelopment/Public Works Department
Montclair Community Development Department
Montclair Fire Department
Montclair Administrative Services Department
Montclair Police Department

Enjoy our history!
—Paul M. Eaton, Mayor

BIBLIOGRAPHY

Besecker, Michael J. 1965–1977. "Highlights in the History of Montclair." *Pomona Valley Historian* 1-13.

Conley, Bernice Bedford. *Monte Vista Incorporated 1956*, special edition. Montclair. 1980.

Guideposts to History, second edition. Sante Fe Federal Savings and Loan Association. 1977.

"Montclair Boasts of a Rich History." *Progress Bulletin*. May 16, 1982.

Montclair Women's Club. *Montclair California Past and Present*. 1962.

Rogers, C. T. "The History of Montclair: From Citrus to Commerce." *Progress Bulletin*. 1967.

INTRODUCTION

The history of Montclair, as with other communities in Southern California, is rich and colorful. Serrano Indians were the earliest known inhabitants of the land that is now Montclair. The name "Serrano," a broad term applied to the band of Native Americans who inhabited the area around the San Gabriel Mountains, is derived from Spanish and means "mountaineers," or more specifically "those of the Sierra." These early inhabitants built a village on the banks of a sycamore tree-lined creek that flowed along a route that is now Mills Avenue.

Like many Southern California Native American bands, the Serrano were incorporated into the Franciscan mission system. Once missionized, they were forced to converse in Spanish and adopt European farming techniques. The process of missionizing resulted in the loss of nearly all early evidence of their aboriginal culture. The entire Serrano population at the time of European contact was small, perhaps as low as 1,500. The tribe had no chief, and subtribes often fought each other. Census information indicates that fewer than 250 Serrano ancestors survive today.

In 1774, Capt. Juan Bautista de Anza, in his exploratory expedition from Mexico to California, named that sycamore tree-lined creek "Arroyo de los Alisos," the Stream of the Sycamores—later renamed San Antonio Creek. Legend has it that Captain de Anza carved his initials on the trunk of a large sycamore standing along the creek bank. This exploratory trip by Anza was the first sizeable land expedition by Europeans into what is now present-day California. The expedition opened a 2,200-mile route across the southwest deserts and so impressed the Spanish Viceroy in Mexico City that de Anza was ordered to return with a colonizing army.

Captain de Anza returned to the area in January 1776 as part of the famous trek that established the Juan Bautista de Anza Trail. He had successfully opened up Alta California (present-day California) for settlement and missions. The trail from Arizona to northern California was considered a strategic link to the northwest frontier of Spain's empire and its claim to California and the territory's important west coast harbors. A revolt of Yuma Indians in 1781 closed the Juan Bautista de Anza Trail, and the Spanish never reopened it, isolating Alta California from the Spanish government in Mexico.

Accompanying de Anza on his 1774 expedition was a Franciscan priest named Francisco Garcés. In his treks throughout California, Father Garcés traveled thousands of miles searching for mission sites. In 1771, he established the route followed by de Anza in 1774. Father Garcés also made first contact with an estimated 24,500 Native Americans in California and Arizona. He was killed in the Yuma Revolt of 1781.

The Montclair area also served as a point along the Old Spanish Trail, an early trade route linking Santa Fe, New Mexico, with Pueblo de los Angelos (Los Angeles). Sections of this route were used for trade; emigration; and the transportation of mules, horses, and Native American slaves. The trail's heyday was between 1830 and 1848. After the Mexican War of 1846–1848, competing routes blazed by America's Army of the West ended use of the trail.

Up until the 1890s, Montclair was little more than grazing land and a watering hole. In 1897, Mrs. Edward Fraser was instrumental in founding "the Township of Marquette," giving the area its first modern name. This signaled the beginning of land development and the formation of a viable community.

In the early 1900s, Emil Firth, a Los Angeles land developer, named the 1,000-acre land tract (that would one day become Montclair) "Monte Vista." All of the tracts were laid out in 10-, 20-, and 40-acre lots with special financing terms to entice the planting of orchards and construction of homes. Settlers moved in shortly after the tract opened in 1907, and the first "modern" settlement within the tract was called Narod. Buildings that made up the settlement included a large orange-packing house, a dry goods store, a hotel, and the Little White Church of Narod.

It was during this period that the Narod settlement emerged as a contributing component of Southern California's economically important citrus industry. Citrus groves dotted the landscape—

the fragrance of orange and lemon blossoms scenting the air. Oranges and lemons had become symbols of promise to Southern California orchard farmers—as powerful as the gold rush, though without the popular image of quick riches; and for the state, the citrus industry was its first economic dynamo, financially more important than the discovery of gold at Sutter's Mill.

Citrus fruit, however, had not always been a visceral part of the Southern California desert landscape. Citrus plants originated in China and first arrived in the Americas with the second voyage of Christopher Columbus to the New World. It took another 300 years before oranges were brought to California to be cultivated, in 1804, at the San Gabriel Mission. But it was the arrival of a mutant, seedless navel orange plant from Brazil in 1873 that revolutionized the region's citrus industry. The mutant navel orange plant found Southern California soil and weather to its liking; and navel orchards thrived to meet a growing national demand for the fruit. Within 20 years, the navel orange had transformed the deserts of Southern California into a Mediterranean oasis.

The completion of three rail lines through the region opened Southern California's citrus market to the rest of the country. The orange was remaking the terrain and the state's economy. Pioneers moved into the area to establish grove farms and participate in the new industry. George H. Reeder, a native to Narod, and son of one of the citrus industry's first navel orange growers, lived his entire life at the Reeder family grove home on Holt Avenue. His wife, Hazel, later joined him. The Reeders continued providing quality navel oranges to the area's citrus packing houses until the industry was hit hard after World War II by smog, soaring real-estate prices, a burgeoning population, freeways, and vandalism. Today the bulk of the navel crop is grown in California's Central Valley, with only a few thousand grove acres remaining in the Inland Empire.

The Monte Vista Land Tract experienced a population boom after World War II, and as in like most southland areas, housing and commercial development replaced citrus groves. Veterans receiving GI benefits for home purchases moved into the area to buy from the abundant supply of affordable housing that was being mass produced by developers. As the population grew, local residents opposed to annexation by a neighboring city formed the Monte Vista Improvement Association with the objective of incorporating the Monte Vista Land Tract. Residents were asked to vote on the incorporation proposal in the April 1956 election.

Incorporation of the City of Monte Vista was approved by a vote of 682 to 455 on April 25, 1956. Members of the first city council included James West, a post control operator and orange grower; Paul Frame, a real estate broker and builder; Miller Buchanan, a poultryman; Glen Wolfe, the proprietor of an equipment sales and rental business; and Dana Pankey, a minister. On the date of incorporation, the City of Monte Vista had a total population of 8,008 spread over 4.2 square miles. On April 28, 1956, the city council appointed Henry Busch to serve as city attorney; and on May 1, the city council determined that its meeting place would be a building owned by Mr. Phil Hurst at 5326 San Bernardino Avenue. This building, the site of a former butcher shop, was in good condition and had a room large enough for a few employees and small city council meetings. The city council set Tuesday, May 8, 1956, as its first official meeting date, with subsequent regular meetings to be held on the first and third Monday of each month. Councilman West, with the help of his family, loaded his pickup truck with a couple of rattan tables and eight chairs from his house and took them to the new city hall to serve as the council dais. Tween Stone loaned the new city some folding chairs from his mortuary for audience seating, and he brought an American flag to the first meeting.

Monte Vista's new leaders accomplished much during the first year of the city's incorporation. A master street-lighting plan was designed; zoning ordinances were adopted; provisions were made for the city's streets to be swept; engineering data was assembled; and a city recreation program was begun. Ben Smith was appointed chief of police; and shortly thereafter, a staff of four patrolmen and one female dispatcher were hired. At the end of its first year of existence, the City of Monte Vista had 10 full-time employees.

The first fire department serving the Monte Vista Land Tract was established by the San Bernardino County Board of Supervisors years in early 1948. In 1949, a $50,000 bond issue was approved to build a fire station and buy equipment. In 1950, the fire station was completed and housed two fire trucks. Three full-time firefighters were employed, and 13 reserves were paid "by the call." Montclair established a municipal fire department in 1964.

During the city's first years of operation, the federal government refused to open a post office in the community because a town with the same name already existed in Northern California. On April 8, 1958, the residents rectified the problem by voting to change the town's name to "Montclair." On July 1, 1958, a branch post office was opened in the Mayfair Market at Central Avenue and Benito Street. Residents were notified to change their return addresses as of September 1, 1958, and mail was distributed through the Ontario Plaza Branch Post Office on Mountain Avenue. In 1964, the post office was relocated to its current location on Benito Street. Over the next two decades, postal delivery problems continued because of overlapping zip codes shared with the cities of Pomona and Ontario. This problem was finally resolved in the late 1980s when the U.S. Postal Service agreed to a single zip code for all of Montclair and the unincorporated areas in the city's sphere of influence.

As early as 1953, the residents of Montclair had the forethought to negotiate a lease-purchase of land on the southeast corner of Benito Street and Fremont Avenue for a civic center. An orange grove at the site generated revenue for the lease payments. On April 25, 1964, a new Montclair Civic Center was dedicated. The complex housed the city's administrative offices and police department. A county branch library was the second building completed on the civic center property.

Since 1952, a county branch library had been located at Monte Vista Elementary School and was open only two days a week. The new library met the community's growing demand for this service. Today the Montclair Branch Library provides traditional services, DVD rentals, vital document services, marriage licenses, and hosts an outdoor patio for weddings.

An important element for community and family life is a good educational system. The growing population required the construction of schools in quick succession. Vernon Junior High School opened in 1956; Margarita Elementary School opened in 1958; and Lehigh Elementary School and Montclair High School followed in 1959. By 1963, Monte Vista Elementary School and Montclair High School needed additions, and Serrano Junior High was built on the west side. State regulations forced the closure of Margarita Elementary School in the late 1990s; however, three new elementary schools—Howard, Ramona, and Montera—opened to address school-age population requirements.

During its early years, Montclair struggled to find a greater tax base to pay for the services offered to residents. In 1964, land developers approached the city with the answer to its revenue concerns—a regional shopping center. Three years later, the first building permits were issued; and on August 3, 1968, 15,000 people attended a Preview Ball for the new mall which contained 875,000 square feet of store space, three major department stores, 64 smaller shops, and parking for 5,000 cars. During its first year of operation, the mall increased the city's sales tax revenues by more than 30 percent. Today Montclair Plaza continues to be one of the most successful regional shopping centers in Southern California.

Now, 50 years after its incorporation, Montclair is a thriving full-service city with a population representative of the ethnic and cultural diversity that is characteristic of Southern California. Although the early years of Montclair were not without its growing pains, this small city has proven it can survive, prosper, and be a leader in the Inland Empire.

William V. Donaldson, Montclair City Administrator from 1960–1965, clearly identified the source of Montclair's fortitude when he said, "The record of the growth of the Montclair area is one that was written by its many dedicated citizens. The transformation from orange groves to a growing city is one of which we can all be proud. It is often easy to forget the sacrifices the citizens have made to affect this change. I think the idea of recording our past so that we may not in the future forget these sacrifices is an excellent one."

One

Montclair in the Making

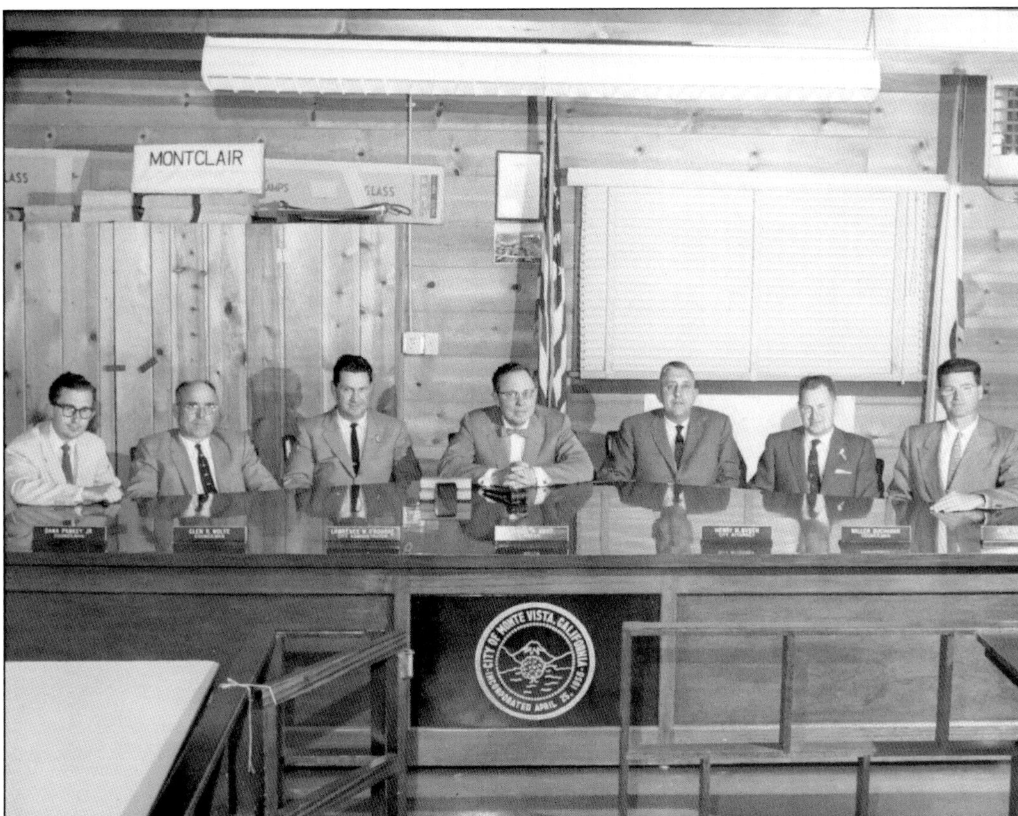

Montclair's First City Council, April 1958. Notice that the city seal displays the name "Monte Vista." The box in the upper left corner of the photograph was the box containing petitions to change the city's name to "Montclair." Pictured, from left to right, are Dana Pankey Jr., councilman; Glen R. Wolfe, councilman; Lawrence W. O'Rourke, city administrator; James M. West, mayor; Henry M. Busche, city attorney; Miller Buchanan, councilman; and Paul V. Frame, councilman.

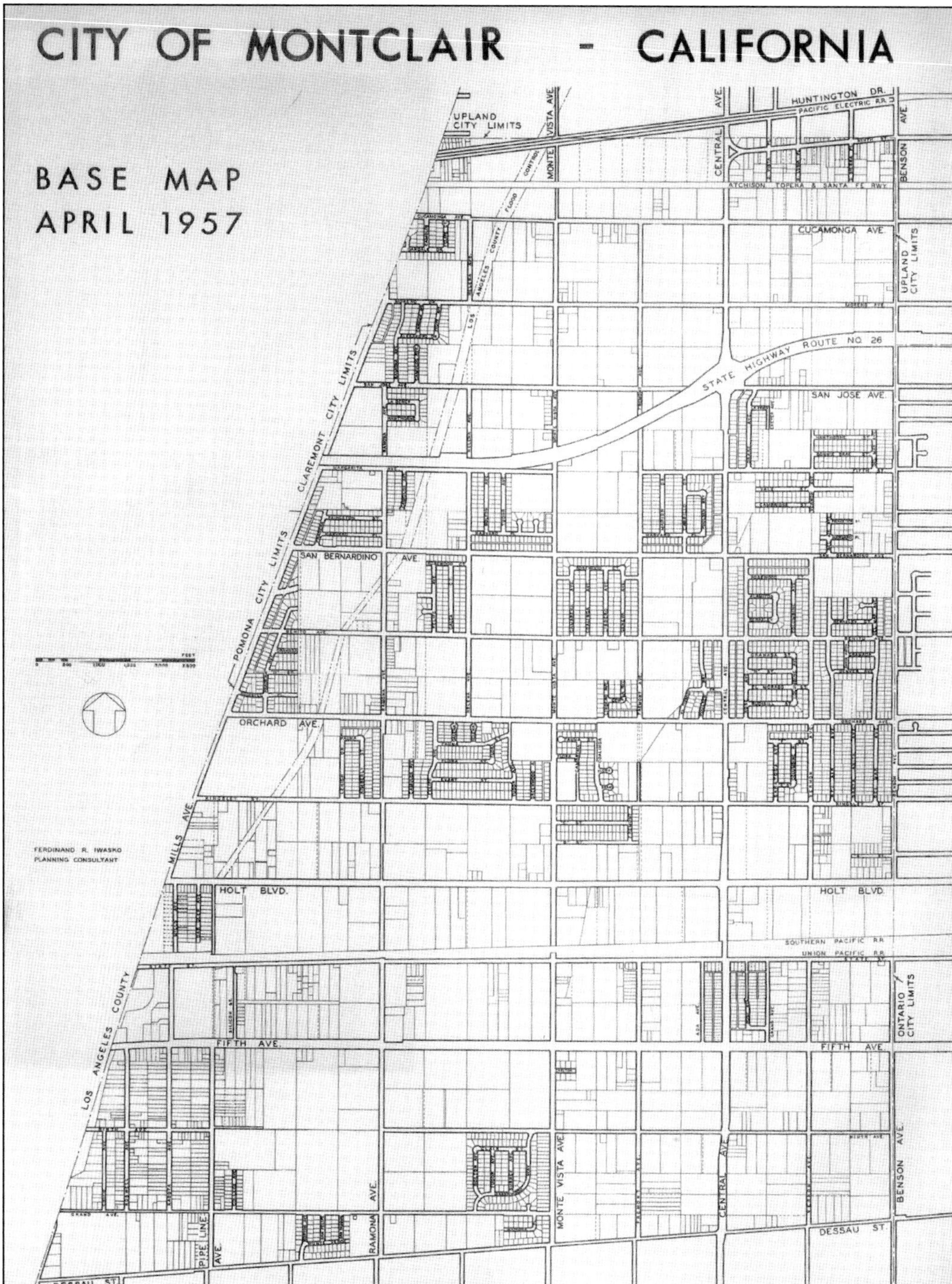

CITY OF MONTCLAIR, BASE MAP, 1957. This map of the City of Montclair depicts the housing tracts occupying Montclair at that time.

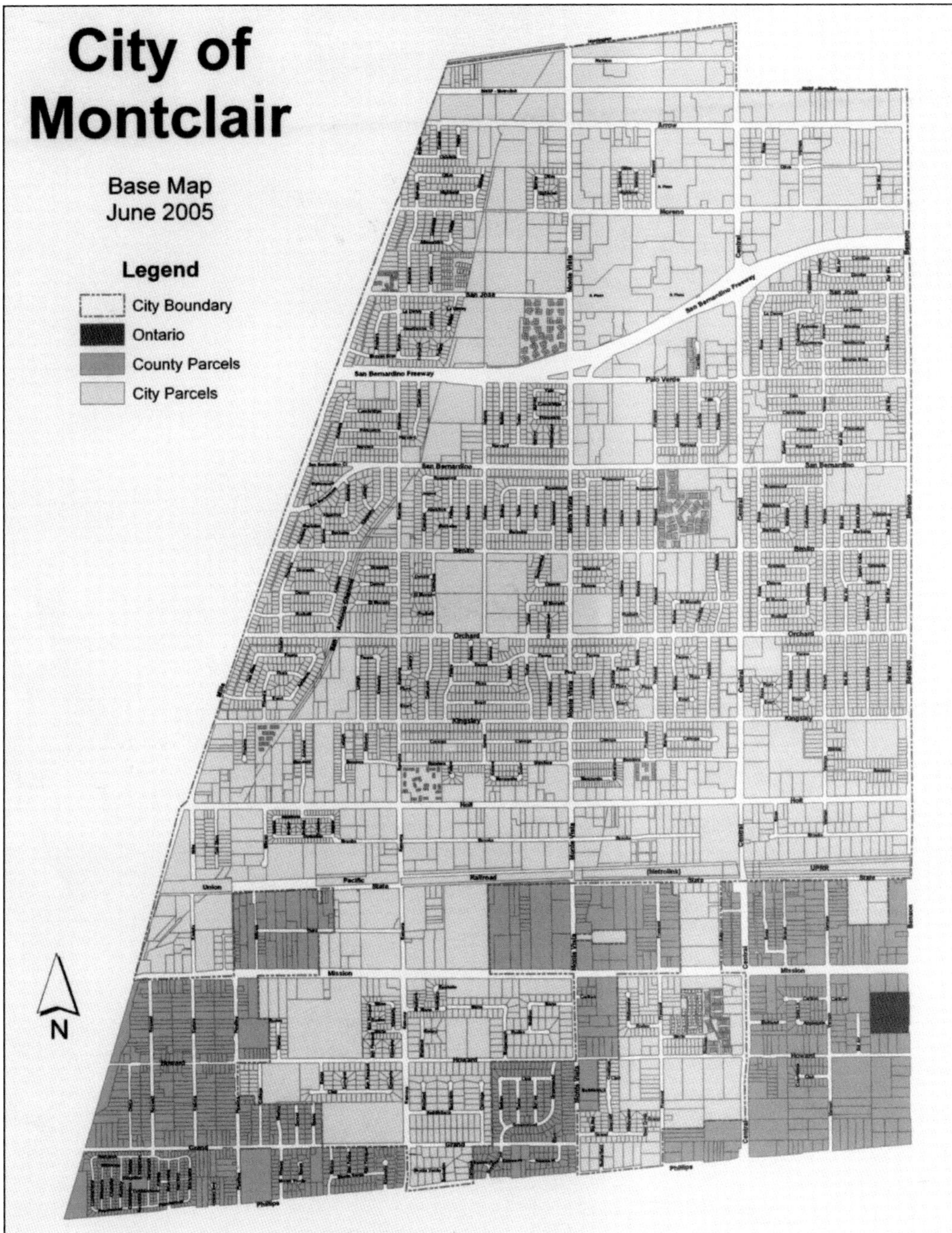

CITY OF MONTCLAIR, BASE MAP, JUNE 2005. A current map of Montclair shows the growth the city experienced over the past 50 years.

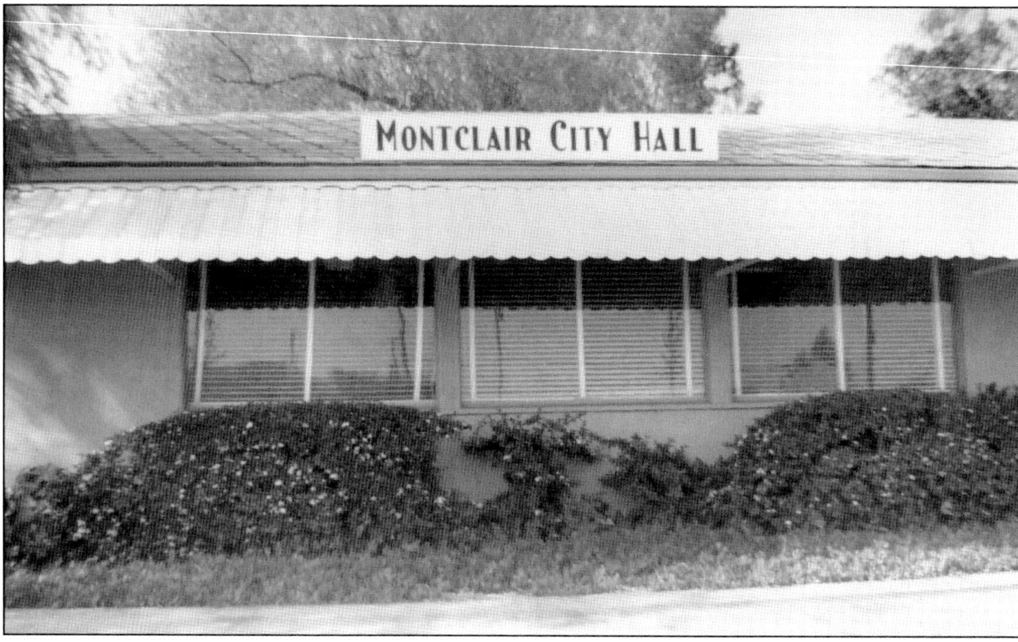

MONTCLAIR'S FIRST CITY HALL, 1961. Council meetings were held at this location on San Bernardino Street until 1963. (Courtesy of Mike Hance.)

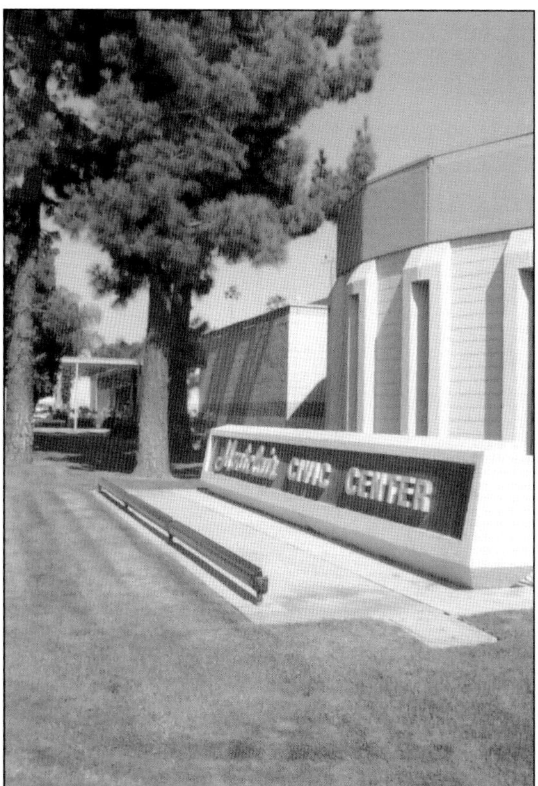

MONTCLAIR CIVIC CENTER, 2005. Today the civic center on Benito Street looks like this.

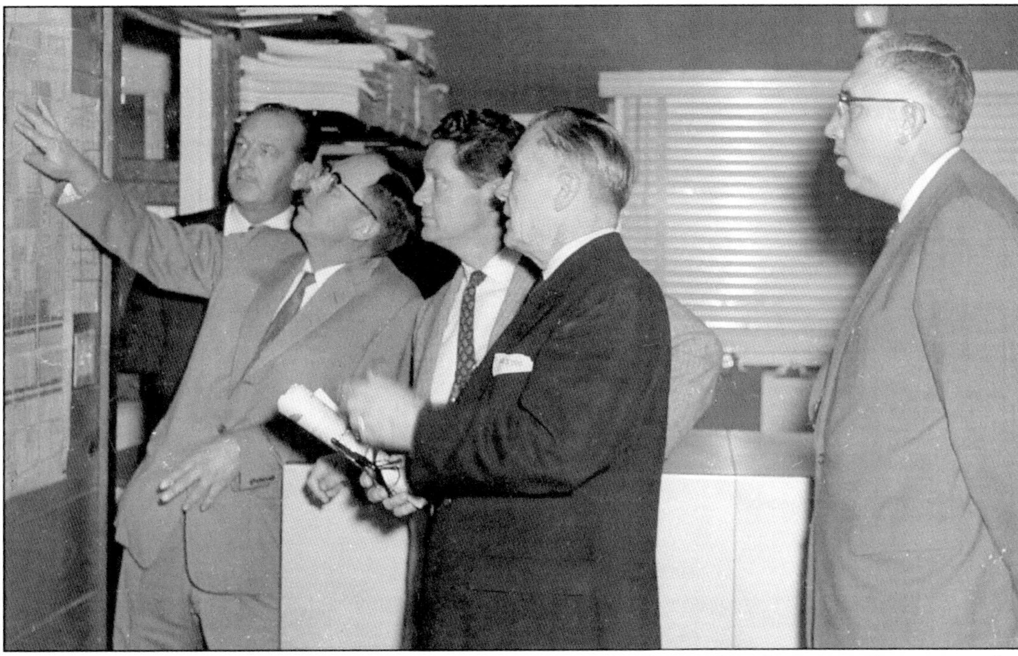

EARLY PLANNING FOR A NEW CITY, NOVEMBER 8, 1957. City officials review the master plan map showing planned future development of the area. Pictured here, from left to right, are Don Bernard, assistant to Congressman Sheppard; Mayor James West; city administrator Larry O'Rourke; Congressman Harry Sheppard; and city attorney Henry M. Busch.

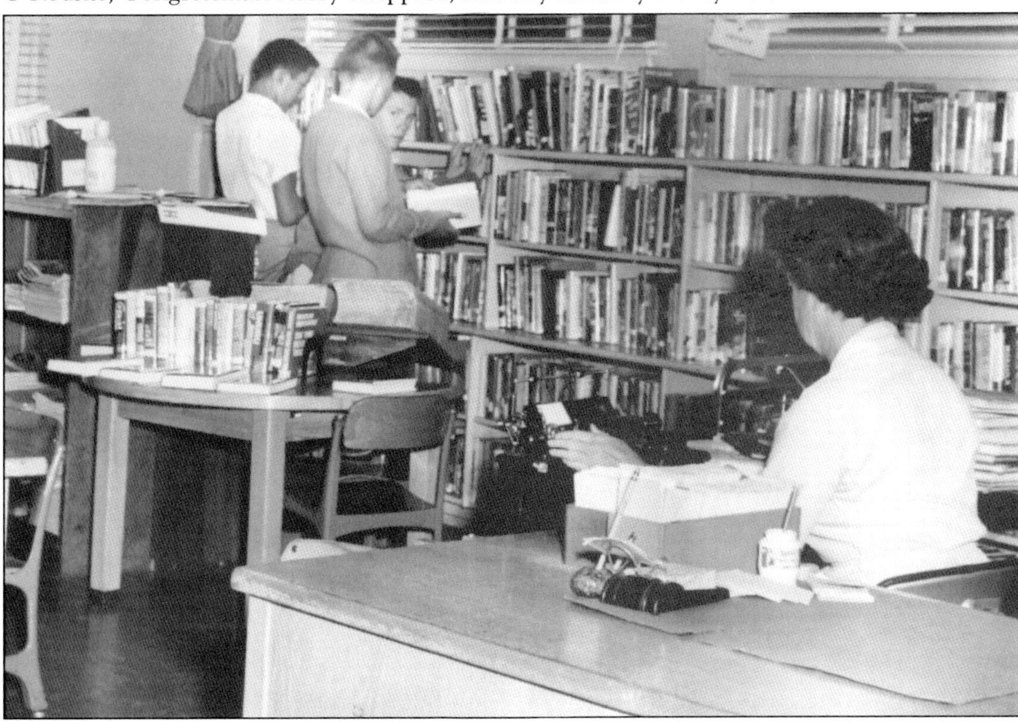

MONTCLAIR'S FIRST LIBRARY, 1950. The first county library in Montclair was located at Monte Vista Elementary School. Seated is the first librarian, Dorothy Berkoss.

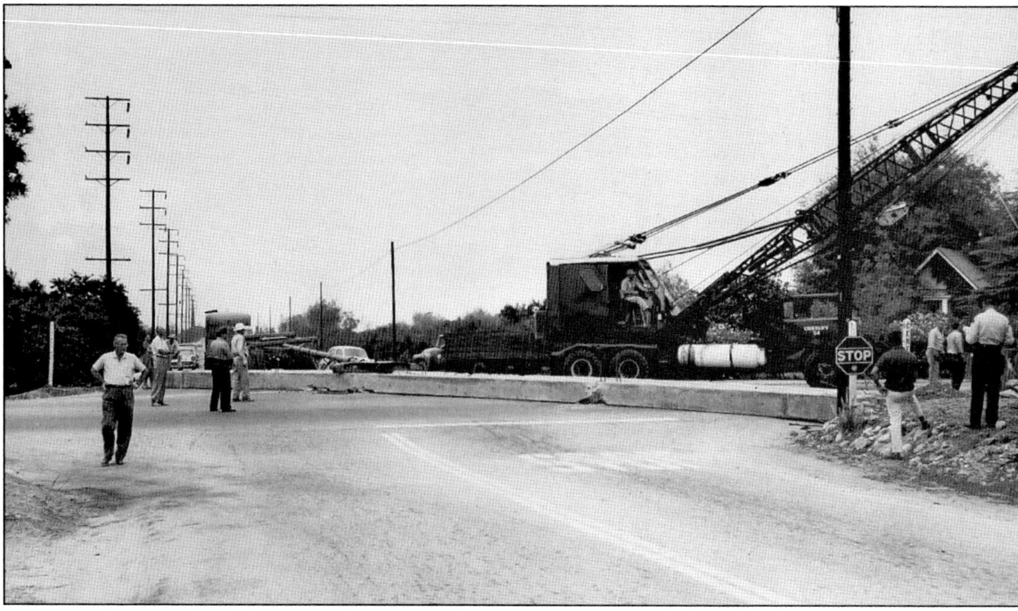

EARLY CITY CONSTRUCTION, C. 1957. This photograph was taken on the corner of Eighth Street (Arrow Highway) and Central Avenue looking west.

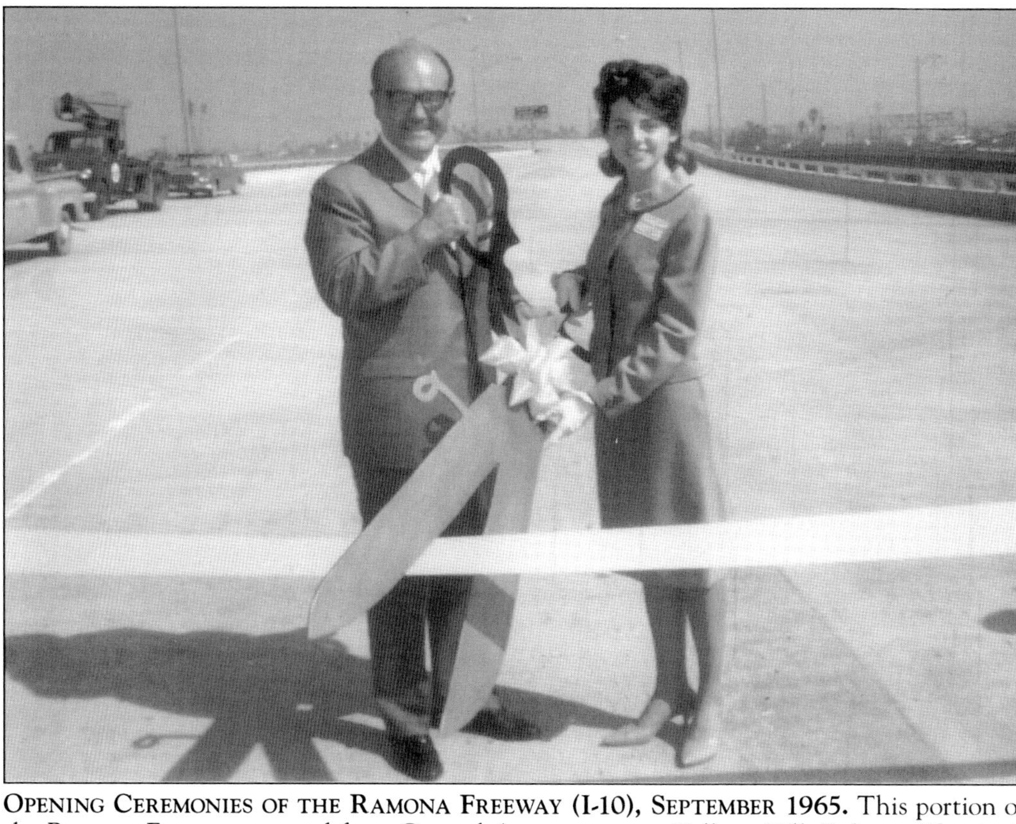

OPENING CEREMONIES OF THE RAMONA FREEWAY (I-10), SEPTEMBER 1965. This portion of the Ramona Freeway spanned from Central Avenue west to Kellogg Hill. Roberta Chavin is cutting the ribbon.

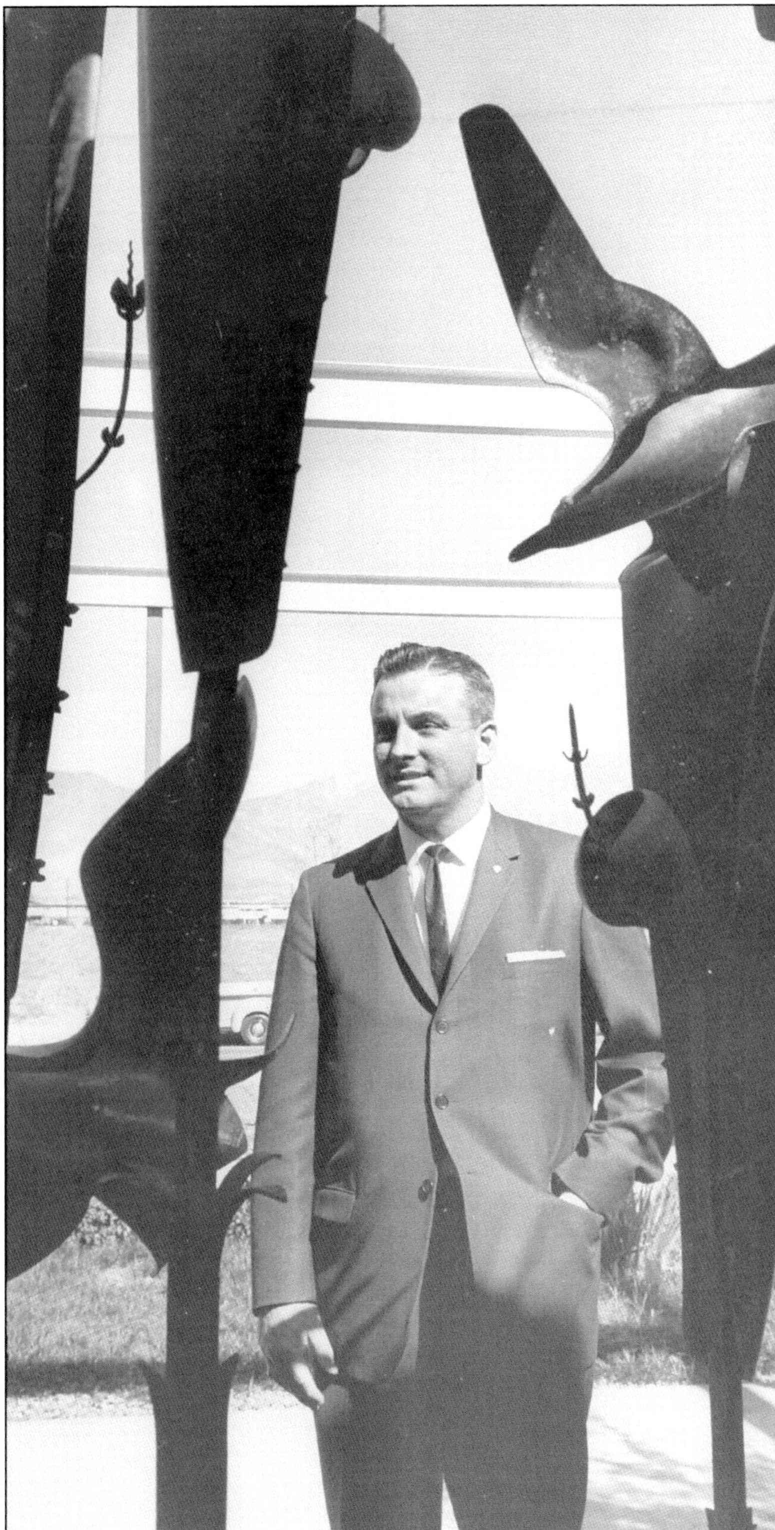

John Svenson's Sculpture, April 1965. Mayor Kenneth Ziebarth stands by John Svenson's bronze and brass sculpture located at the civic center. The sculpture was dedicated at the city's ninth-anniversary event.

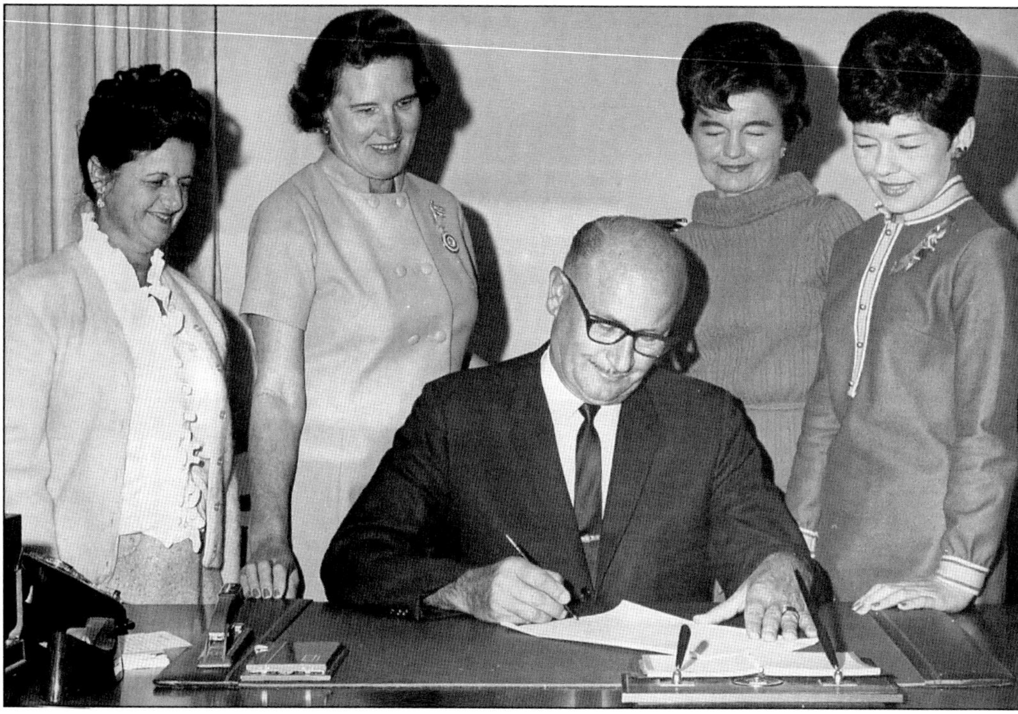

MEMBERS OF THE MONTCLAIR BUSINESS AND PROFESSIONAL WOMEN'S CLUB, C. 1967. Members stand by while Mayor Hayes signs a proclamation declaring October 21–27 National Business and Professional Women's Week in Montclair. Witnessing the event, from left to right, are Mrs. Eileen McPherson, personnel development chairman; Mrs. Mary Novelli, civic participation chairman; Mayor Hayes; Mrs. Gladys Carlson, vice president; and Mrs. Elezabeth McClure, president.

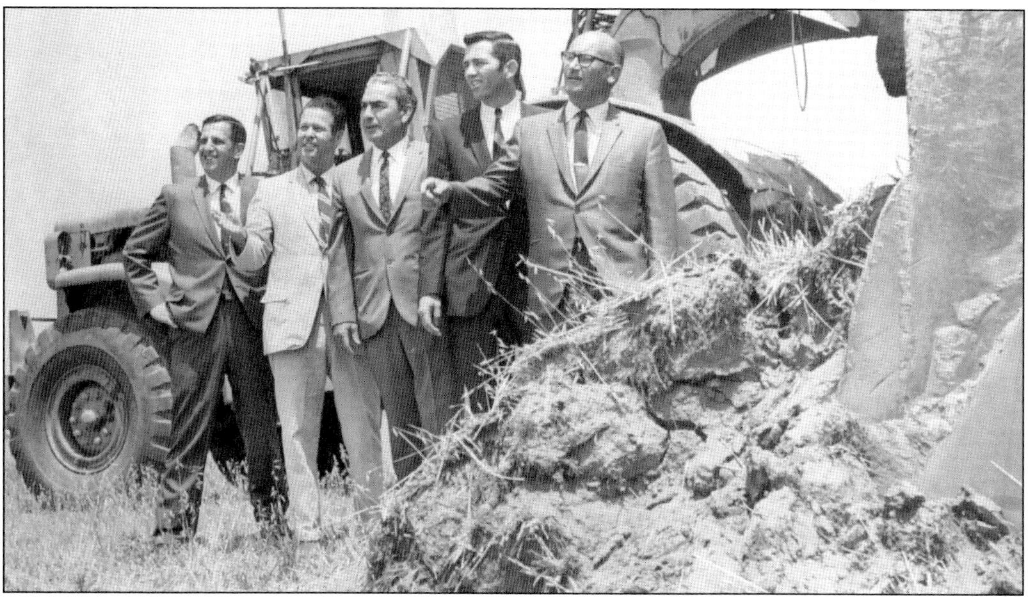

GROUNDBREAKING OF POMONA FREEWAY, C. 1966. On hand for the groundbreaking ceremonies, from left to right, were Lou Cassani; Montclair councilman Paul Jones; Tony Zangi; Lyle Snow; and Harold Hayes, mayor of Montclair. In 1969, construction began on this portion of the freeway.

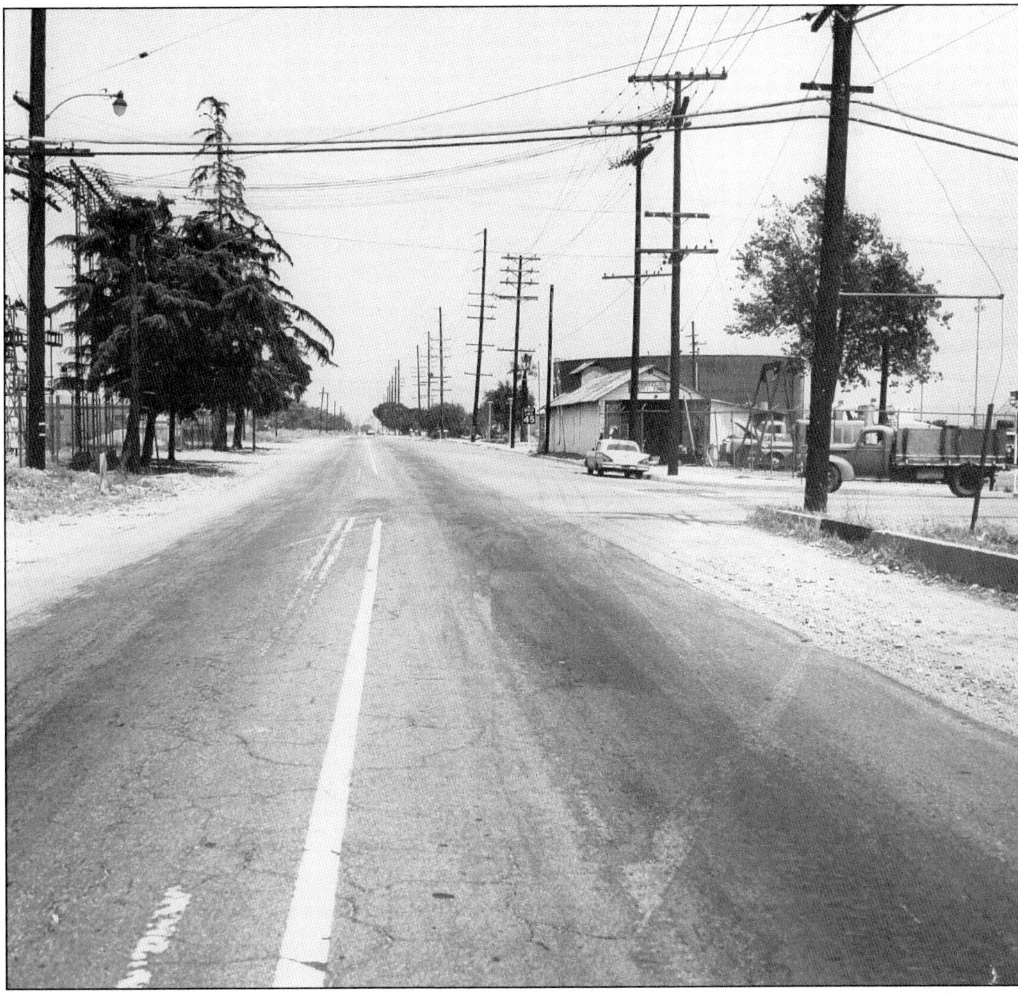

MONTCLAIR CITY CORPORATE YARD, C. 1966. Pictured here is the original City Yard that was located on the southeast corner of Arrow Highway and Monte Vista Avenue. This building was demolished in November 1967 to build Fire Station No. 1. The City Yard houses a portion of the Public Works Department offices, and its employees are responsible for street maintenance, installing new signage, vehicle maintenance, park maintenance, flood control lines, tree maintenance, sewer maintenance, graffiti abatement, and street sweeping services.

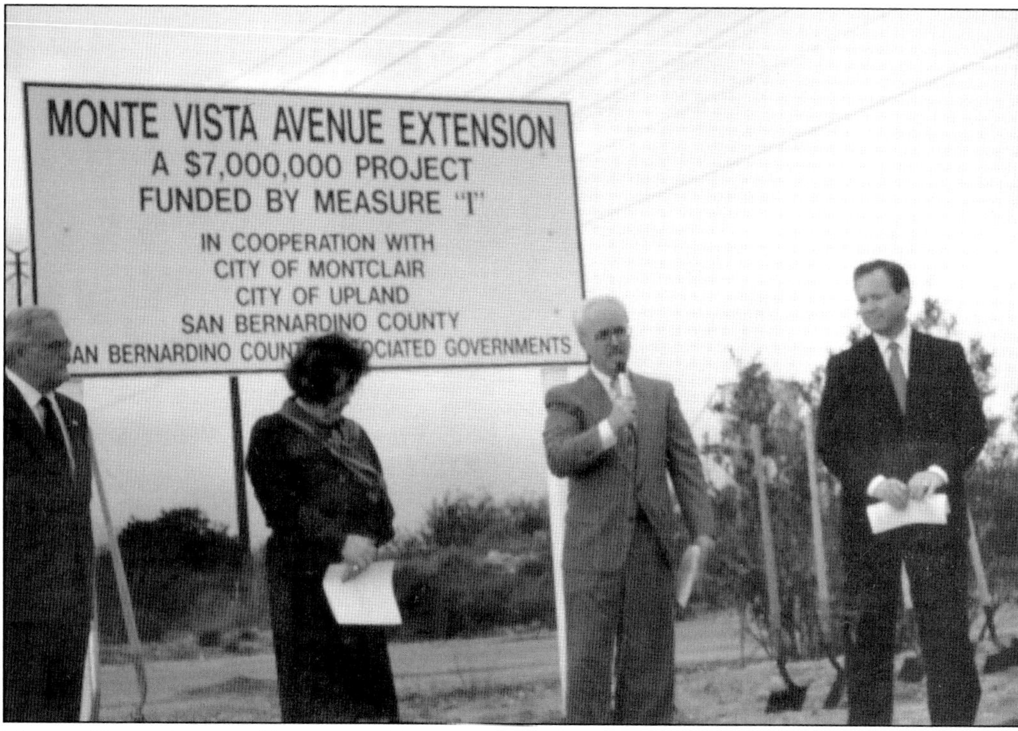

MONTE VISTA AVENUE EXTENSION GROUNDBREAKING, 1991. In order to ease traffic congestion on nearby thoroughfares and provide a significant regional arterial link between the I-10 and future California 210 freeways, Monte Vista Avenue was extended north of Arrow Highway to Foothill Boulevard. (Courtesy of the Montclair Chamber of Commerce.)

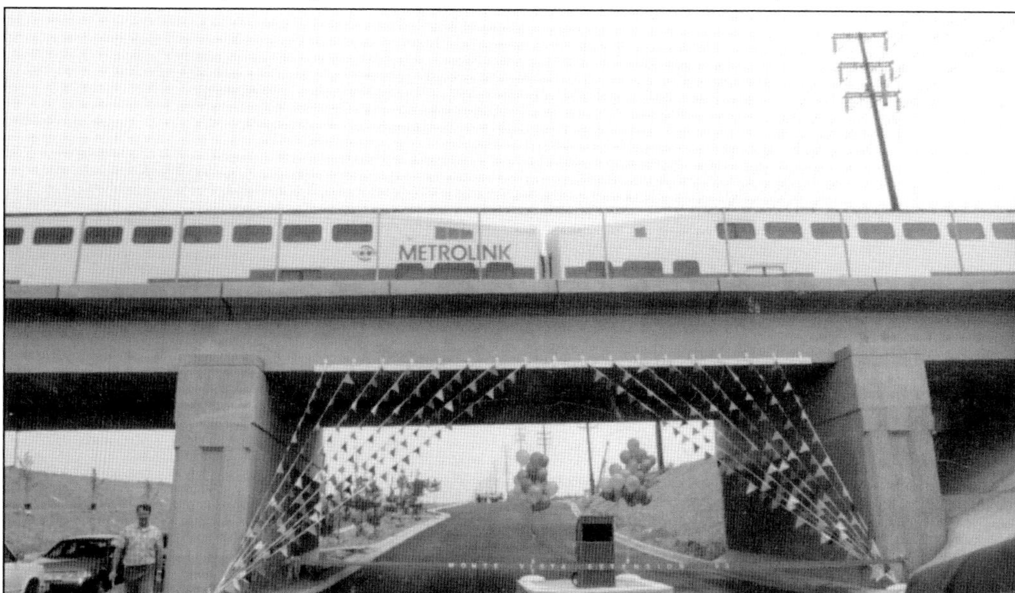

MONTE VISTA UNDERPASS DEDICATION, 1993. Ceremonies were held in honor of the opening of the new Monte Vista Avenue underpass. The Montclair High School band can be seen in the background ready to commemorate the event.

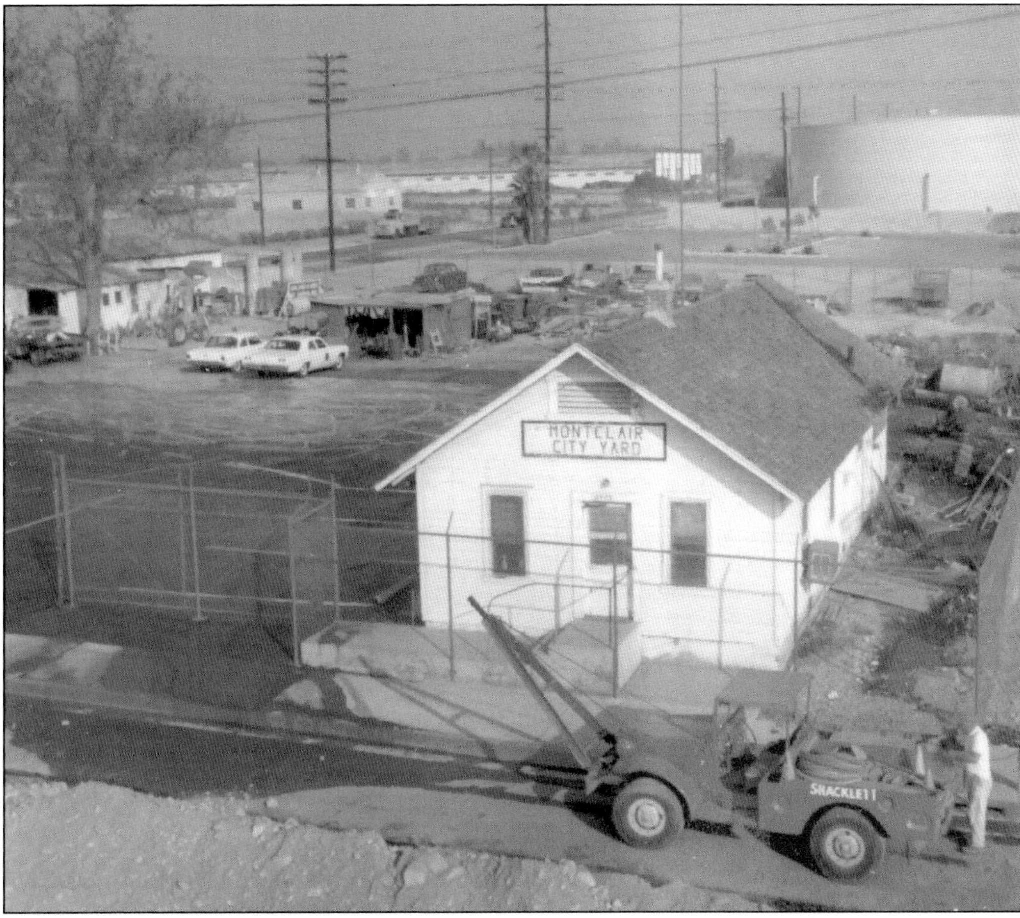

ORIGINAL CITY YARD ON MONTE VISTA AVENUE AT ARROW HIGHWAY, NOVEMBER 20, 1967. This photograph was taken shortly before the building was demolished and construction of Fire Station No. 1 began.

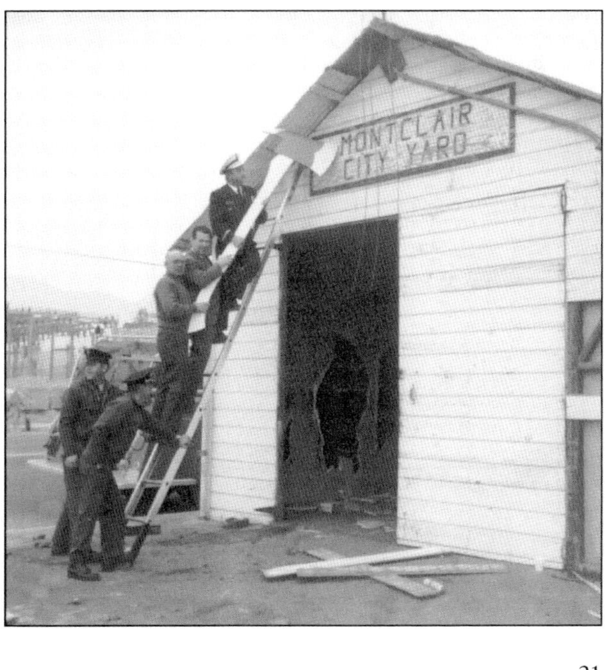

GROUNDBREAKING FOR FIRE STATION NO. 1, NOVEMBER 20, 1967. This marked the beginning of the groundbreaking ceremonies on the site where Fire Station No. 1 would be built. Helping out, from left to right, are two unidentified firemen, an unidentified man, councilman Paul Jones, and fire chief Harold Duncan.

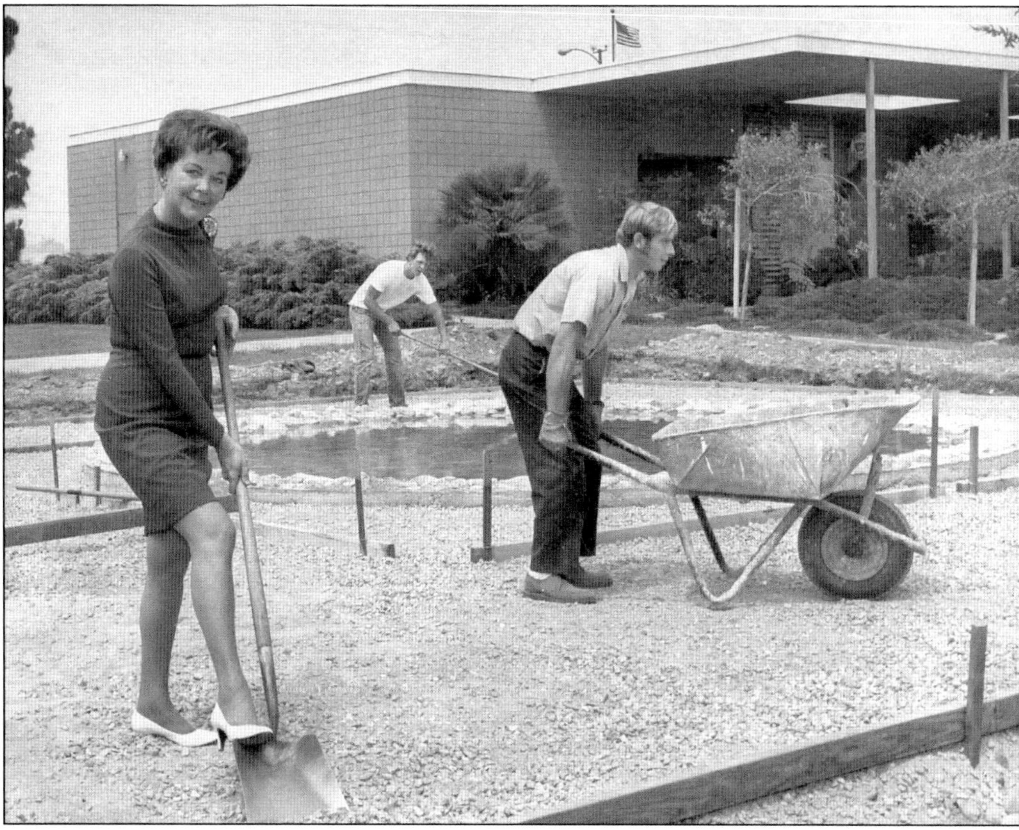

LANDSCAPING OF ANTIQUA GARDEN, 1971. This garden is located on the south side of city hall at the Montclair Civic Center. City clerk Barbara D. Williams and two unidentified men help with the garden landscaping.

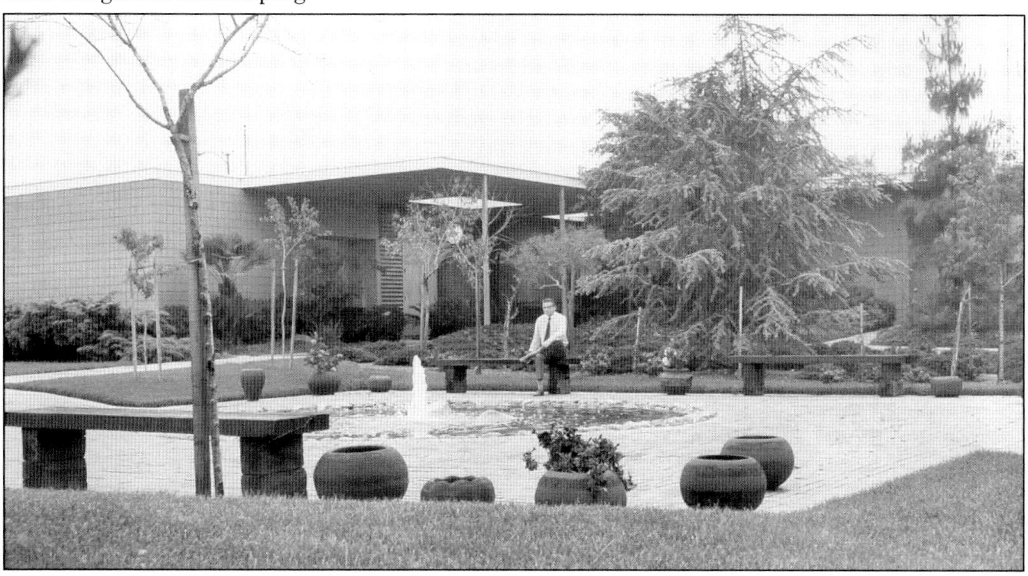

MONTCLAIR CITY HALL, 1971. Ron Eggerston, Montclair director of building and planning, is seen here looking at the fountain and pool of the Antiqua Garden.

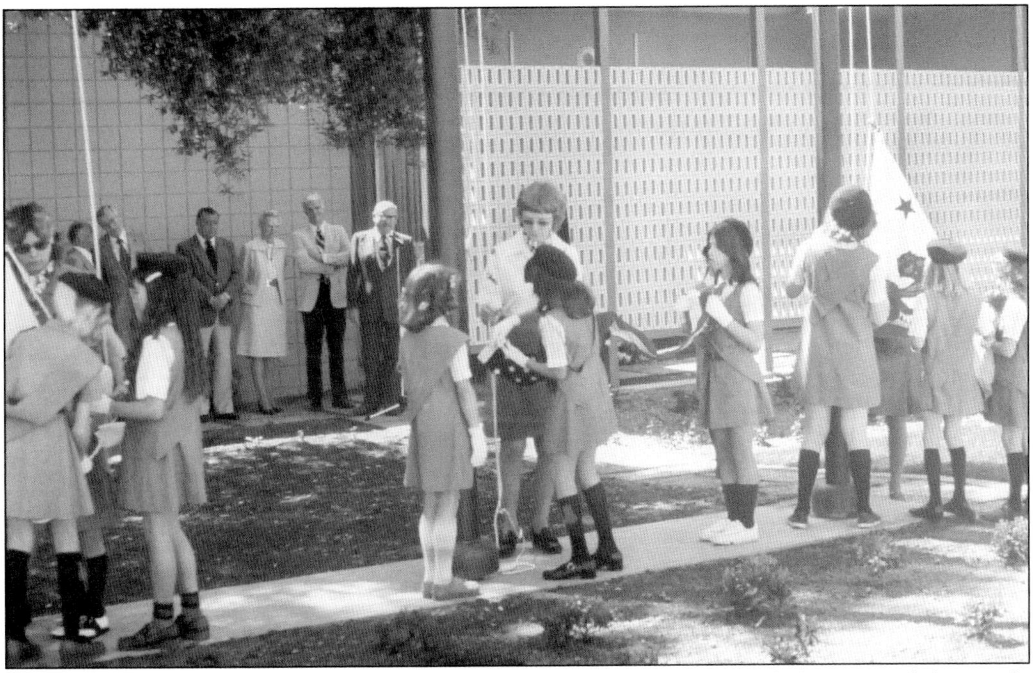

Civic Center Dedication, 1978. Local Girl Scouts help in the dedication of the newly remodeled civic center.

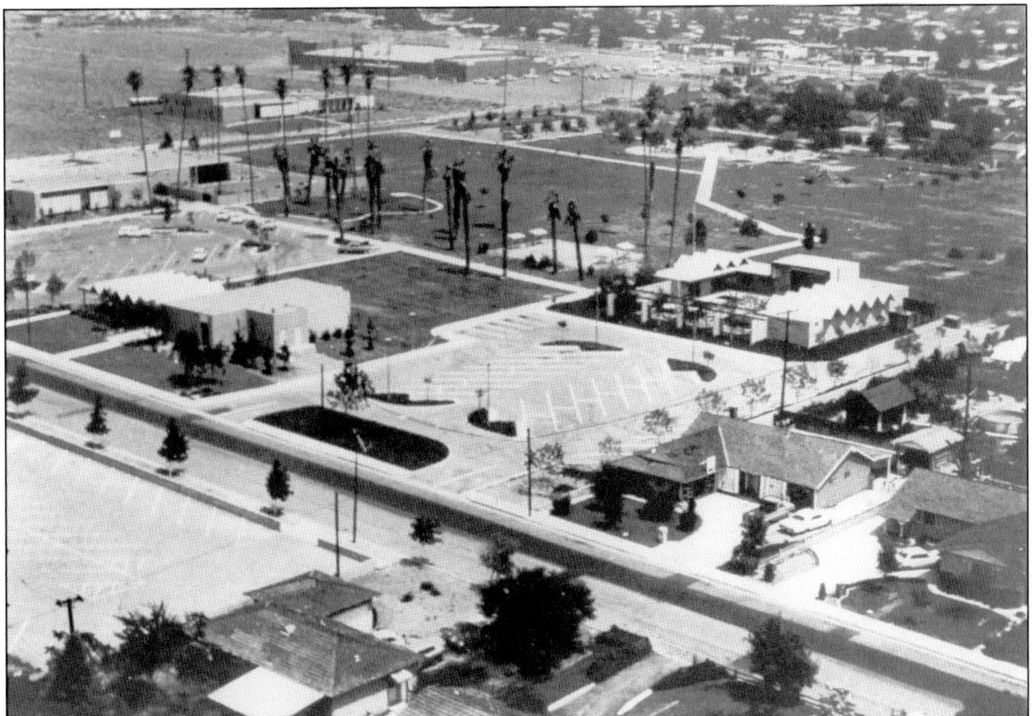

Montclair Civic Center, c. 1970. This is an aerial view of the civic center as it stood for most of the 1970s.

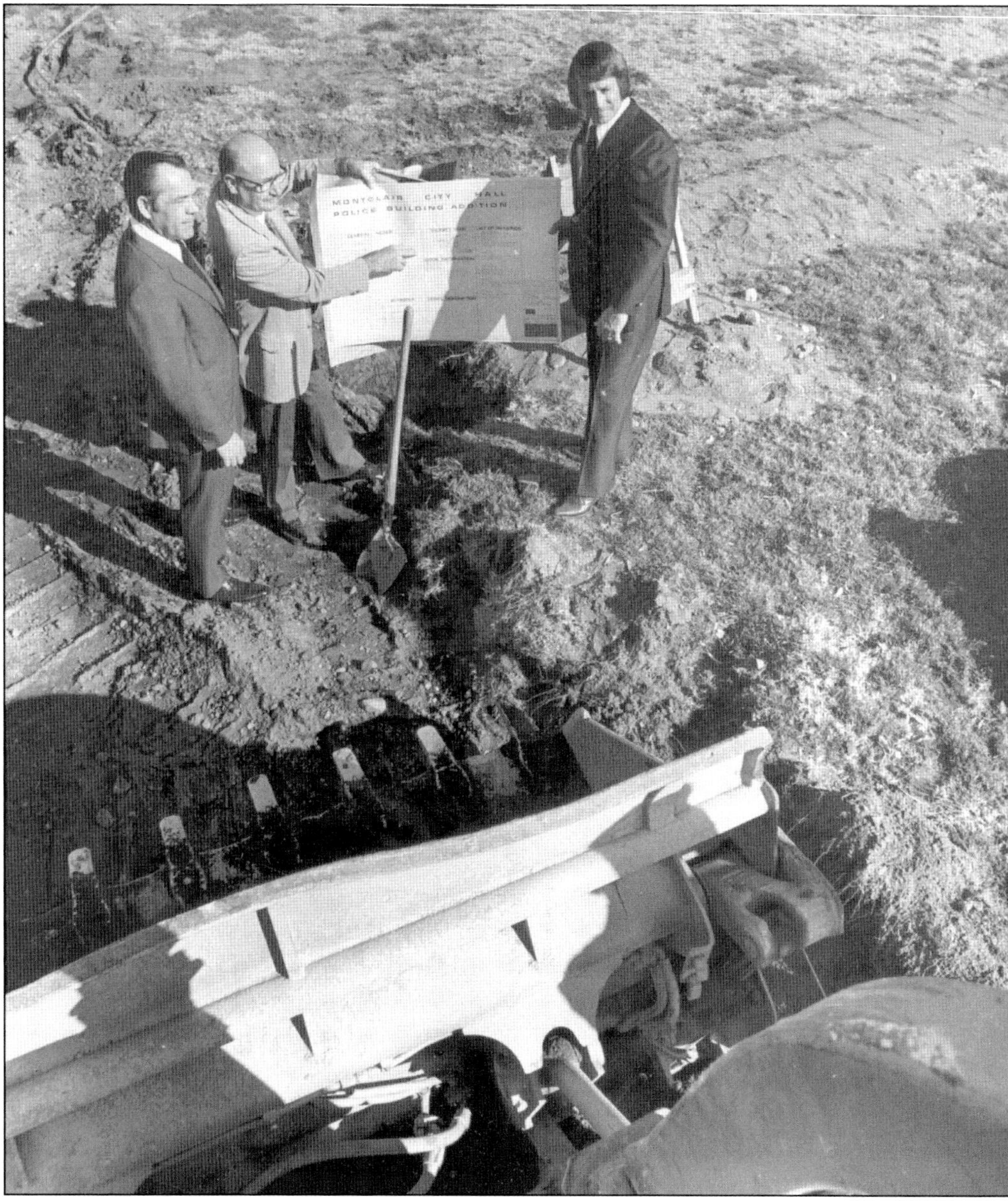

POLICE STATION EXPANSION UNDERWAY, C. 1972. It did not take long for the police department to fill its offices at the civic center to capacity. This photograph was taken at the groundbreaking ceremonies for the police facility expansion. Pictured here, from left to right, are Chief Ray McLean, Mayor Harold Hayes, and an unidentified man.

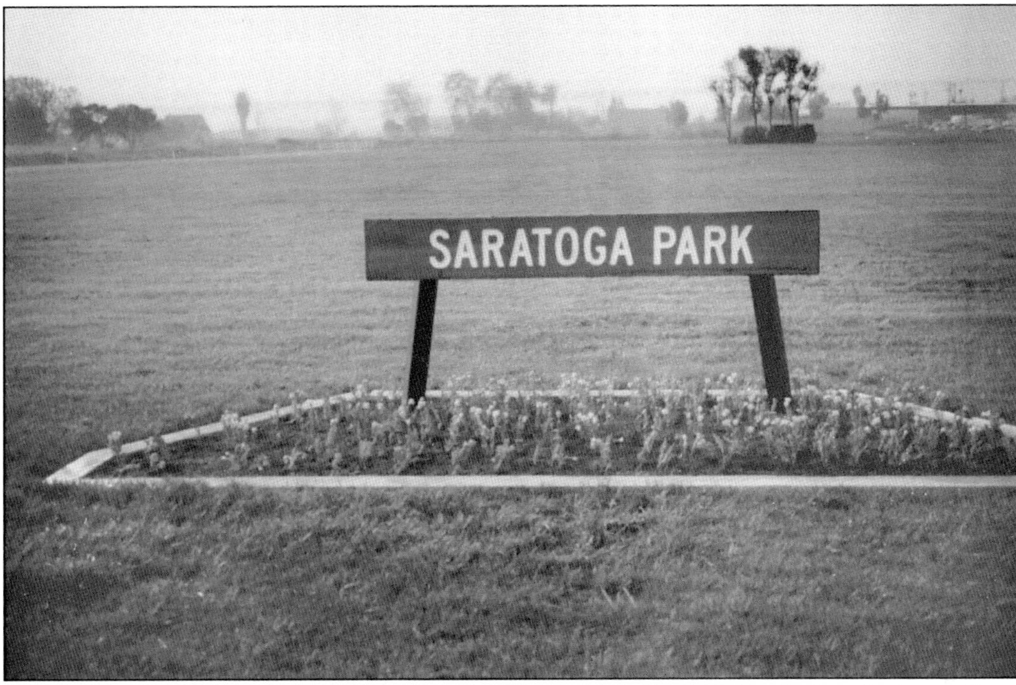

SARATOGA PARK, C. 1980. This photograph of Saratoga Park was taken before the baseball and soccer fields were installed.

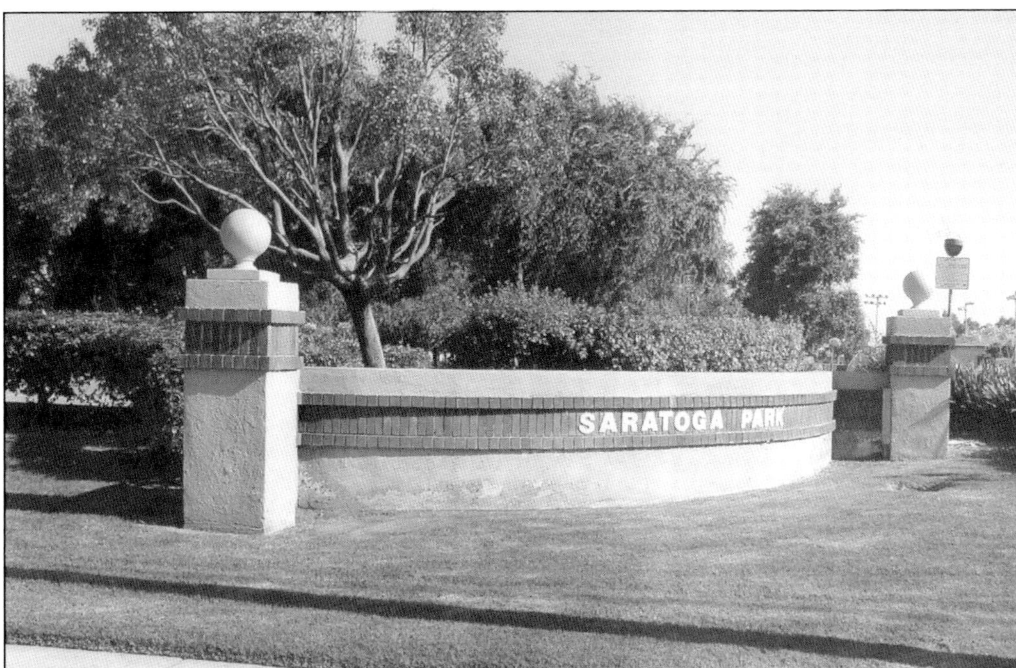

SARATOGA PARK, 2005. Pictured here is Saratoga Park as it stands today. Located on the corner of Kingsley Street and Vernon Avenue, the park has received many improvements over the years, including the addition of four lighted baseball fields, basketball courts, sand volleyball courts, picnic benches, playground equipment, drinking fountains, and two parking lots.

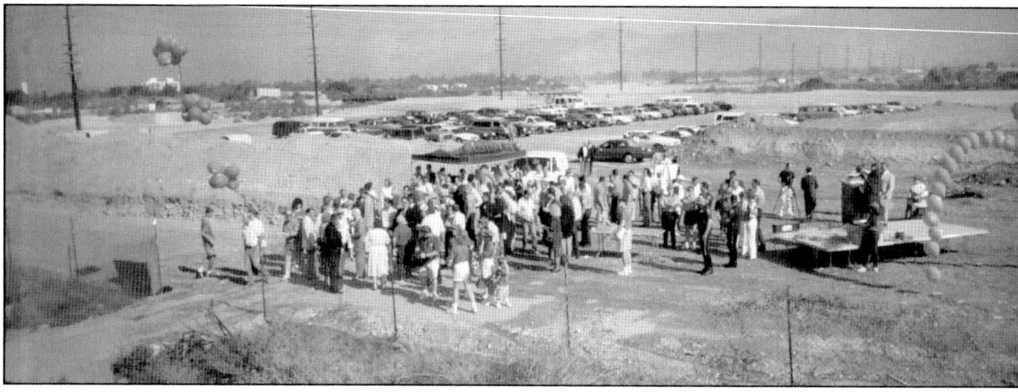

METROLINK OPENING CEREMONY, FEBRUARY 20, 1993. The Metrolink opening ceremony and public open house were held at the area now known as the Montclair Transcenter. (Courtesy of Charlotte Hayes.)

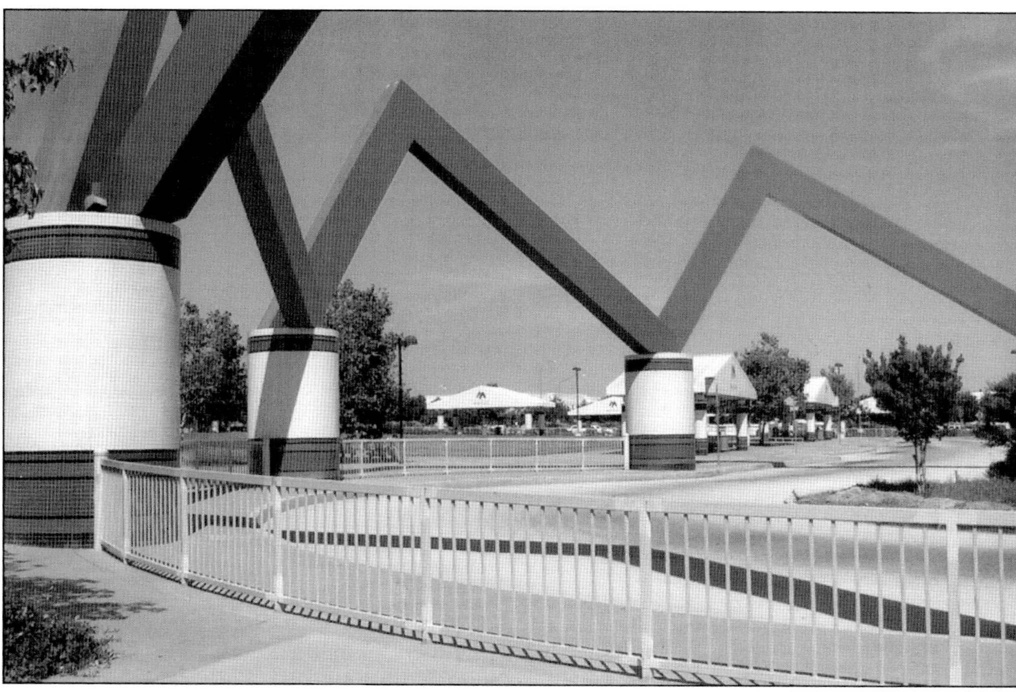

MONTCLAIR TRANSCENTER, 2005. The Transcenter is home to the Metrolink station, Omnitrans, and Foothill Transit bus services. It also serves as a park-and-ride facility and the future home of a Metro Gold Line station.

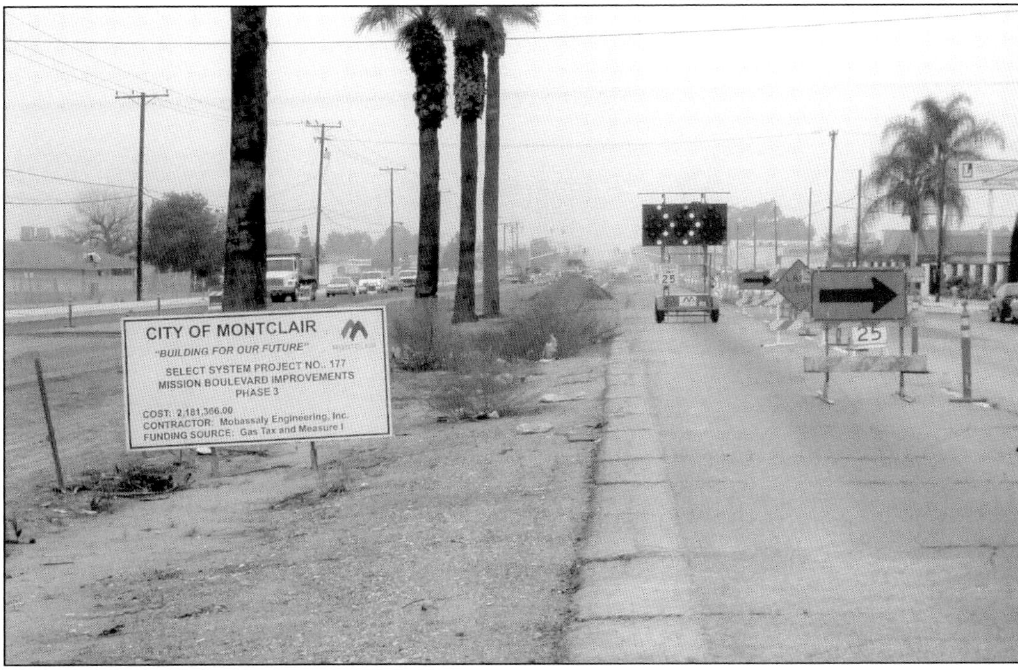

MISSION BOULEVARD IMPROVEMENTS, 2002–2003. After several months of construction, the Mission Boulevard improvements were completed. This project included significant pavement rehabilitation and replacement, median construction, storm drain work, and signal modifications. Work began on this project in 2002 (above) and was completed in 2003 (below).

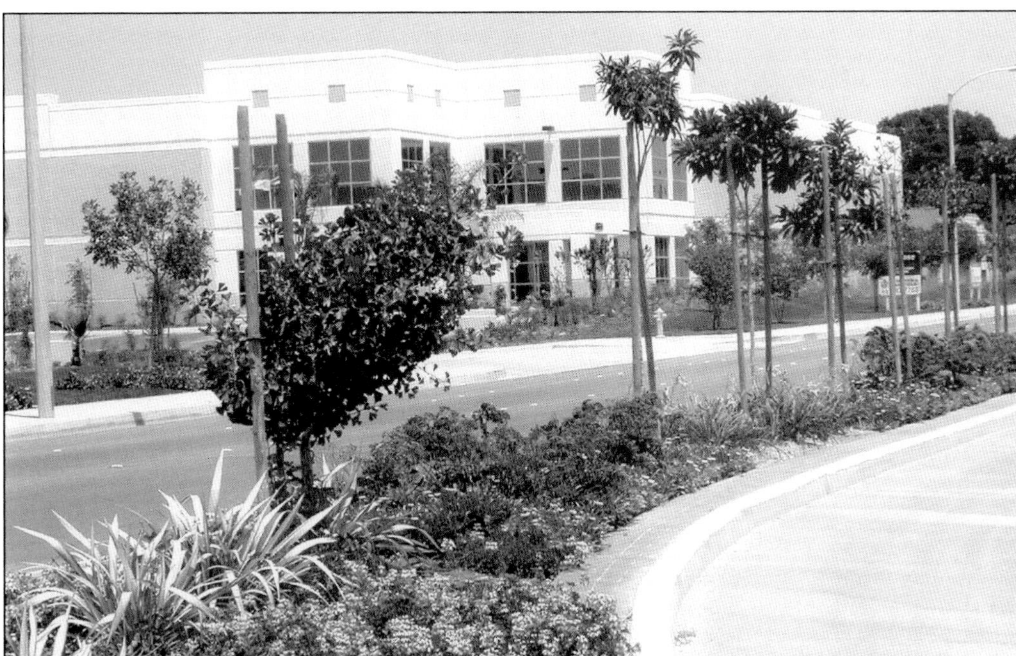

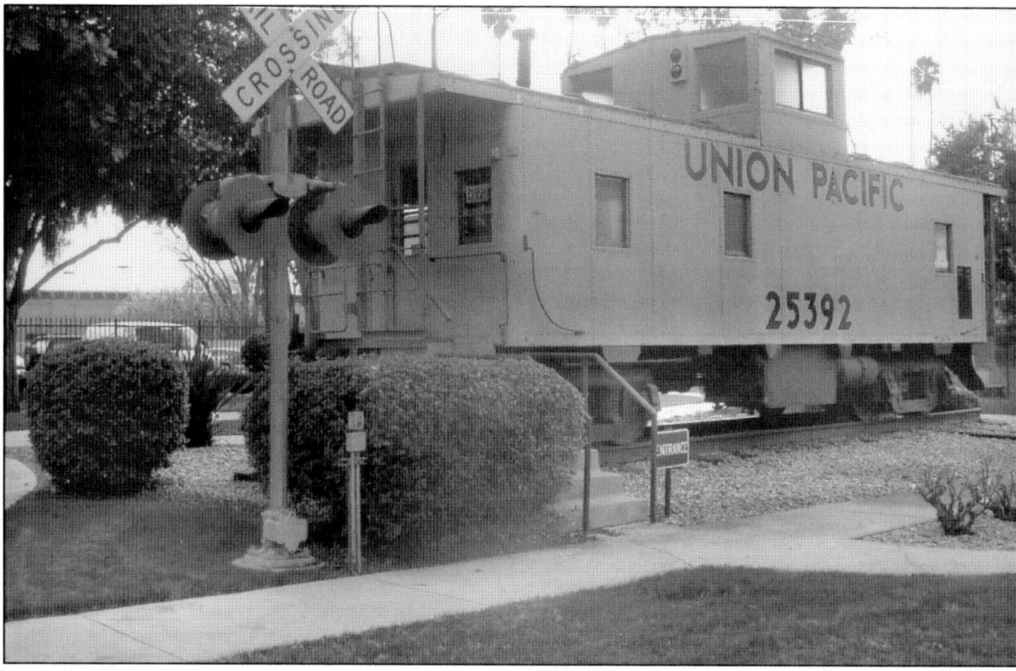

UNION PACIFIC 25392 CABOOSE, 2004. In 1986, this caboose was donated to the City of Montclair by the Union Pacific Railroad. It stayed in Alma Hoffman Park until 2004, when it was moved to Freedom Plaza to make way for a skate park.

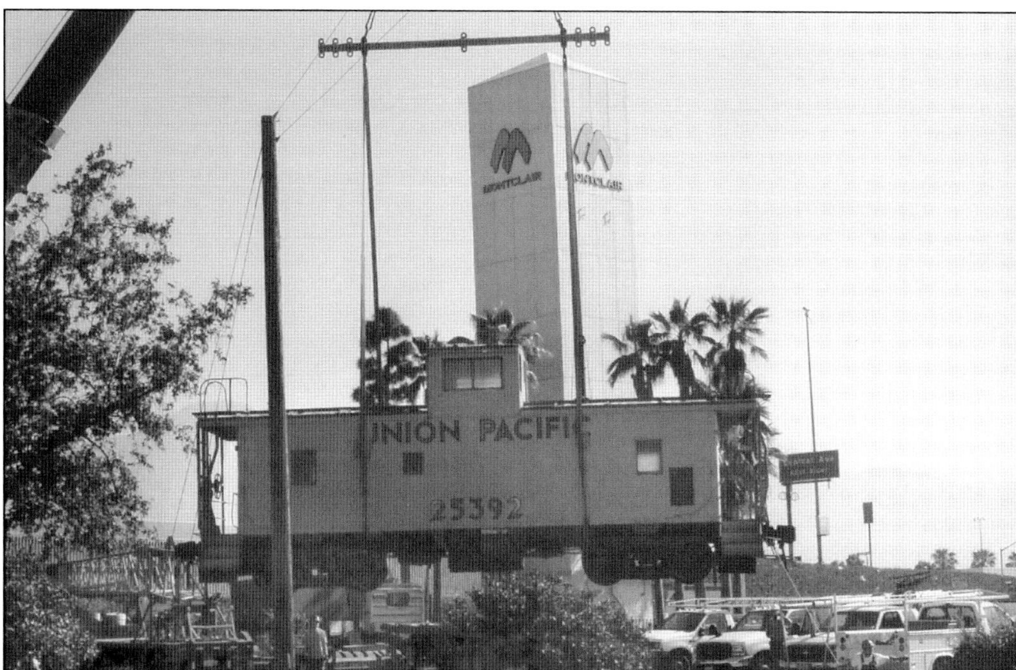

CABOOSE AT FREEDOM PLAZA, MAY 2004. This photograph shows the caboose being installed at its new home at Freedom Plaza.

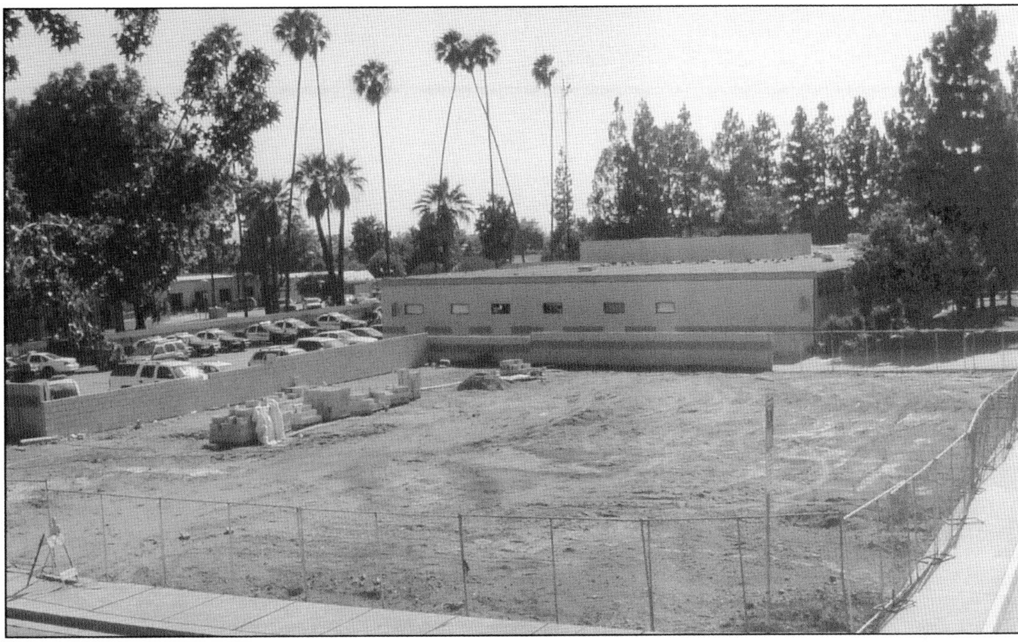

SKATEBOARD PARK PREPARATIONS, MAY 2004. The site where the caboose was located is leveled and prepared for skate park construction.

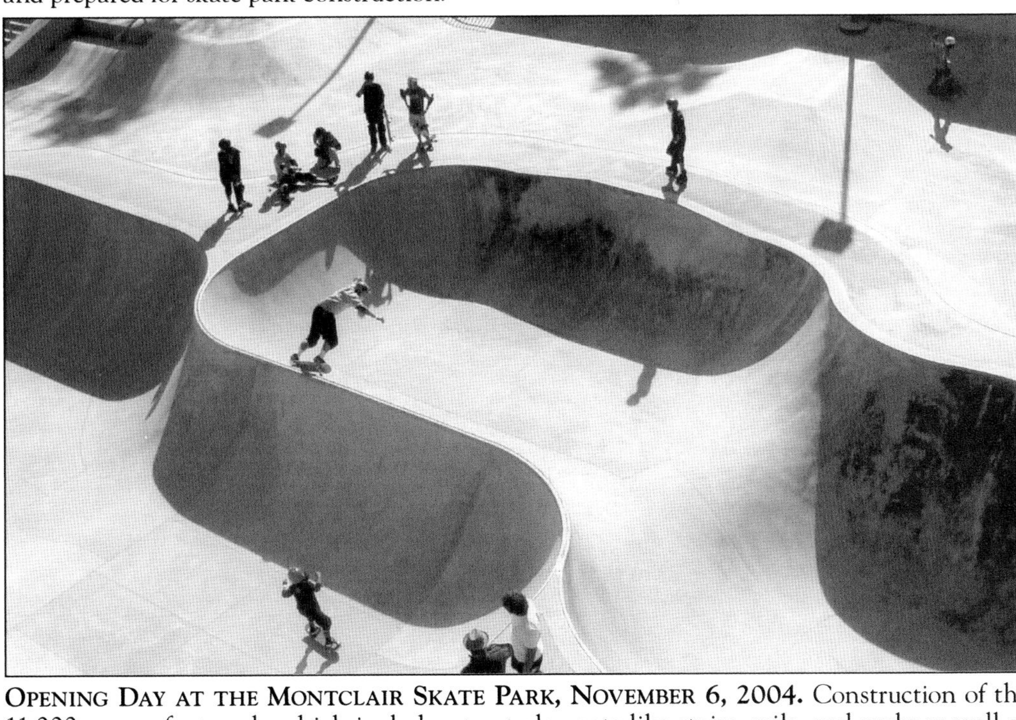

OPENING DAY AT THE MONTCLAIR SKATE PARK, NOVEMBER 6, 2004. Construction of the 11,000-square-foot park, which includes street elements like stairs, rails, and curbs as well as two large bowls, was completed in November 2004. Opening ceremonies included demos by skateboarding legends Steve Alba, Micke Alba, Lance Mountain, Christian Hosoi, Pat Nogho, and Steve Olson. Since its opening, other skateboarding professionals such as Tony Hawk and Andy MacDonald have been seen boarding at the park.

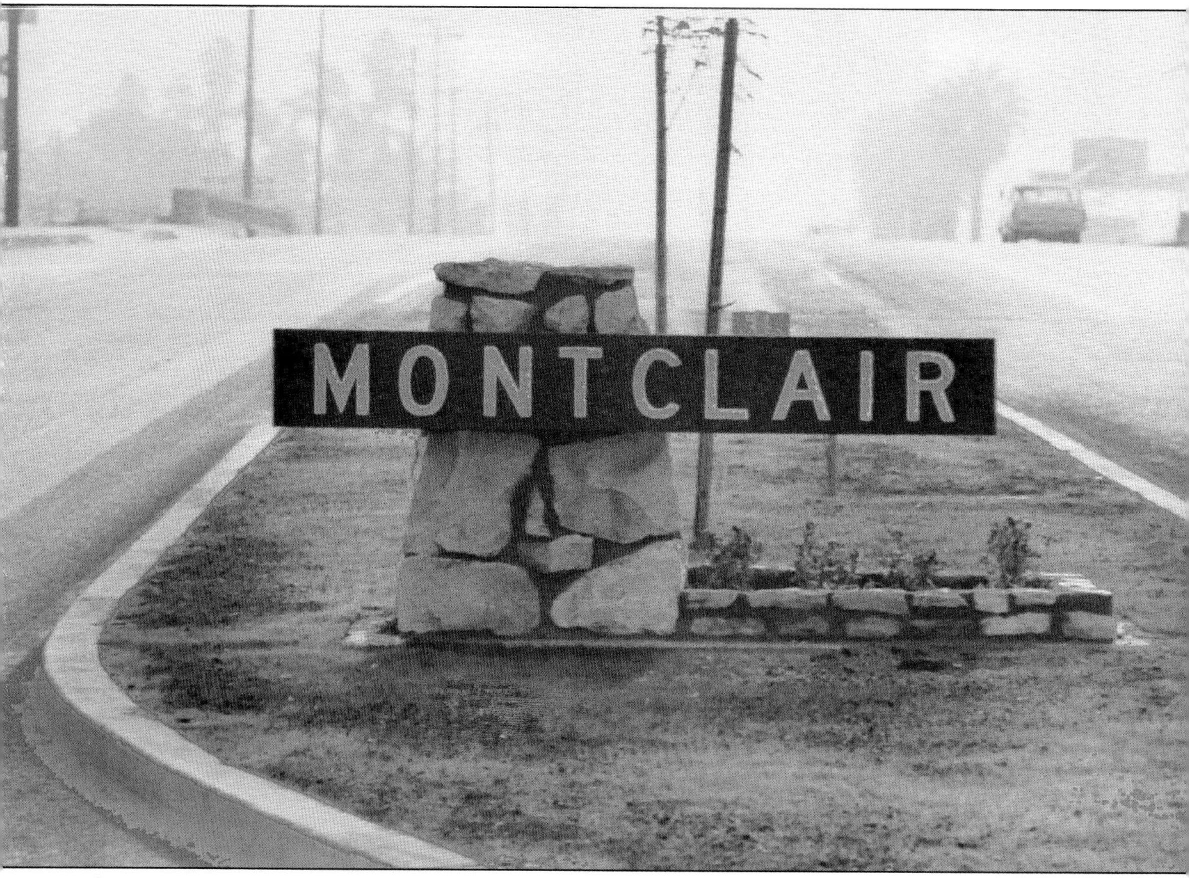

CITY OF MONTCLAIR ENTRANCE SIGN, C. 1970. To help motorists recognize city boundaries, entrance signs were placed on major streets.

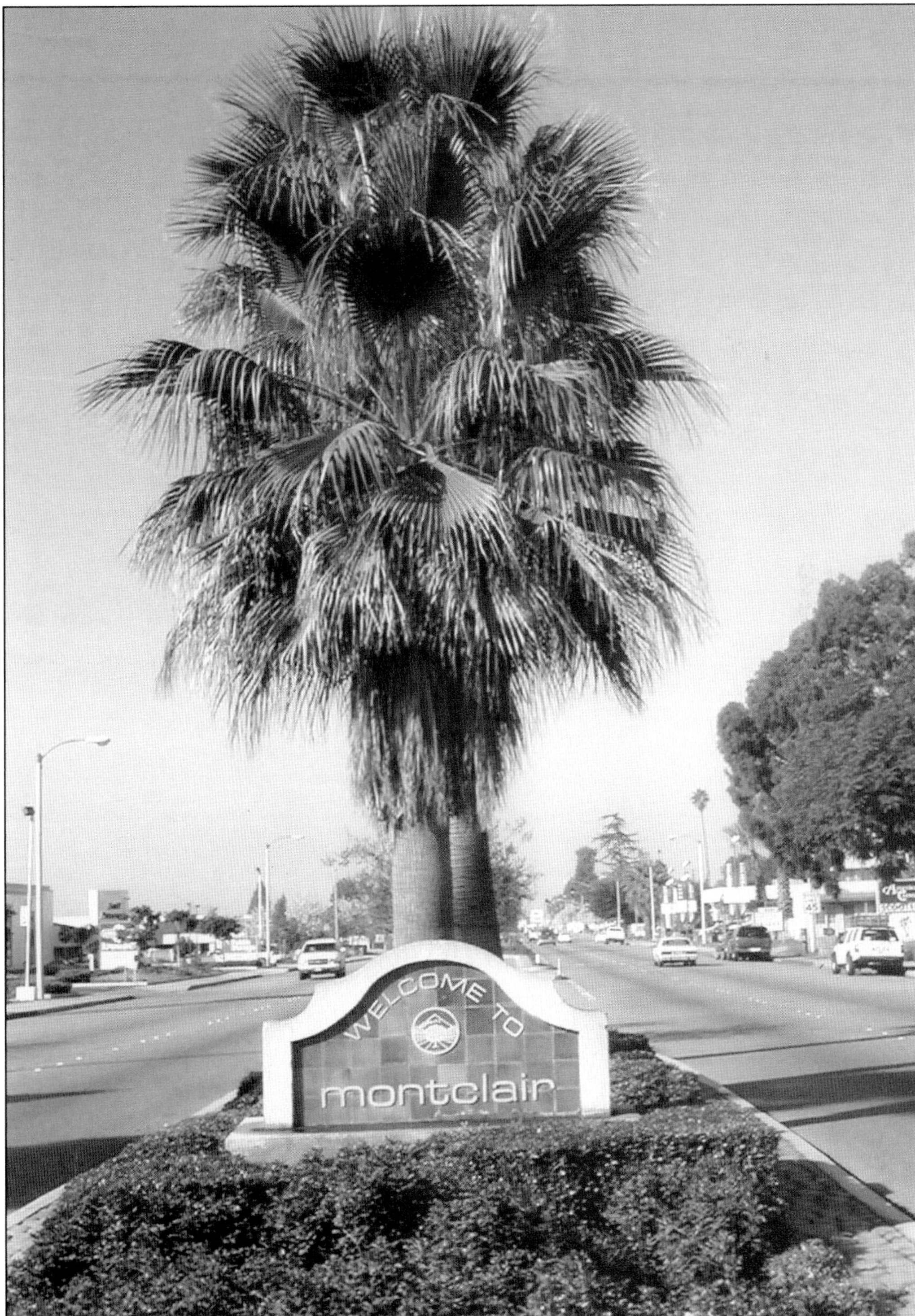

City of Montclair Monument Sign, 2005. New monument signs have replaced the original entrance signs throughout the city.

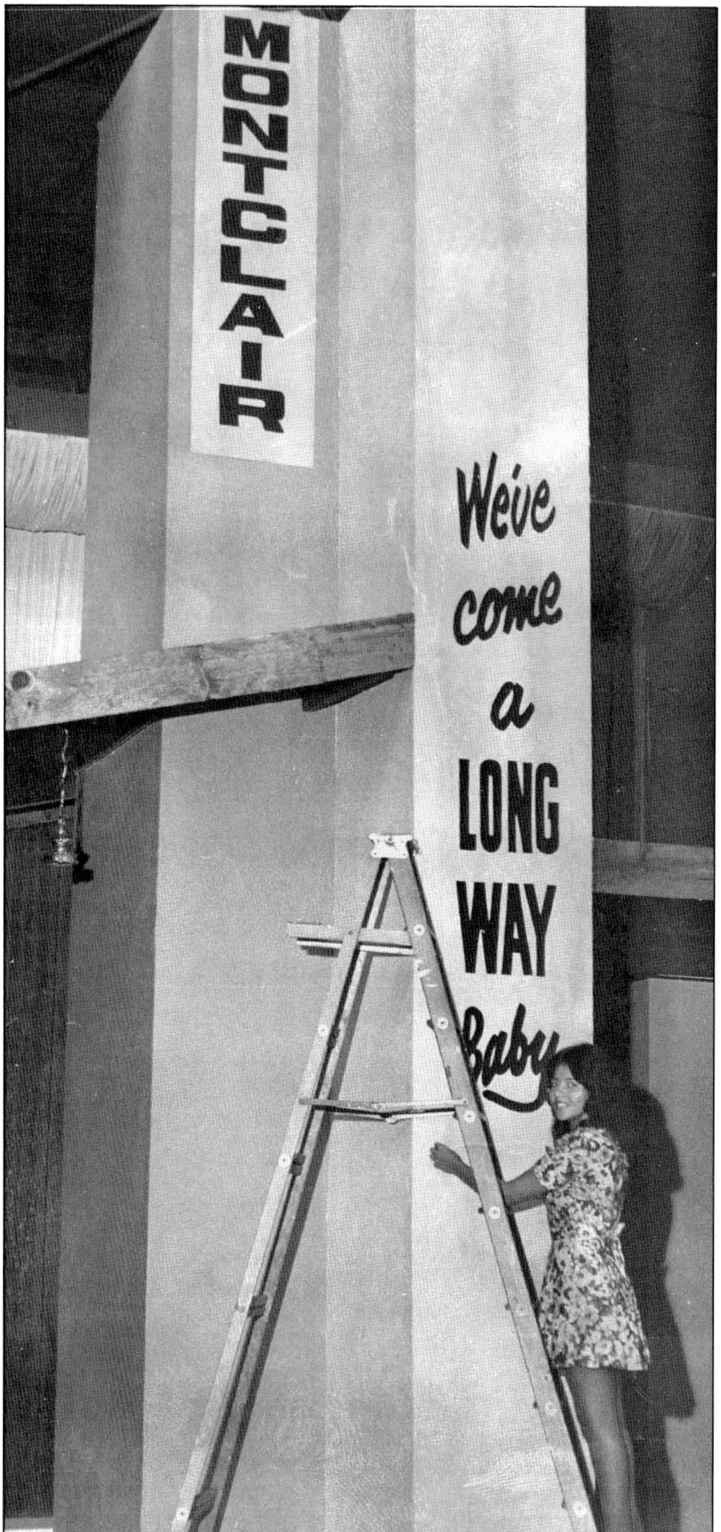

"WE'VE COME A LONG WAY BABY," 1973. This was the Montclair Chamber of Commerce display at the 1973 Los Angeles County Fair. Pictured here is Joanne Garcia.

Two

PROGRESS THROUGH BUSINESS

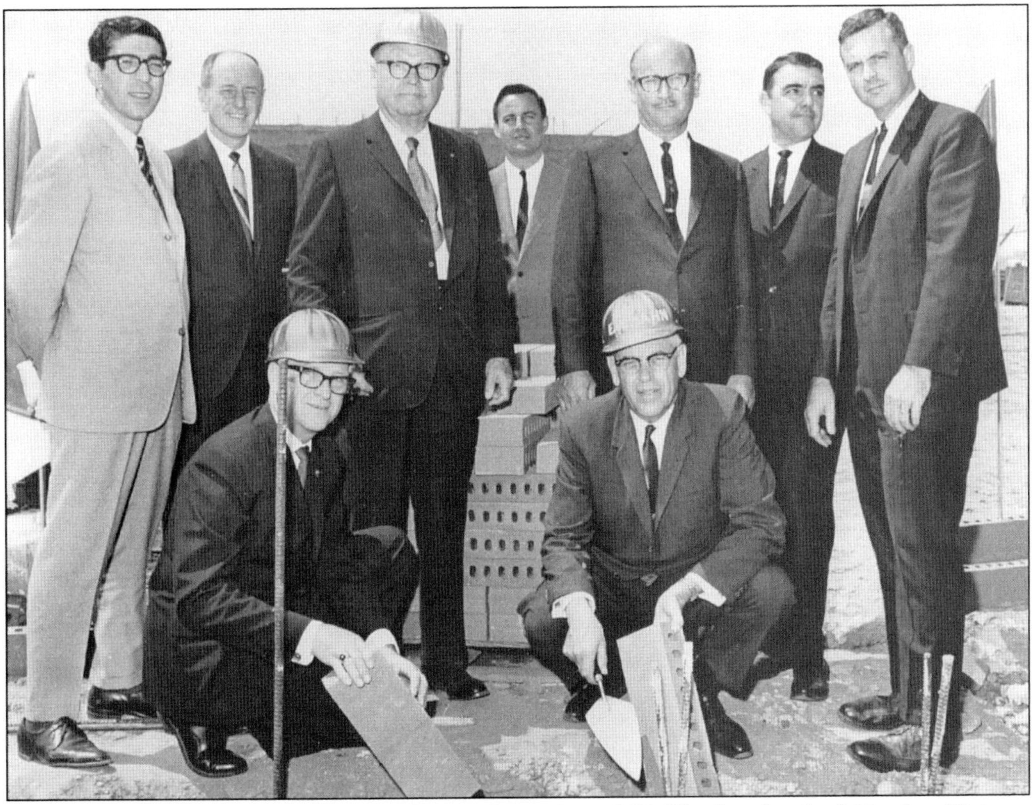

FIRST BRICK OF CROCKER-CITIZENS BANK, JUNE 21, 1967. The first brick of Crocker-Citizens Bank was ceremoniously laid on the corner of Moreno Street and Central Avenue by, from left to right, (first row) Mayor Ernest Rowley and S. Edgar Lauther, executive vice president of the bank; (second row) city administrator Mike Graziano; Ernest W. Hahn, developer and general contractor; Samuel K. Rindge, former chairman of the board of Crocker-Citizens Bank; Tim Moore of Coldwell-Banker; councilman Harold Hayes; Charles Kober, architect; and councilman Leonard Soper.

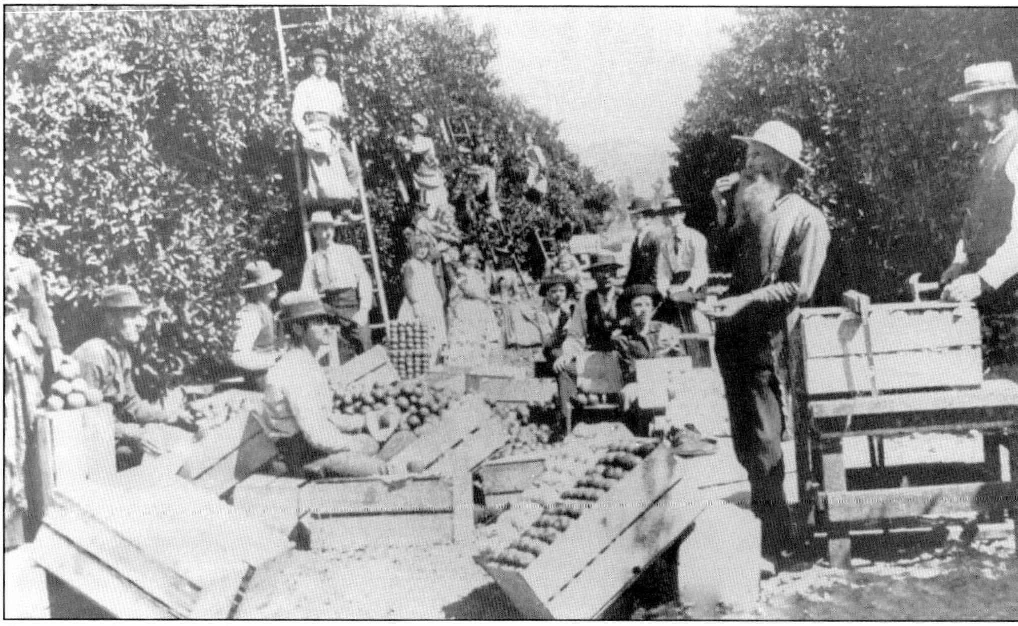

ORANGE GROVES. The citrus industry is a bygone way of life in Montclair and a large part of San Bernardino County. This photograph shows a typical orange grove in the early 20th century. (Courtesy of Monte Vista Water District.)

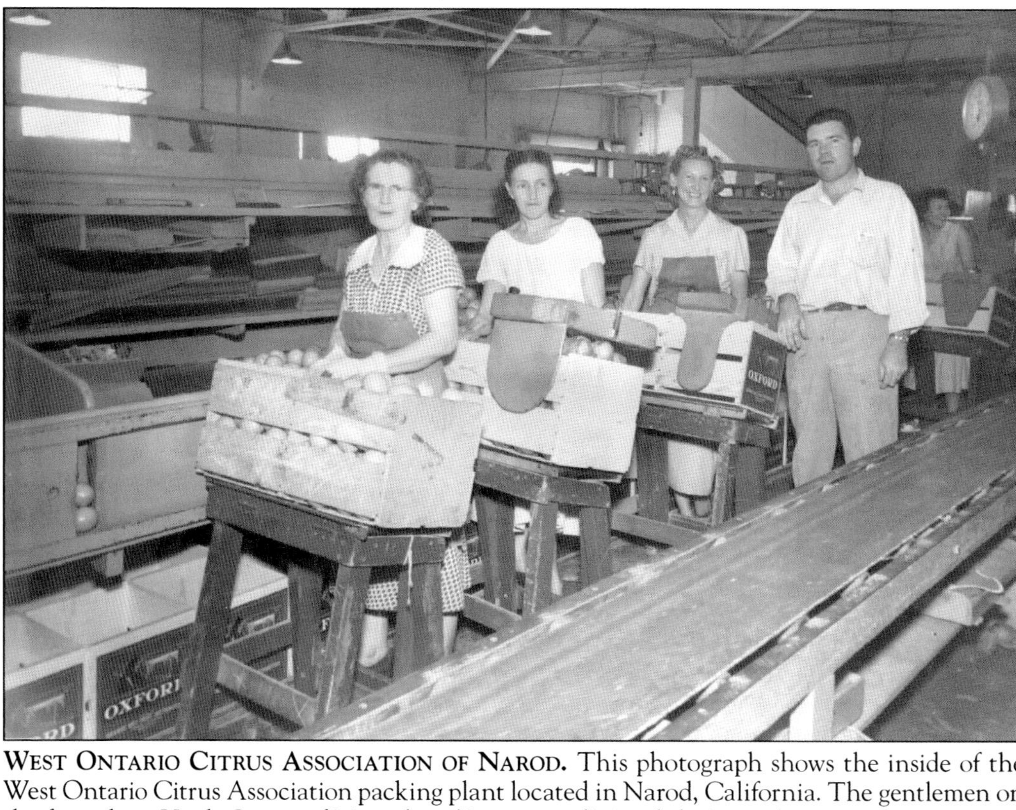

WEST ONTARIO CITRUS ASSOCIATION OF NAROD. This photograph shows the inside of the West Ontario Citrus Association packing plant located in Narod, California. The gentlemen on the far right is Hugh Guinn of Montclair. (Courtesy of Meredith Guinn.)

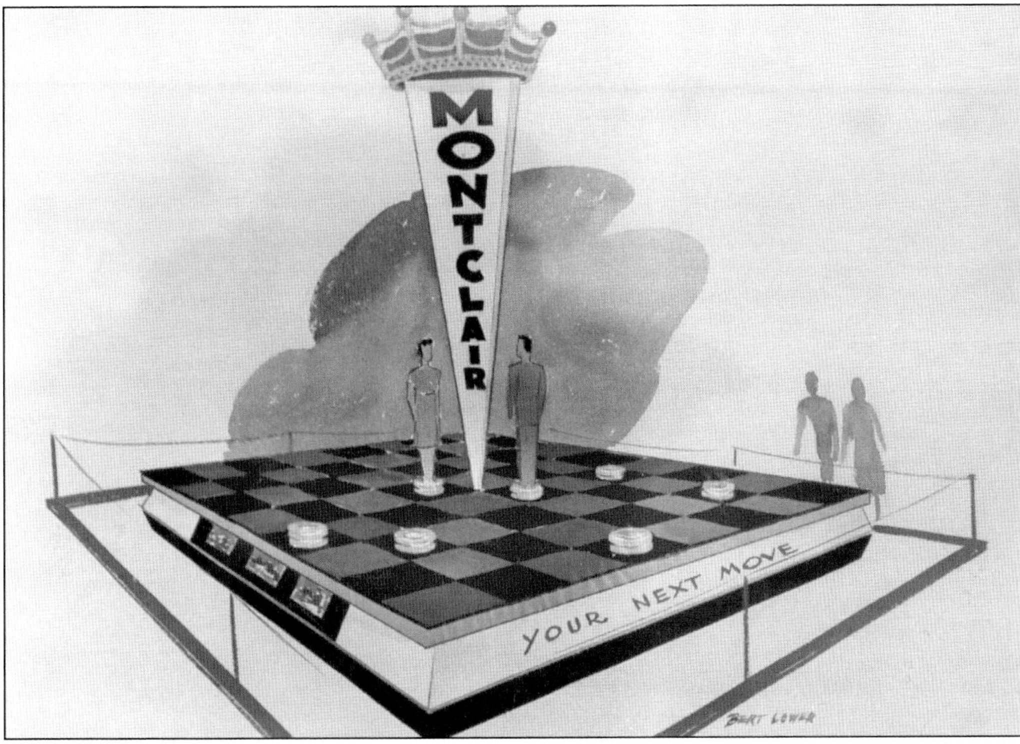

MONTCLAIR, YOUR NEXT MOVE, 1959. To help bolster the local economy in Montclair, the Montclair Chamber of Commerce and Montclair Kiwanis Club jointly displayed this exhibit at the Los Angeles County Fair. The "Your Next Move" conceptual drawing by Bert Lowell could be seen at the 1959 fair.

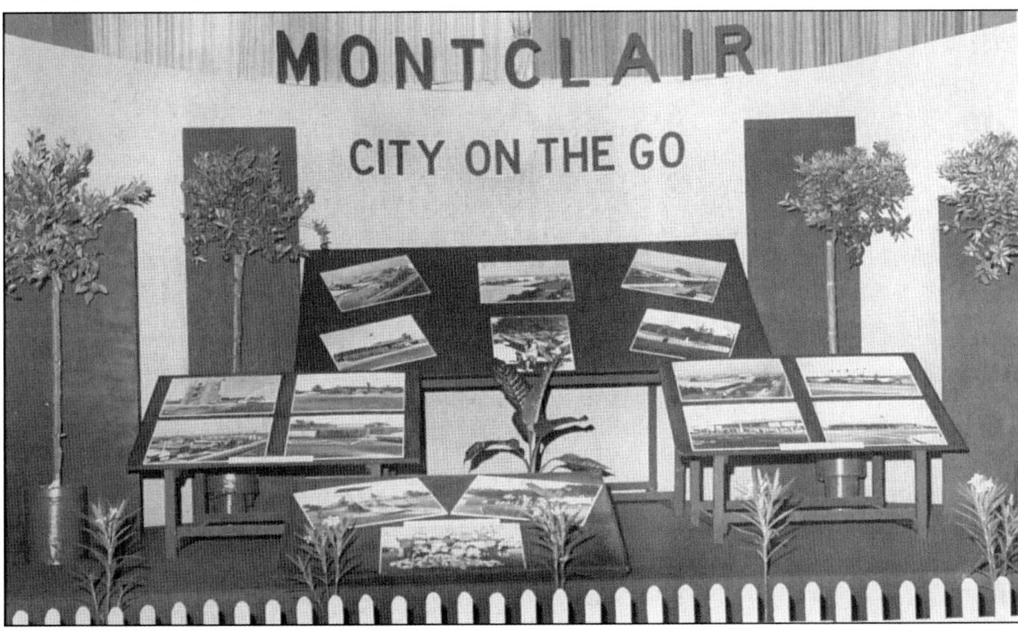

MONTCLAIR CITY ON THE GO, 1973. Pictured here is the 1973 Montclair Chamber of Commerce Los Angeles County Fair display.

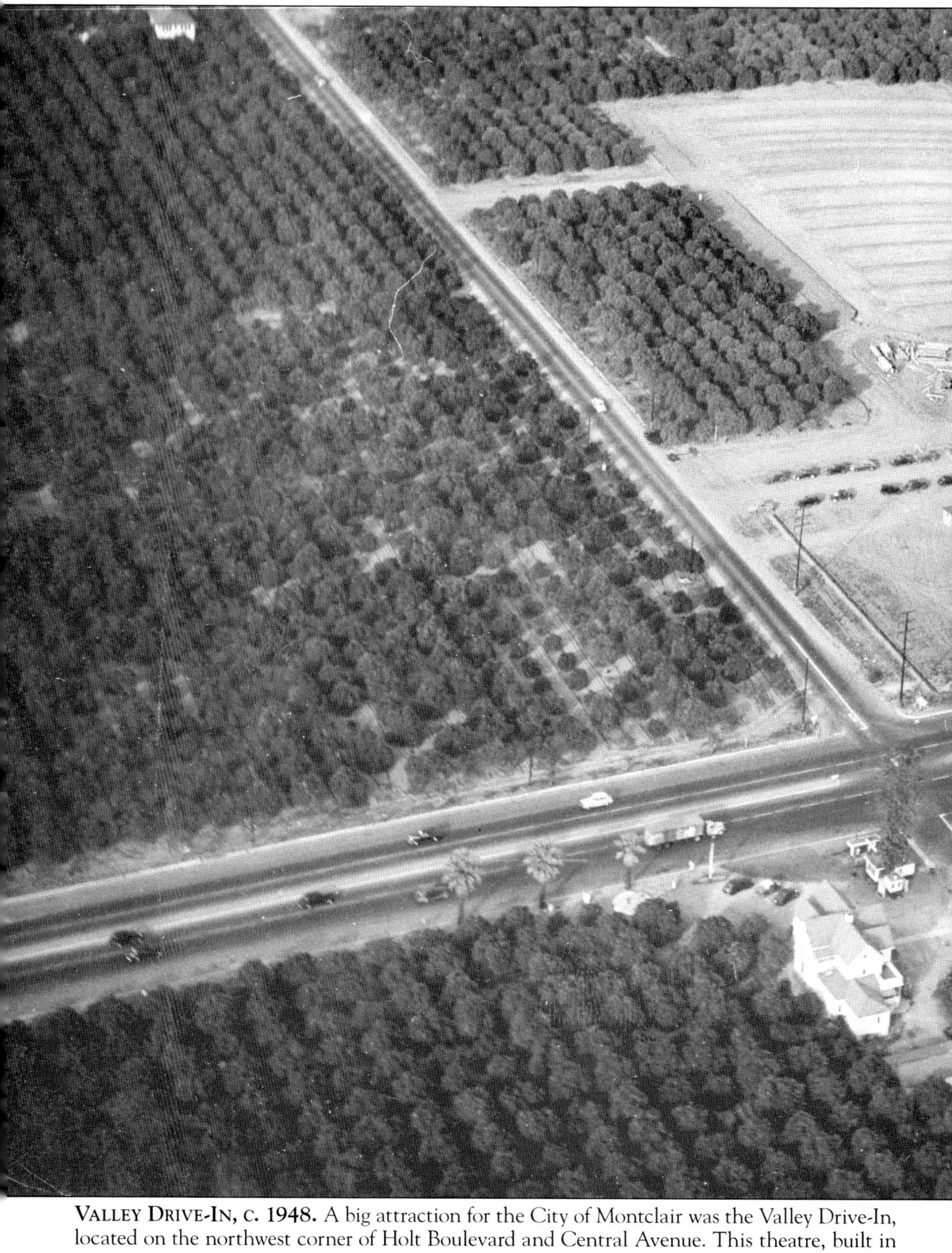

VALLEY DRIVE-IN, C. 1948. A big attraction for the City of Montclair was the Valley Drive-In, located on the northwest corner of Holt Boulevard and Central Avenue. This theatre, built in

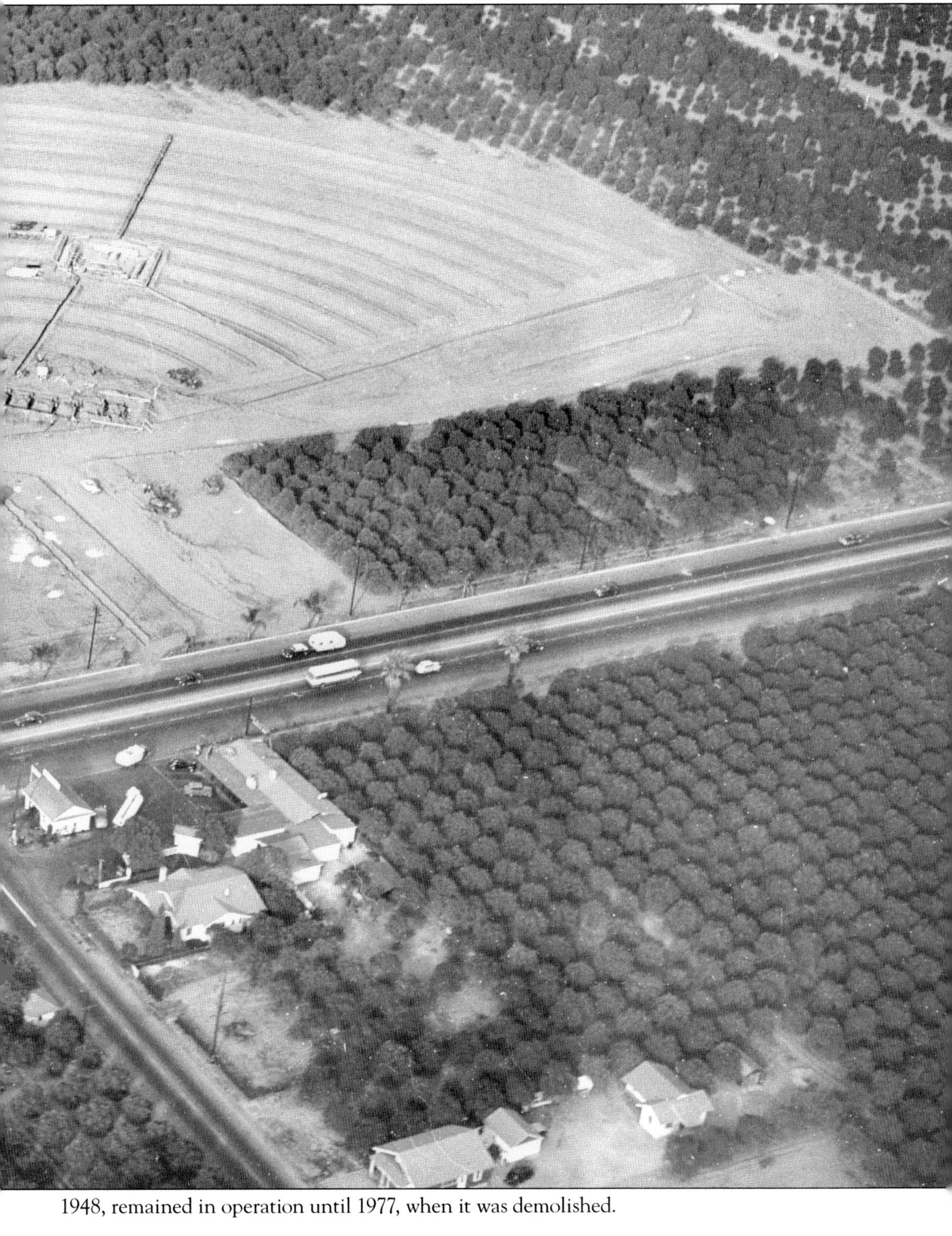

1948, remained in operation until 1977, when it was demolished.

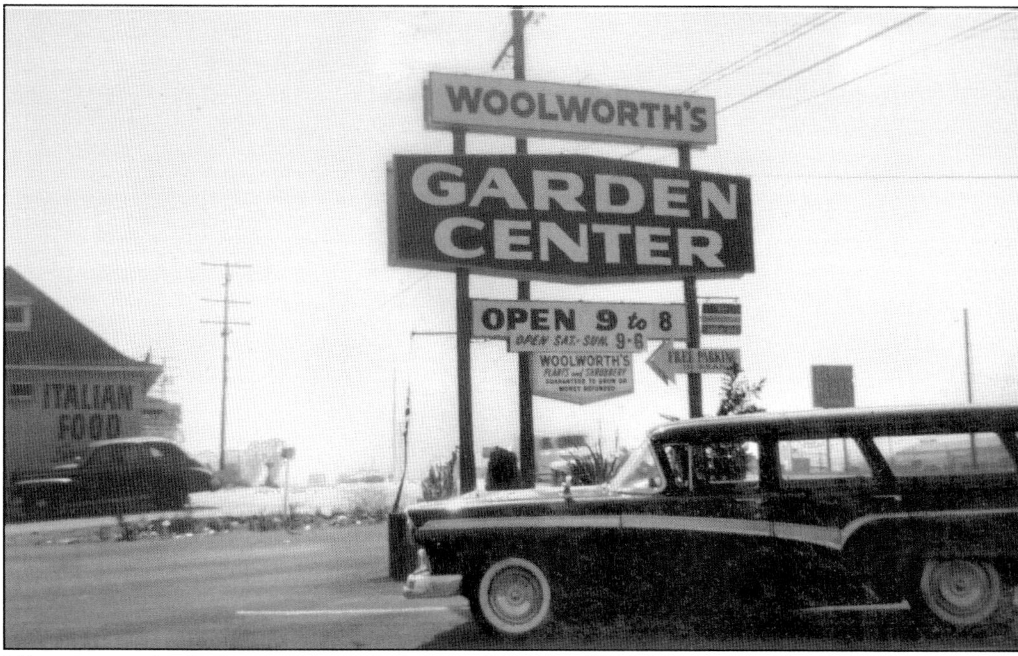

WOOLWORTH'S GARDEN CENTER, JUNE 1961. Woolworth's Garden Center was one of the many businesses in Montclair that served both local and neighboring communities. (Courtesy of Mike Hance.)

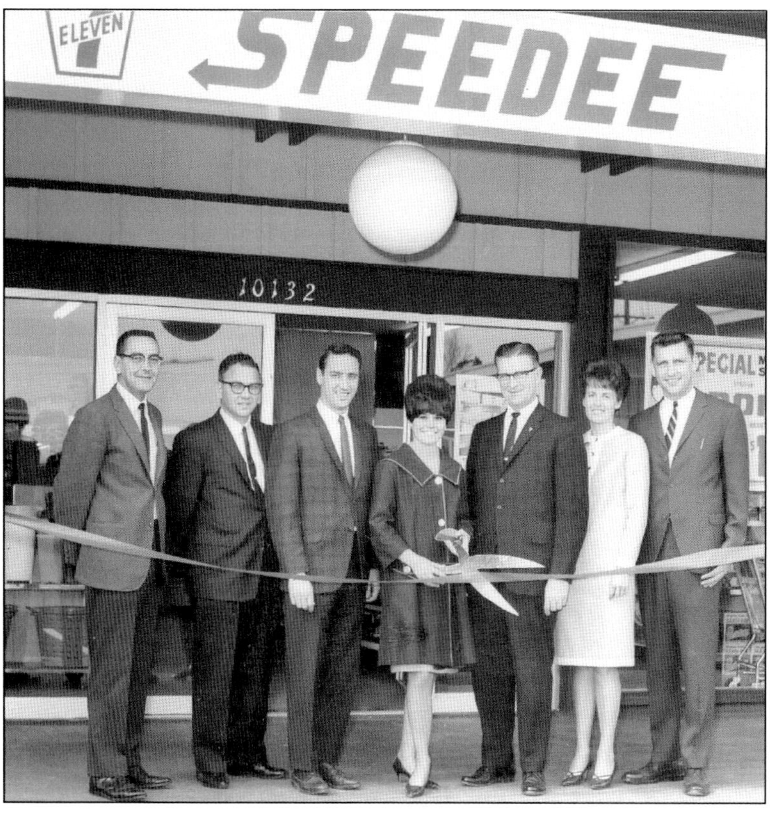

GRAND OPENING, 7-ELEVEN. Located on the corner of Central Avenue and Orchard Street, this business was centrally located and represents one of the many businesses drawn to this city.

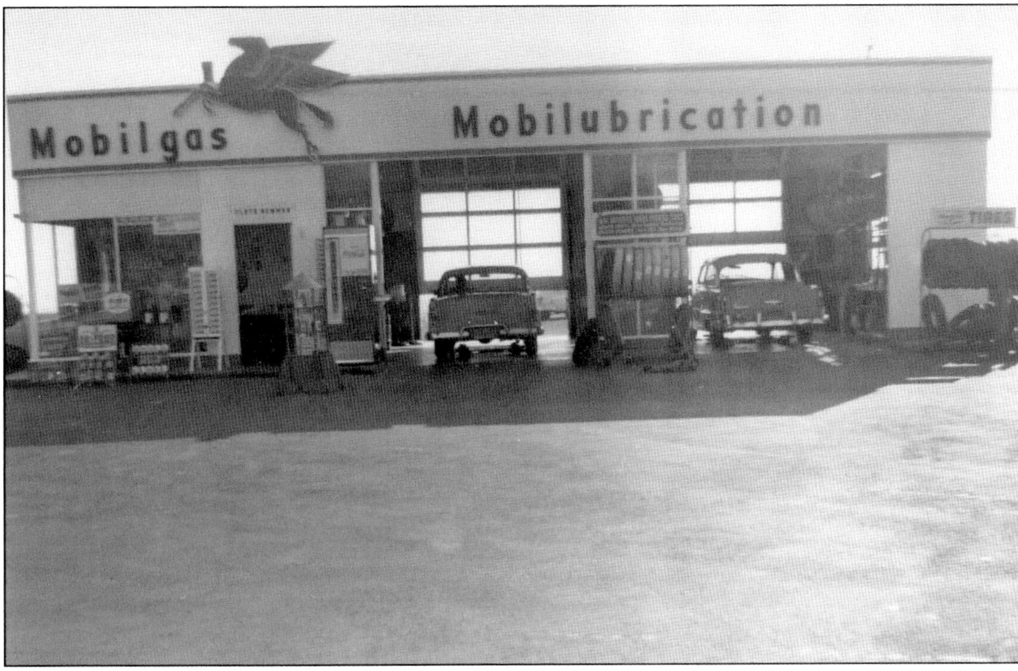

MOBILGAS STATION, APRIL 1961. This gas station, located on Central Avenue, serviced many Montclair residents' vehicles. (Courtesy of Mike Hance.)

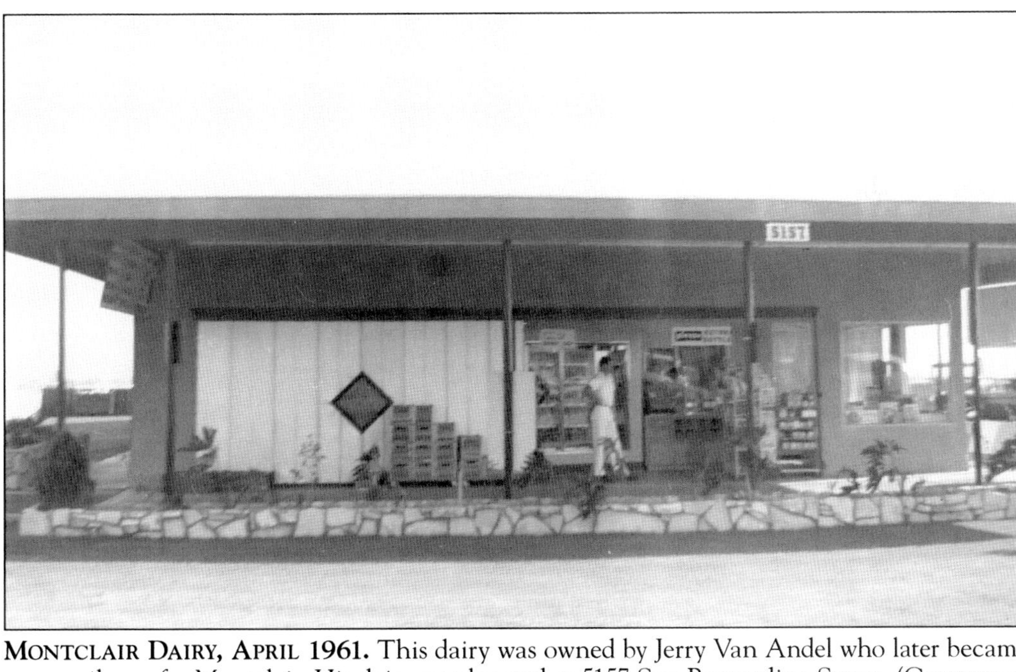

MONTCLAIR DAIRY, APRIL 1961. This dairy was owned by Jerry Van Andel who later became a councilman for Montclair. His dairy was located at 5157 San Bernardino Street. (Courtesy of Mike Hance.)

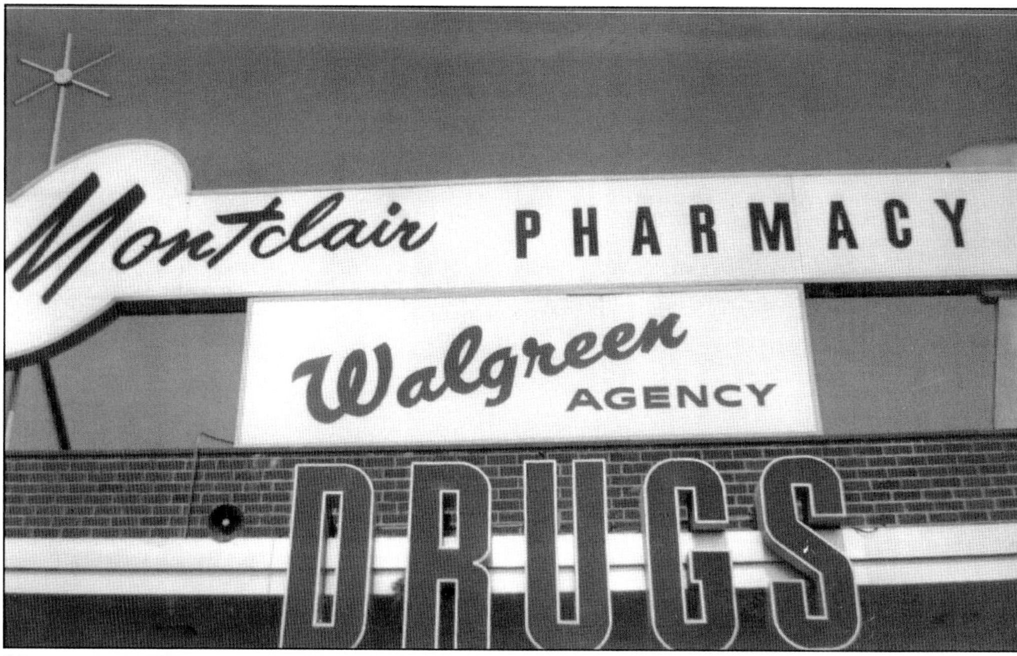

Montclair Walgreen Drug Store, June 1961. The Montclair Walgreen drug store was located at 9870 Central Avenue. (Courtesy of Mike Hance.)

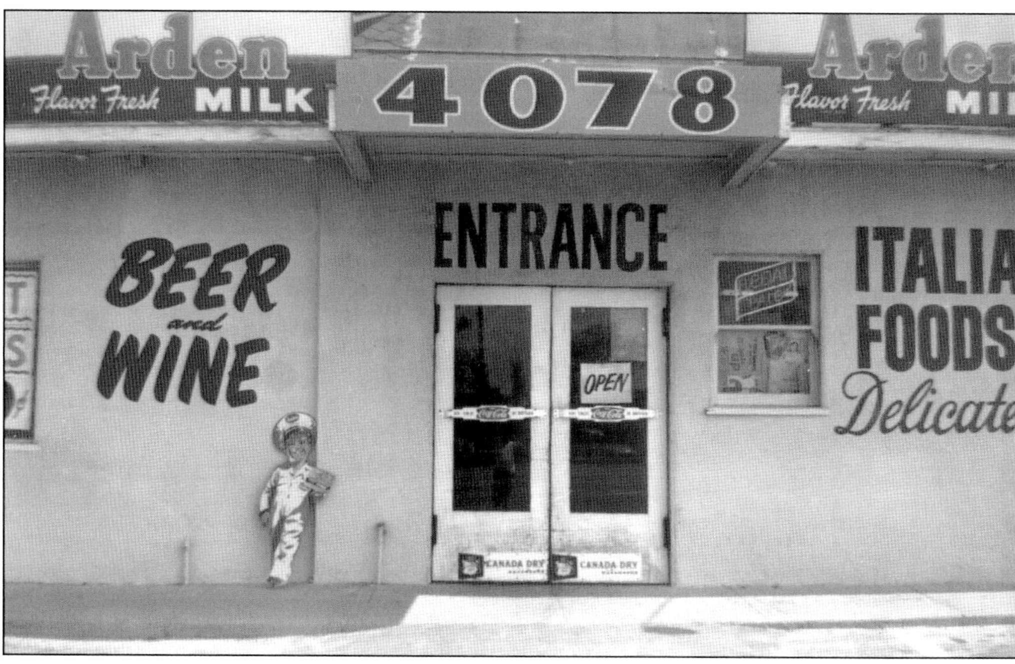

Arden Market, June 1961. Arden Market was located at 4078 Central Avenue. (Courtesy of Mike Hance.)

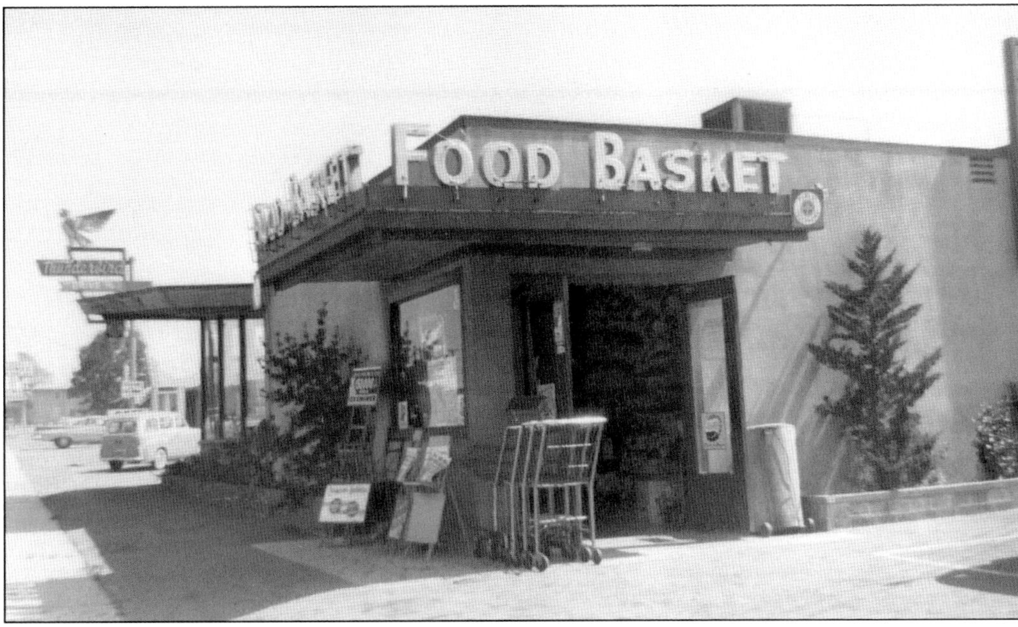

FOOD BASKET, JUNE 1961. The Food Basket store was located at 9681 Central Avenue and served as one of the premier grocery stores for this area. (Courtesy of Mike Hance.)

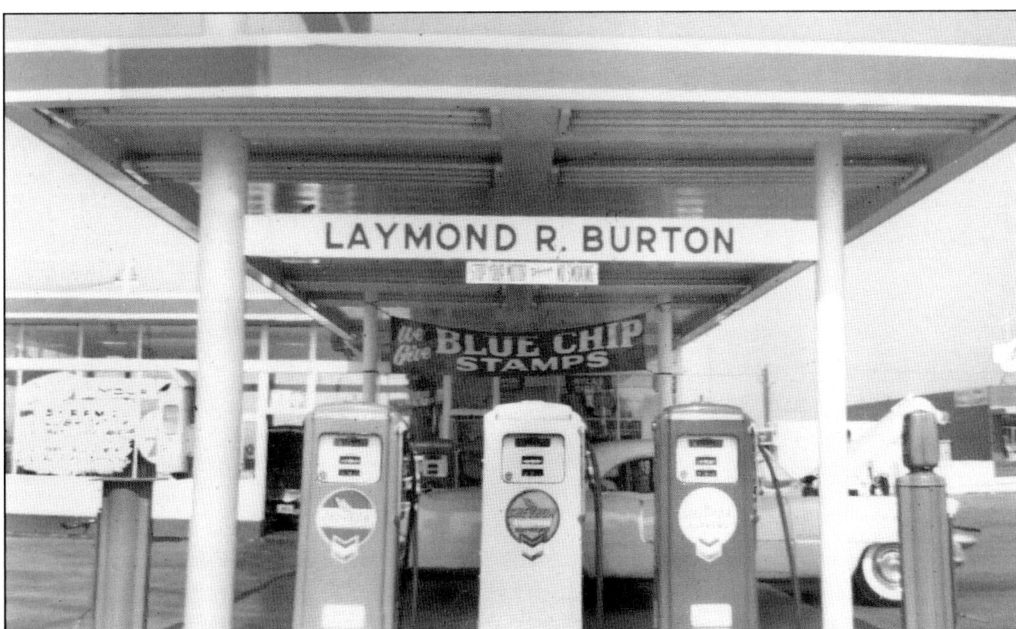

LAYMOND R. BURTON CHEVRON GAS STATION, JUNE 1961. This gas station was located on Central Avenue next to the Montclair Pharmacy. (Courtesy of Mike Hance.)

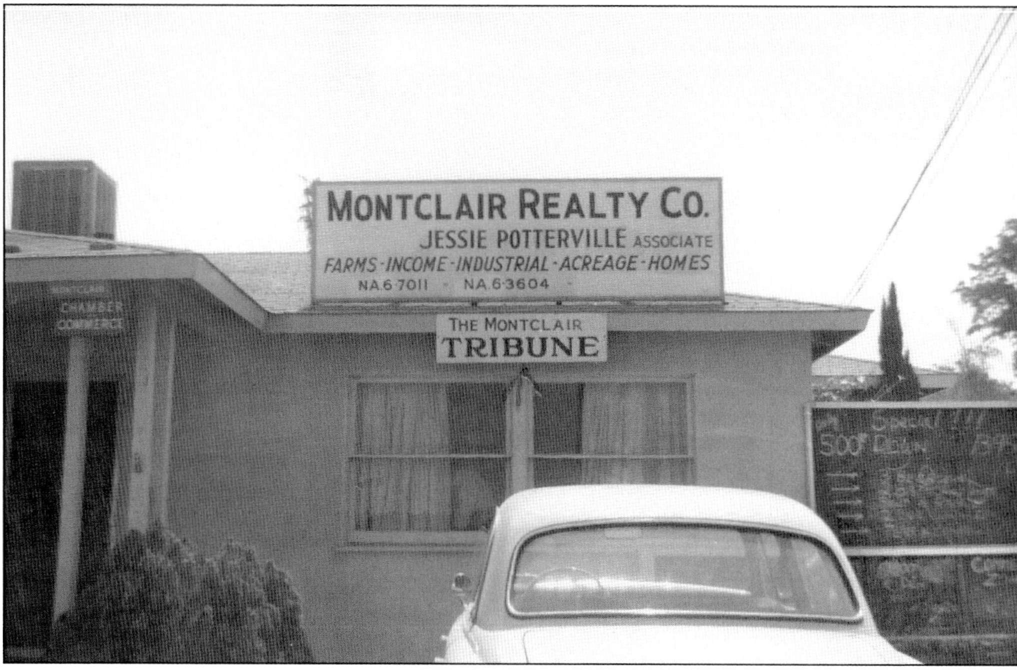

Business Complex, June 1961. This building, located at 9661 Central Avenue, housed the *Montclair Tribune*, Montclair Chamber of Commerce, Montclair Realty Company, Jack C. George Insurance, and Paul V. Frame's real estate company. (Courtesy of Mike Hance.)

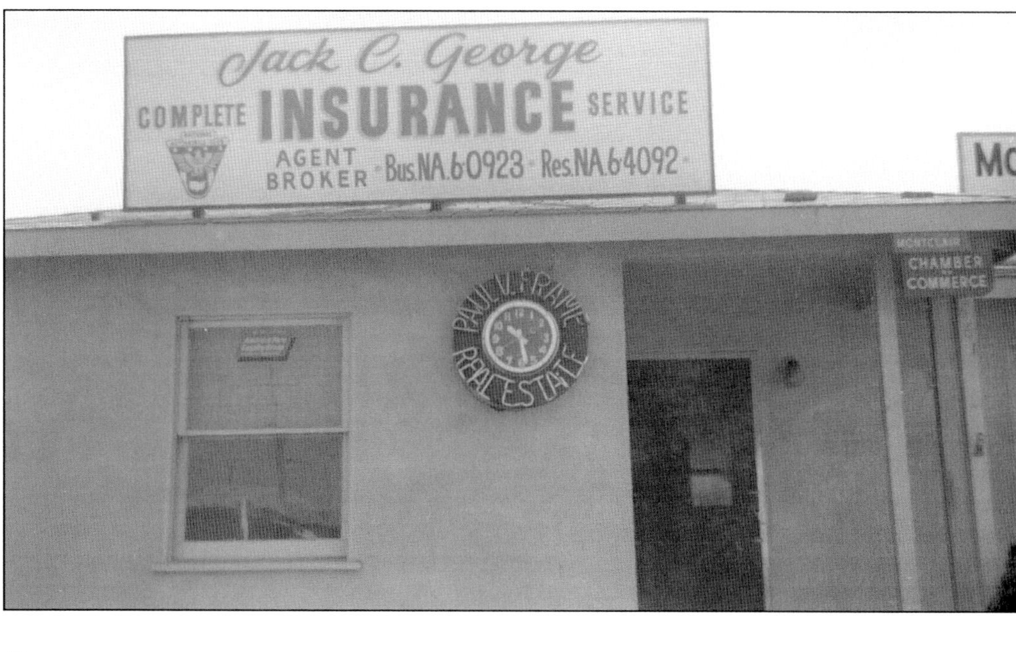

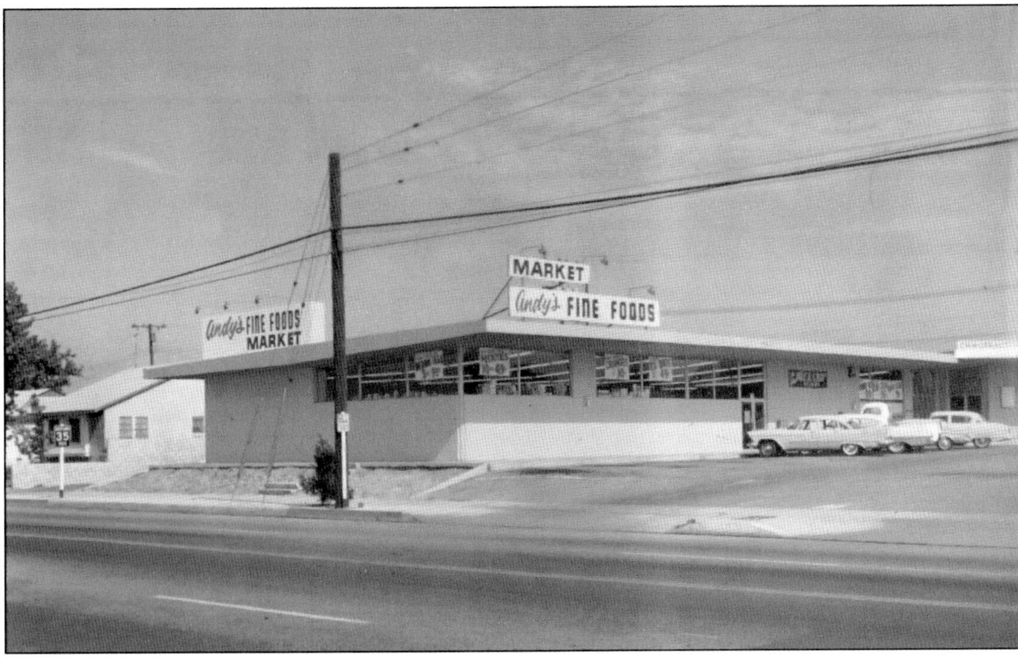

ANDY'S FINE FOODS MARKET, c. 1960s. Andy's was located on the northwest corner of Central Avenue and San Bernardino Street. The signs in the windows advertise potatoes at 10 pounds for 49¢. Other prices advertised in a 1963 newspaper include ground beef at 3 pounds for $1, 5 pounds of sugar for 49¢, margarine at 6 pounds for $1, and top sirloin steak at $1.39 per pound.

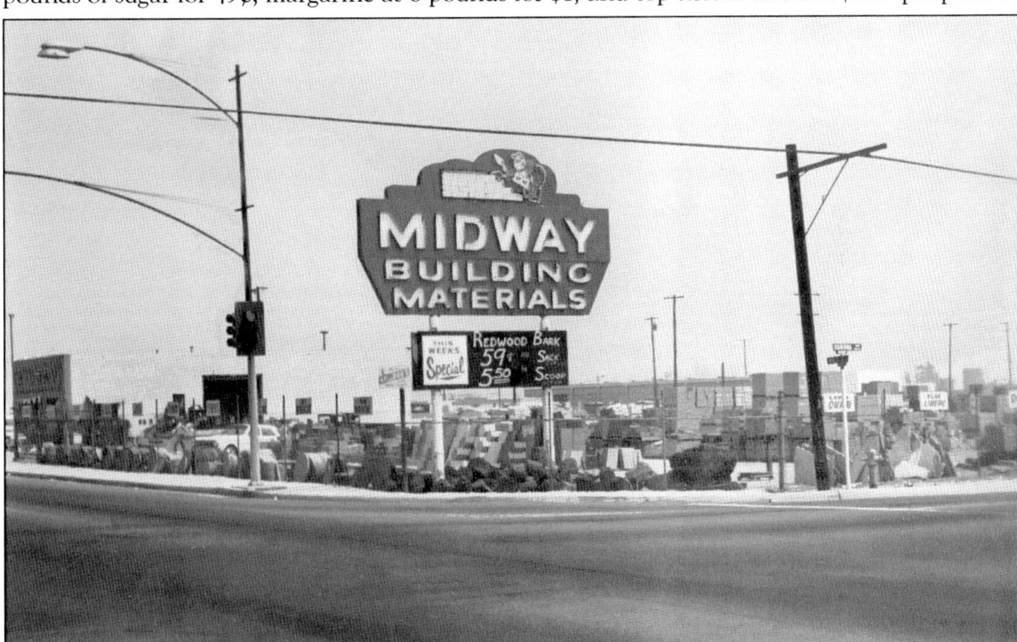

MIDWAY BUILDING MATERIALS. Midway Building Materials was located on the corner of Ramona Avenue and Holt Boulevard for 45 years. Although Midway closed in 1998, this sign is now on display at the Museum of Neon Art in Los Angeles. Holding a brick in one hand, the neon mason appears to raise and lower a hand gripping a pink trowel.

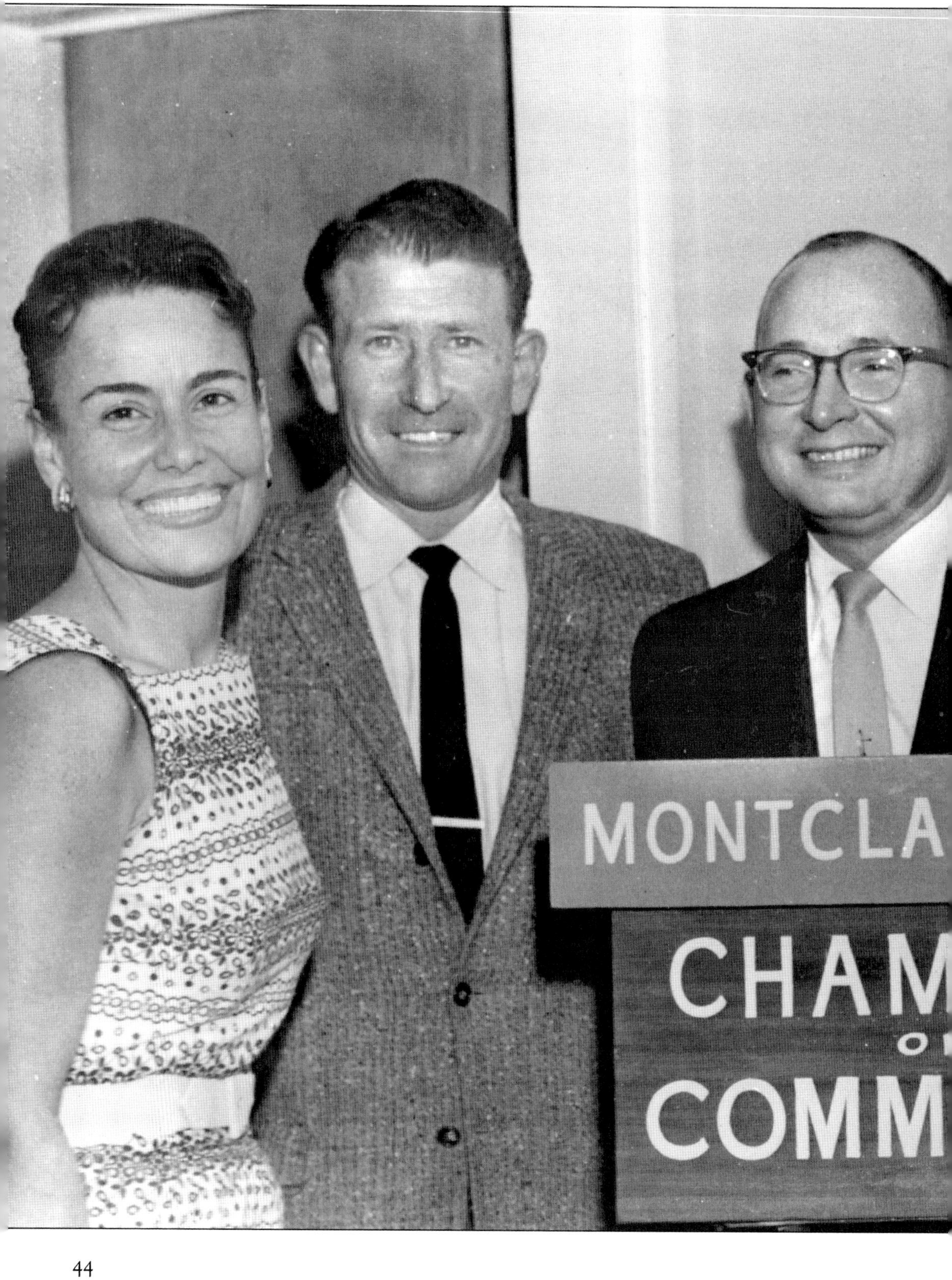
MONTCLA
CHAM
O
COMM

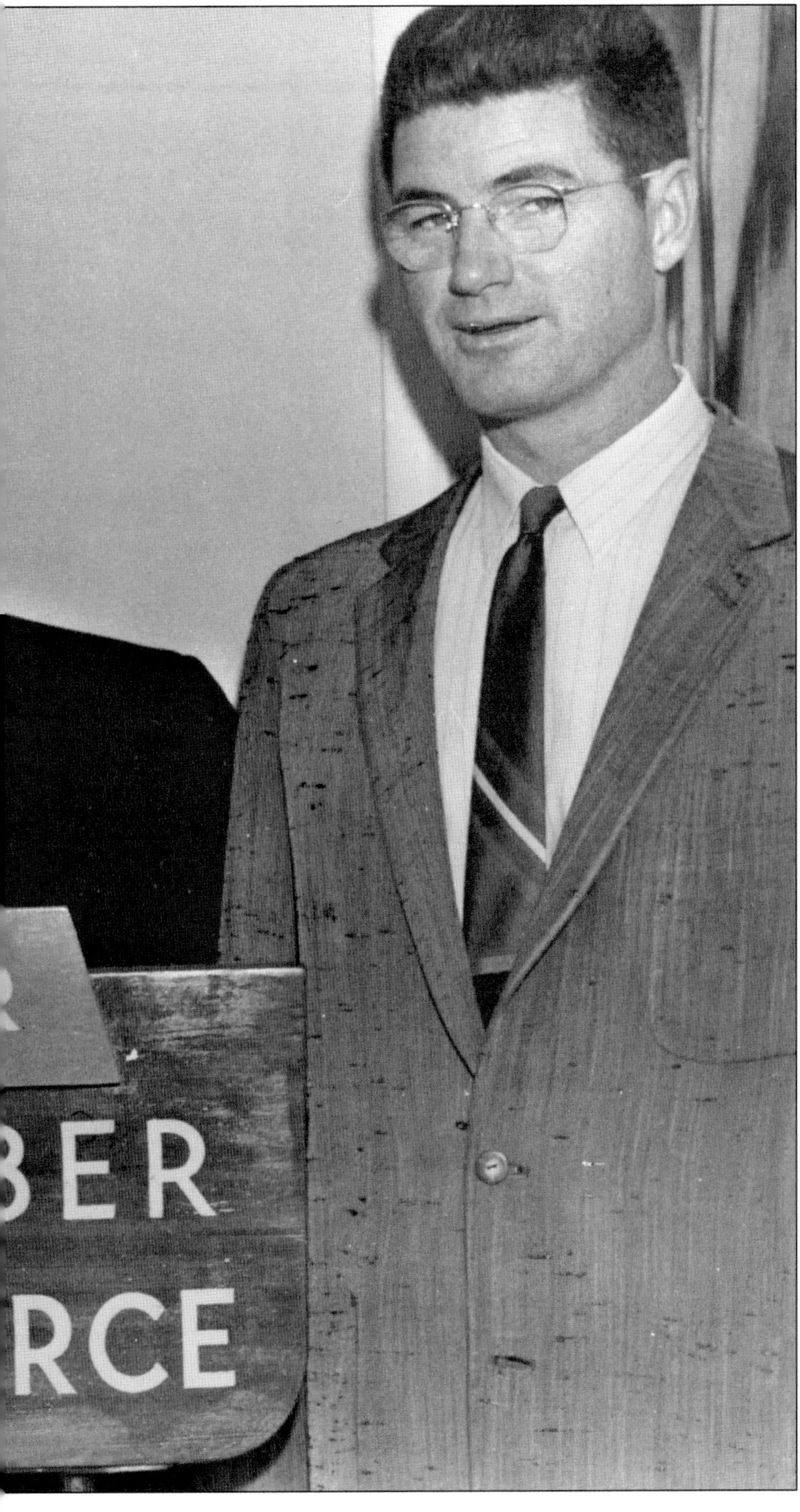

MONTCLAIR CHAMBER OF COMMERCE, OCTOBER 27, 1960. The Montclair Chamber of Commerce celebrates its move to new office space, located at 9661 Central Avenue. Pictured, from left to right, are Mrs. Kitty Hood, Jack George, Mayor Robert Lock, and councilman Paul Frame.

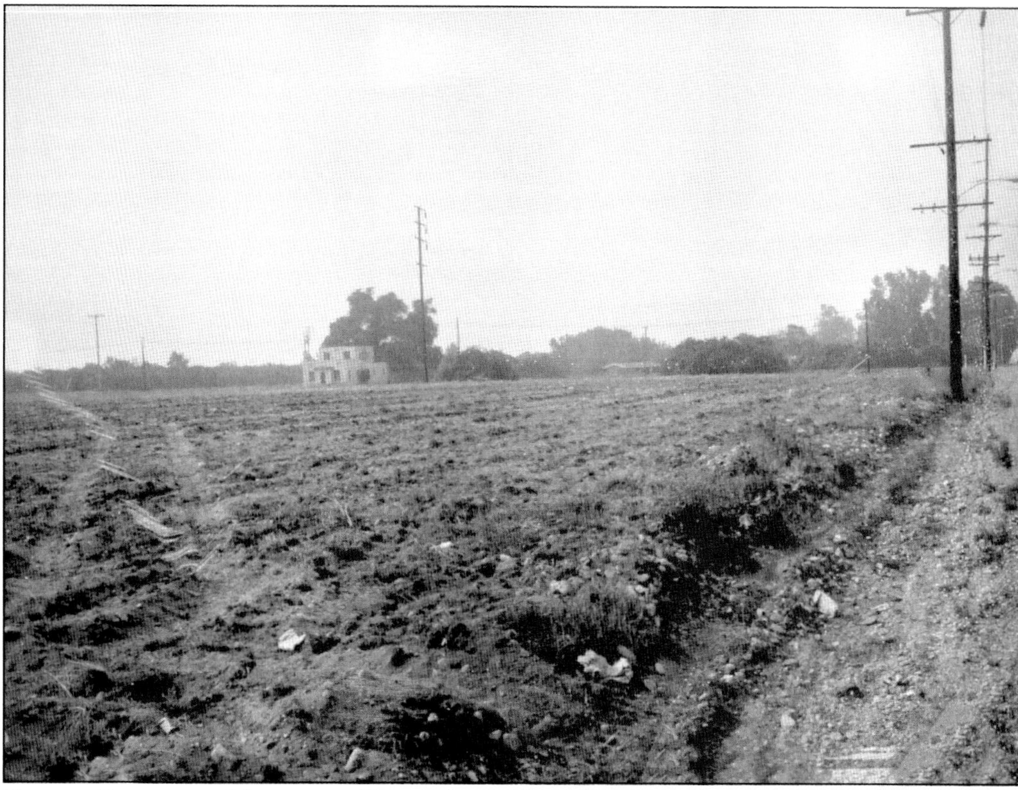

FUTURE SITE OF THE MONTCLAIR PLAZA, JUNE 15, 1966. These photographs are of the northeast corner of Monte Vista Avenue and San Jose Street, the future site of the Montclair Plaza. In the field are orange trees piled for burning.

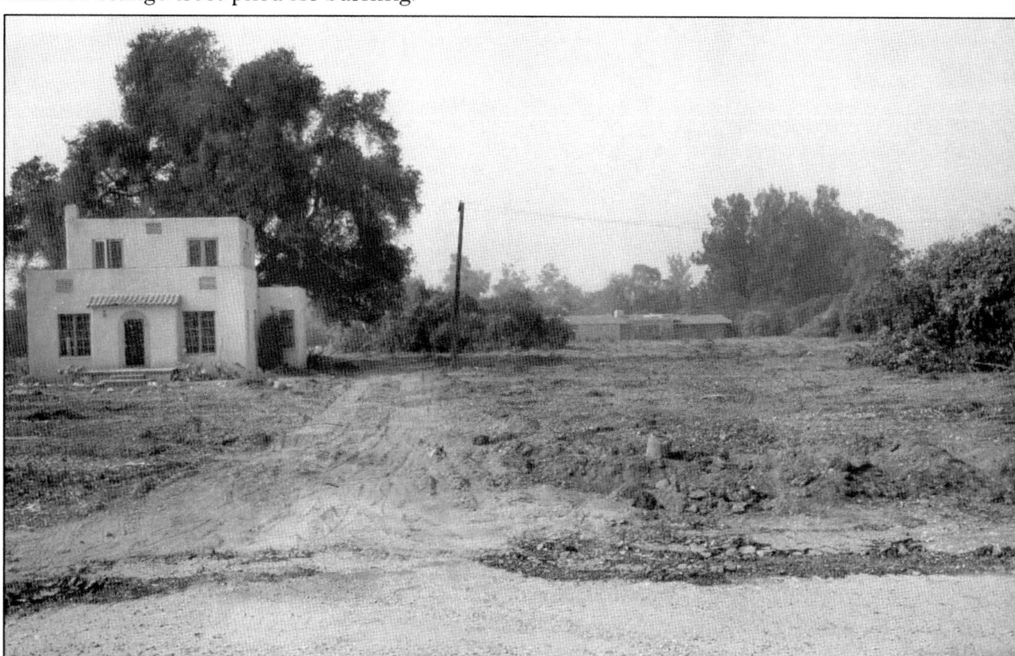

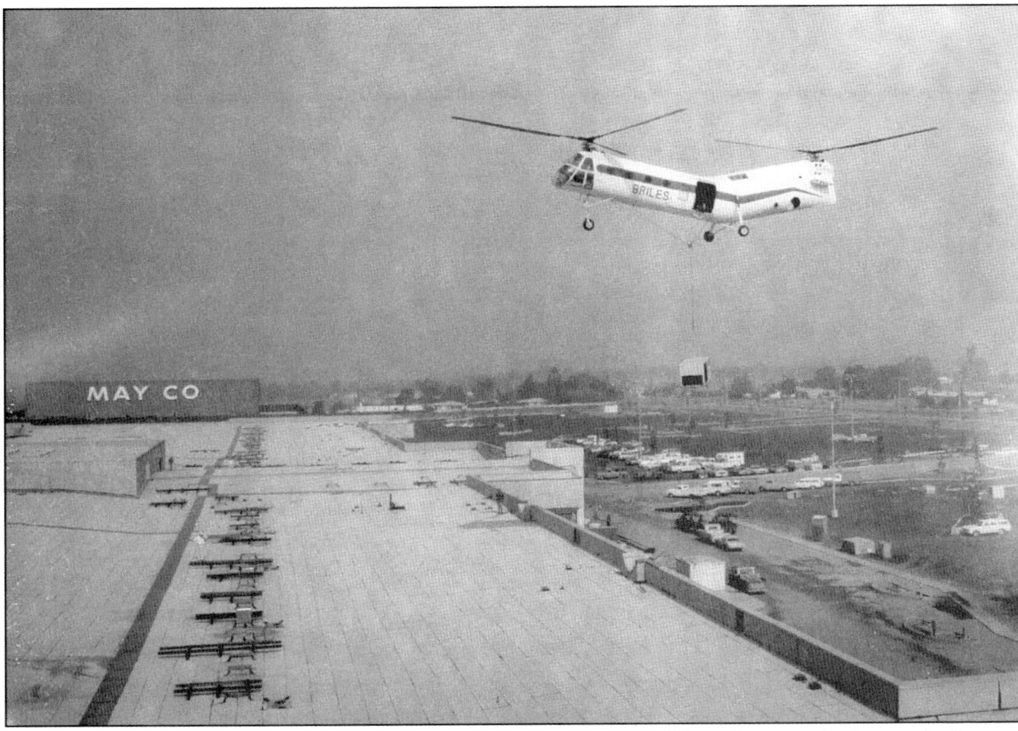

BRINGING IN THE AIR CONDITIONING UNITS, MAY 29, 1968. This photograph shows a helicopter placing the air conditioning units on the almost completed Montclair Plaza.

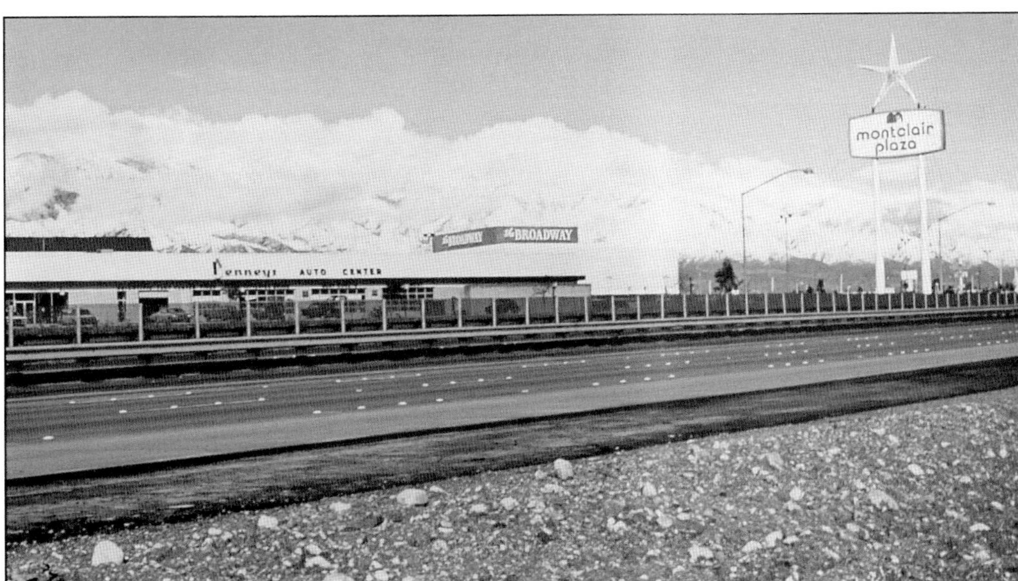

MONTCLAIR PLAZA, 1970. With the picturesque snowcapped San Gabriel Mountains as a backdrop, this photograph shows the completed Montclair Plaza.

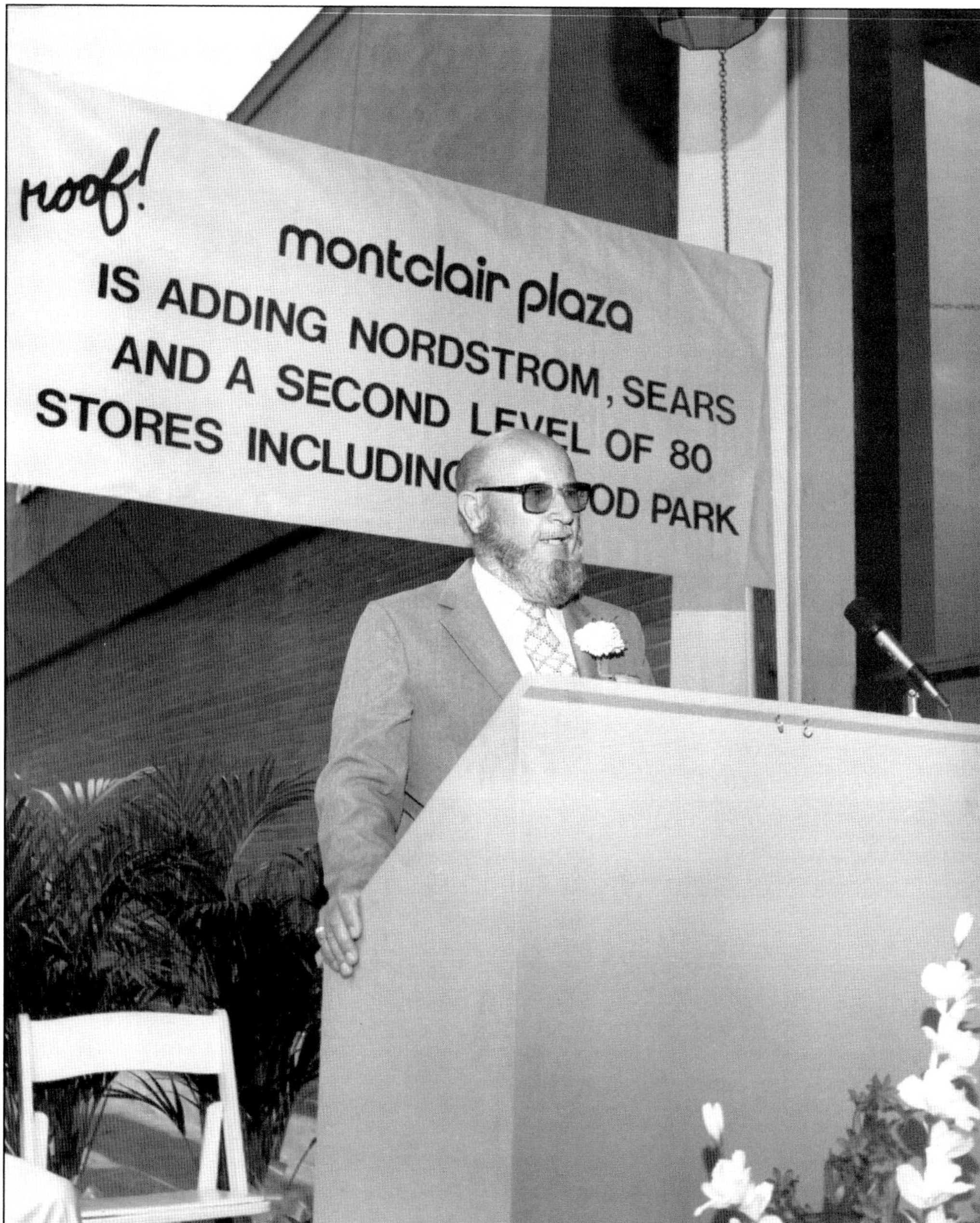

RAISING THE ROOF, C. 1985. Mayor Harold Hayes is seen here speaking about the second level that would be added to the Montclair Plaza. This campaign was called "Raising the Roof." (Courtesy of Charlette Hayes.)

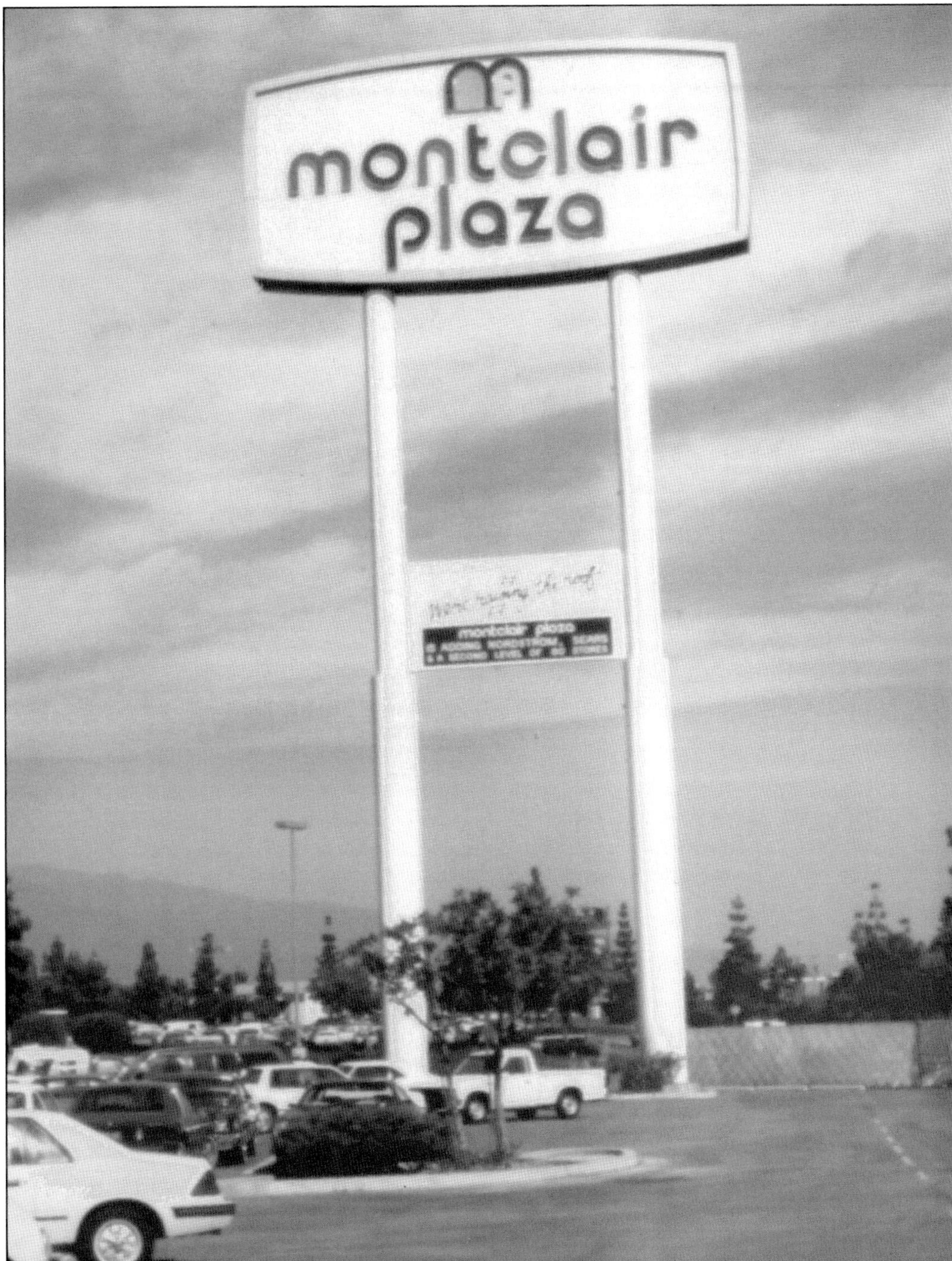

MONTCLAIR PLAZA SIGN, C. 1985. This is the second sign the Montclair Plaza donned. Between the posts is an announcement for the "Raising the Roof" campaign.

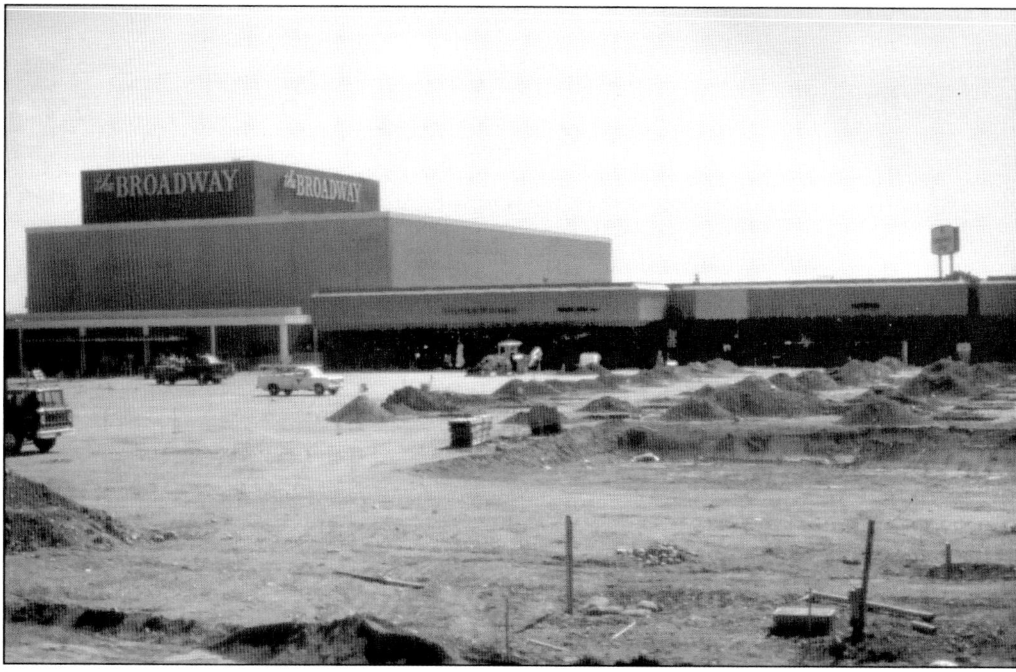

MONTCLAIR PLAZA, C. 1985. Construction is getting ready to begin on the second story addition of the Montclair Plaza.

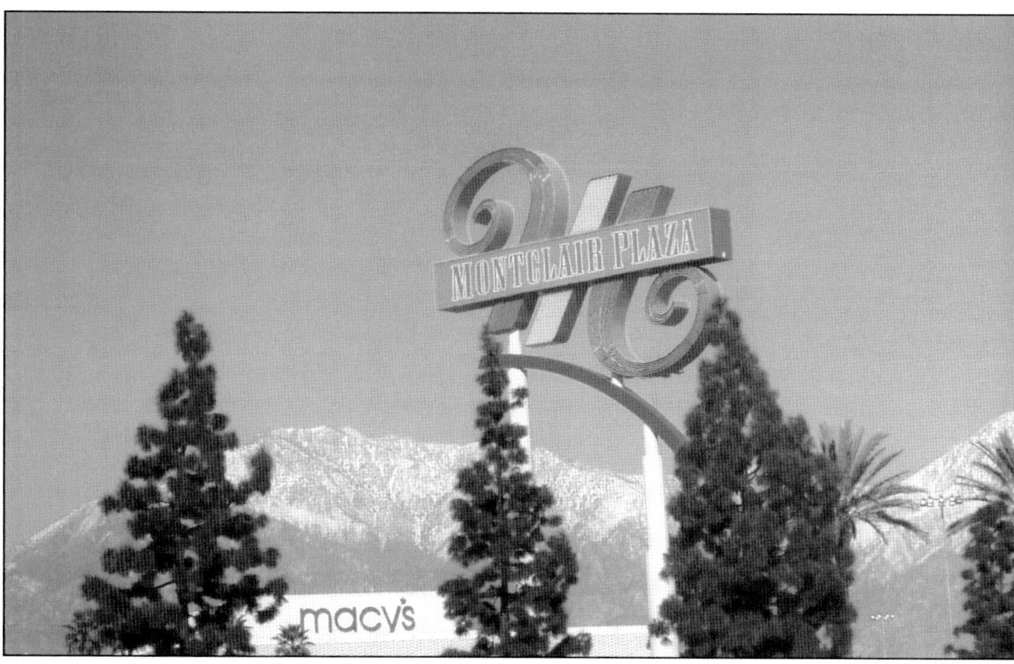

MONTCLAIR PLAZA SIGN, 2004. A view of the Montclair Plaza sign as it is seen from the I-10 Freeway.

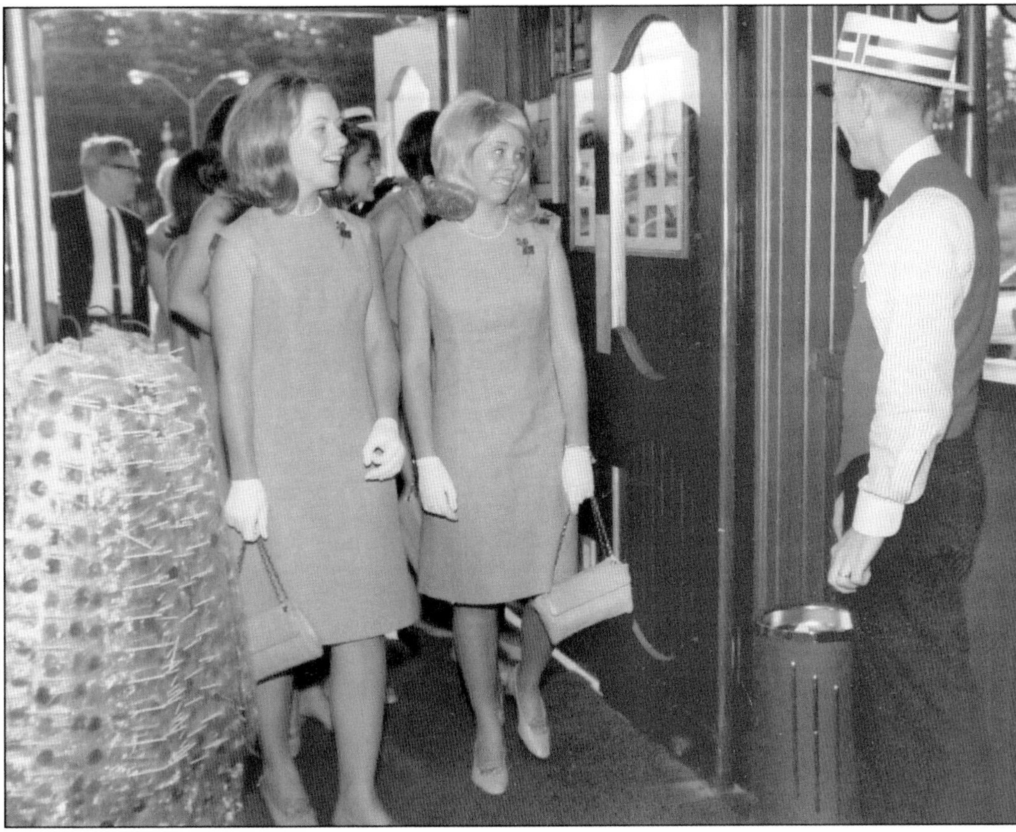

FARRELL'S ICE CREAM PARLOUR RESTAURANT, JUNE 1967. Montclair beauty queens help with the grand opening festivities of Farrell's Ice Cream Parlour Restaurant. Farrell's was located in the northwest corner of the Montclair Plaza parking lot.

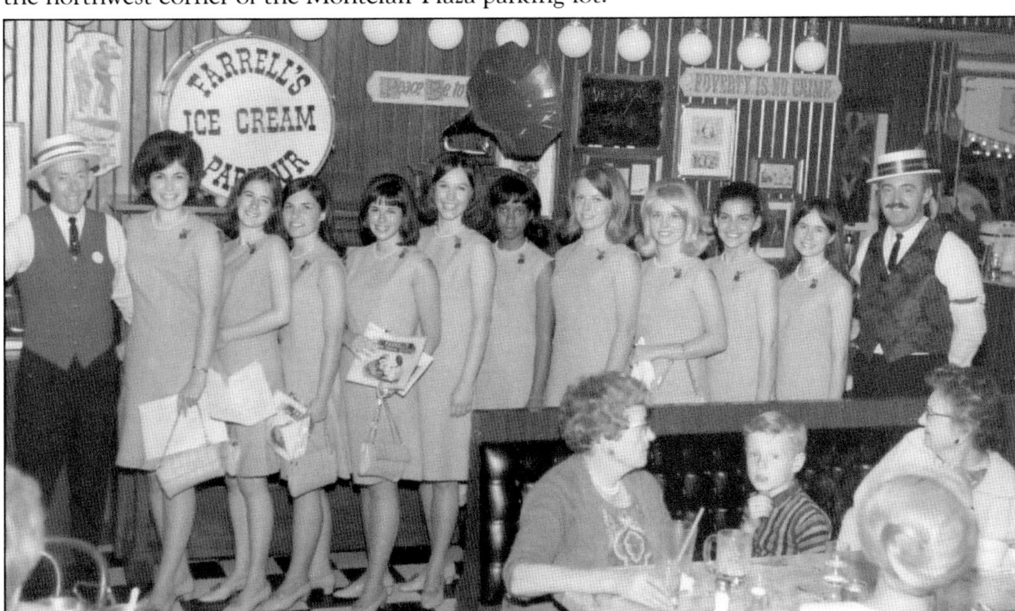

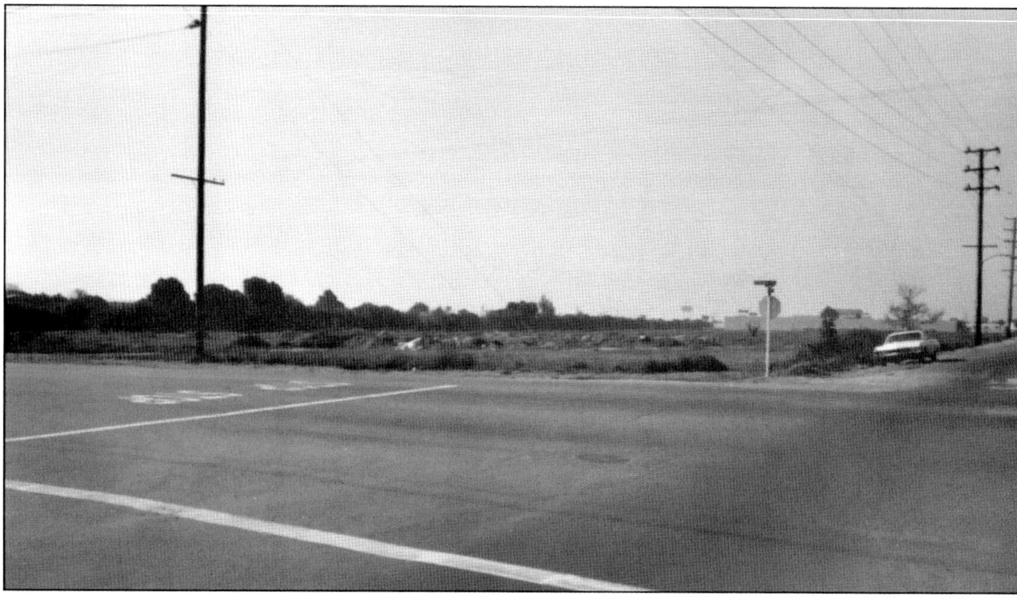

OPEN LAND, JANUARY 10, 1977. This is Moreno Street at Benson Avenue looking at the southwest corner. This spot first housed the Grand Prix Raceway and is now home to Giant RV.

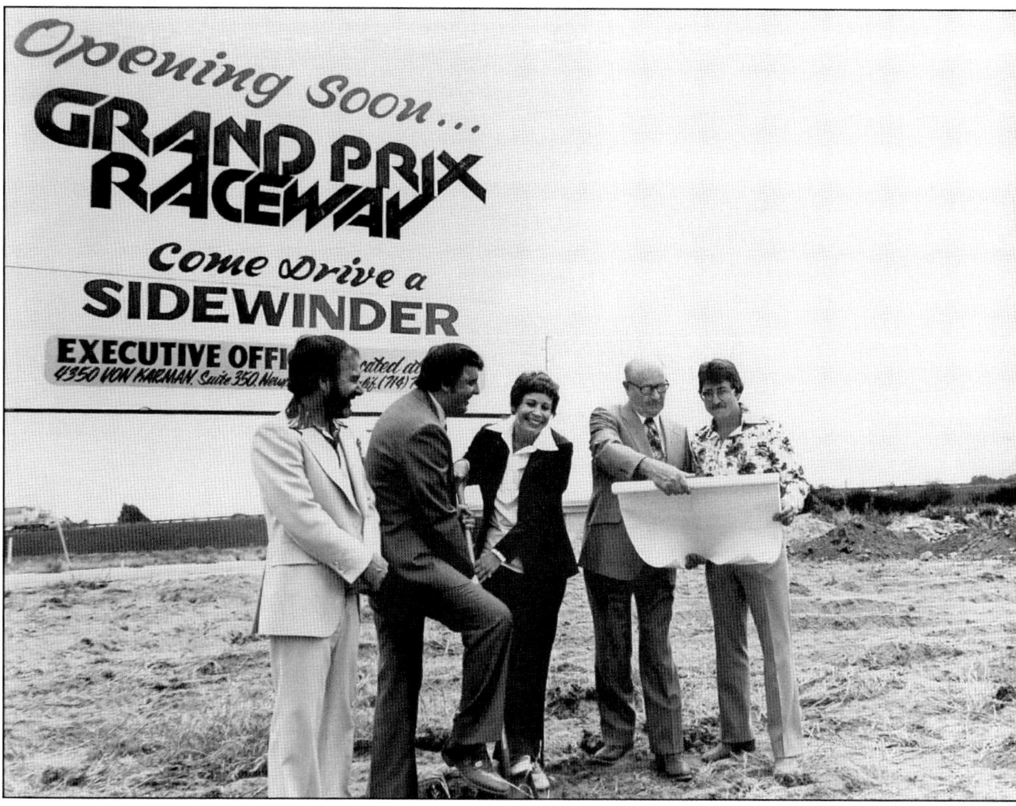

GROUNDBREAKING OF THE GRAND PRIX RACEWAY, C. 1977. The once vacant land on the southwest corner of Moreno Street and Benson Avenue would soon be home to the Grand Prix Raceway. (Courtesy of the Montclair Chamber of Commerce.)

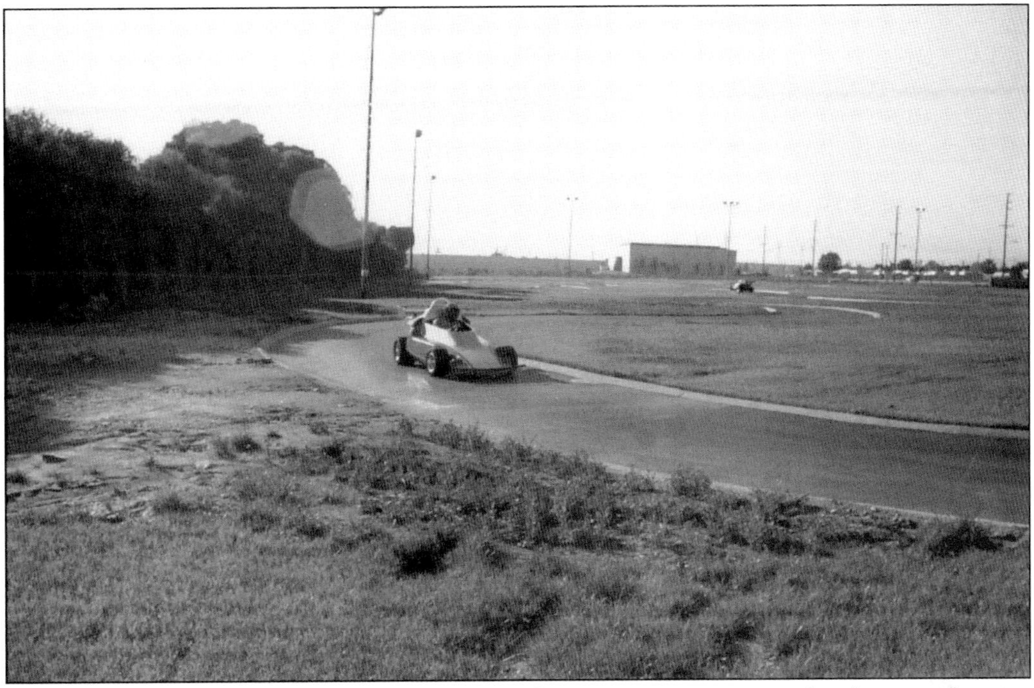

GRAND PRIX RACEWAY, NOVEMBER 15, 1977. Once in operation, many locals enjoyed racing the cars at the Grand Prix Raceway.

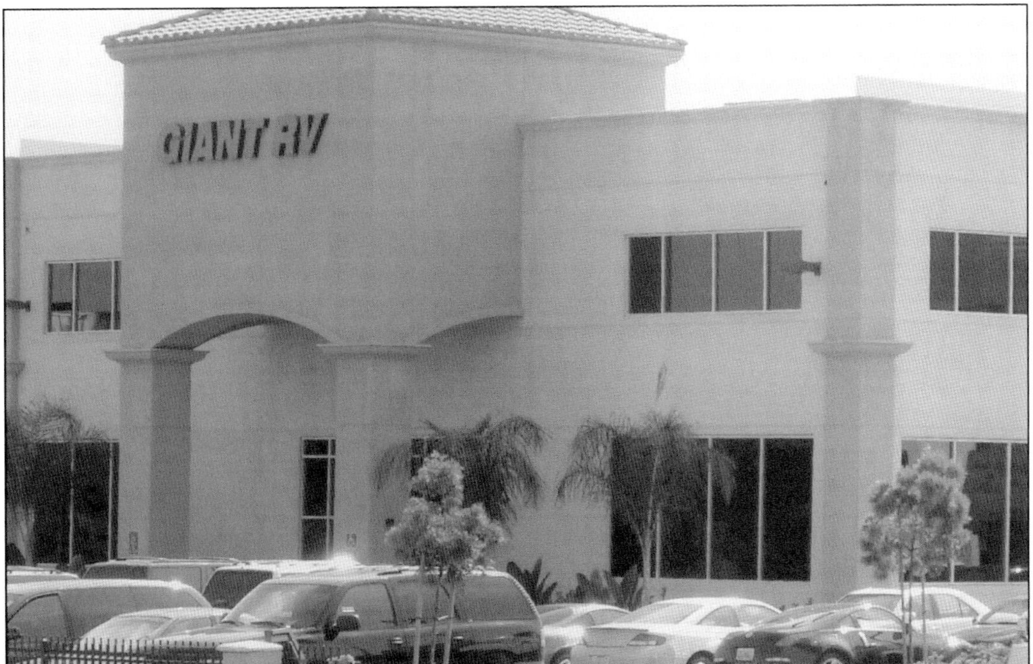

GIANT RV, 2005. The land once occupied by the Grand Prix Raceway is now a Giant RV, California's largest dealer of recreational vehicles.

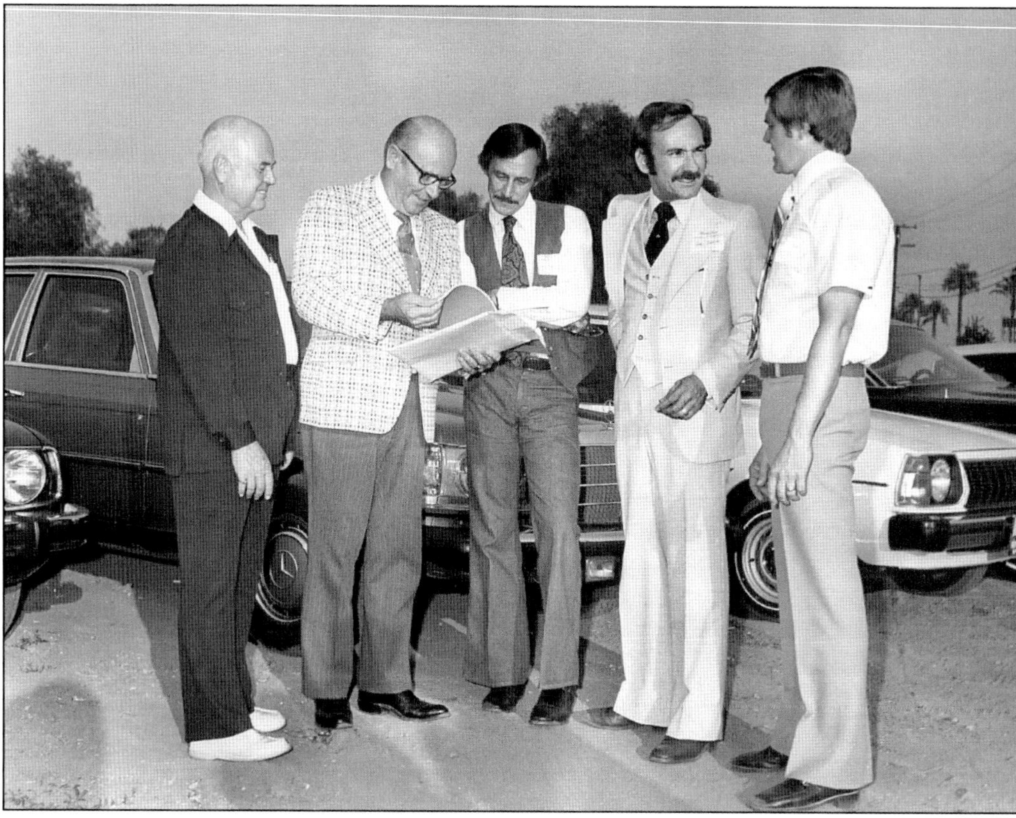

BUSINESS IN MONTCLAIR, C. 1970. Members of the Montclair Chamber of Commerce discuss future business growth with Mayor Harold Hayes (second from the left). (Courtesy of the Montclair Chamber of Commerce.)

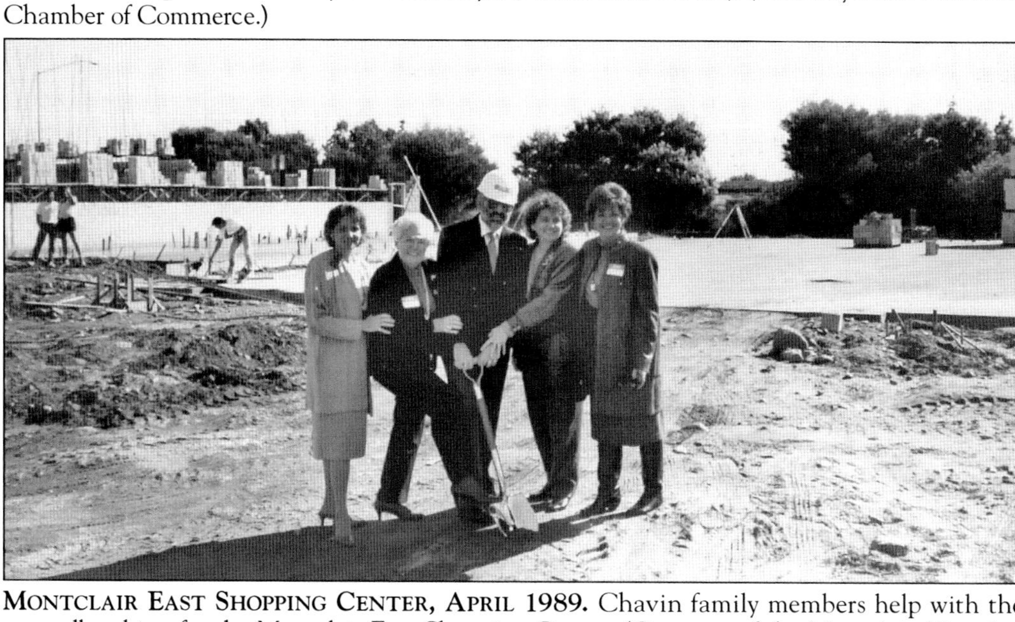

MONTCLAIR EAST SHOPPING CENTER, APRIL 1989. Chavin family members help with the groundbreaking for the Montclair East Shopping Center. (Courtesy of the Montclair Chamber of Commerce.)

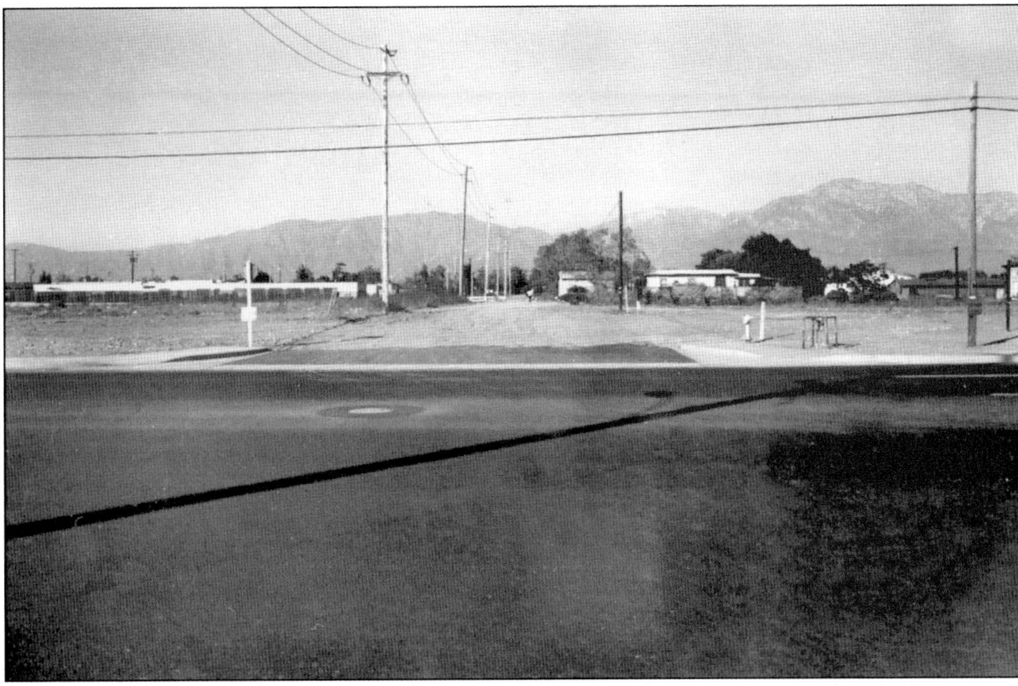

VIEW ON MORENO STREET, NOVEMBER 15, 1977. This photograph was taken looking north on Vernon Avenue from Moreno Street. The photograph below shows what this corner looks like today.

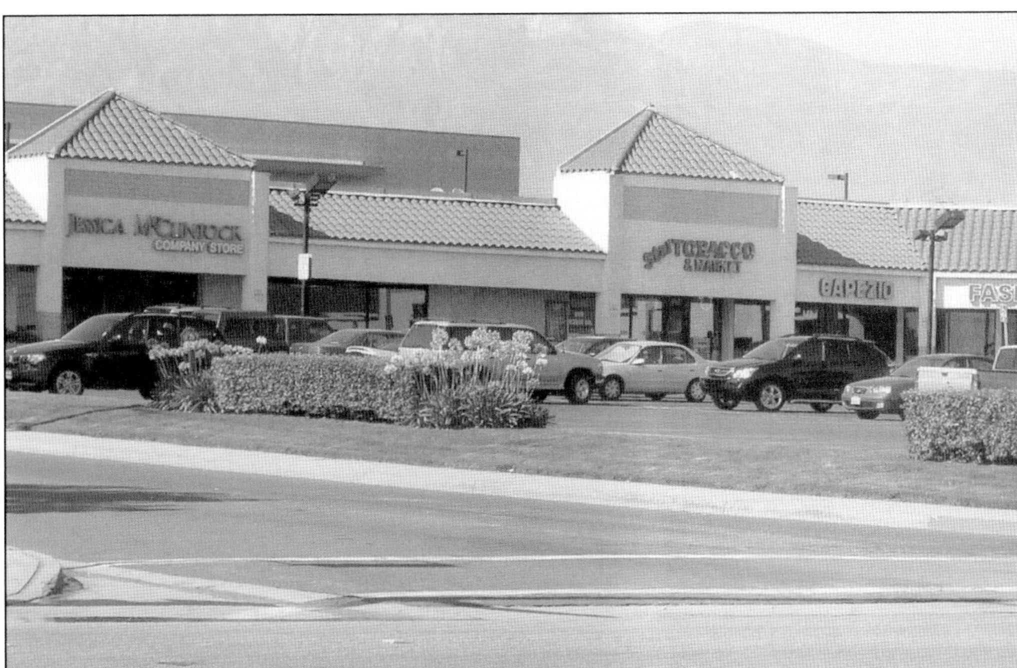

RETAIL DEVELOPMENT, JUNE 2005. What was once vacant land, as seen above, today houses some of the retail development located in Montclair.

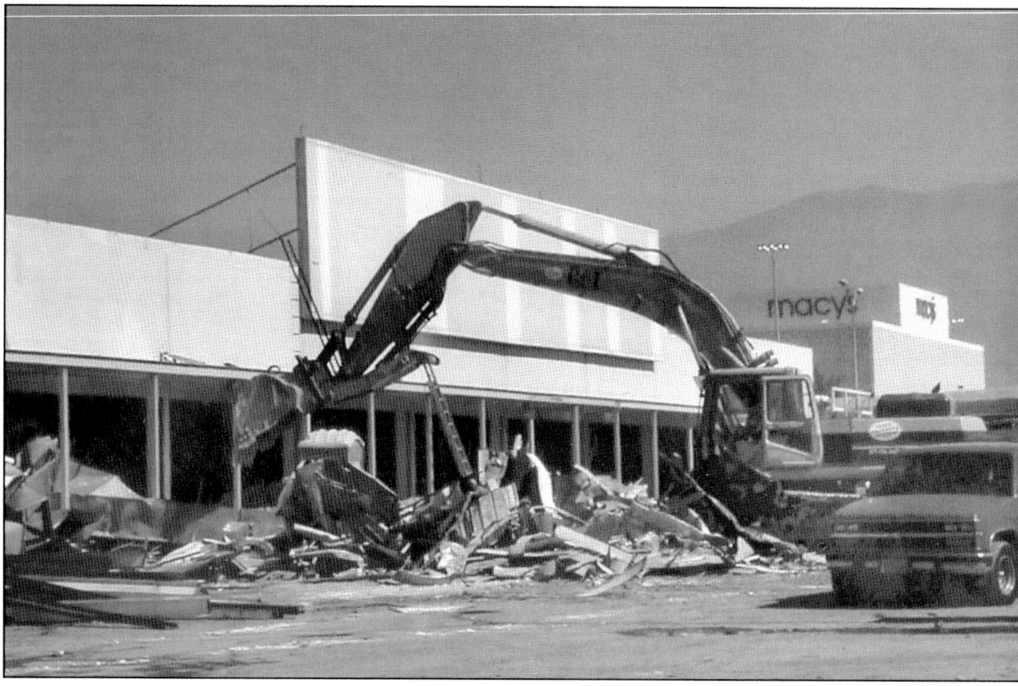

PROGRESS IN MONTCLAIR, 2005. Kmart, which originally opened in 1964, was demolished in 2001 (above) to clear the way for a new Costco Wholesale store (below) to be built. Costco is located on the northwest corner of Palo Verde Street and Central Avenue.

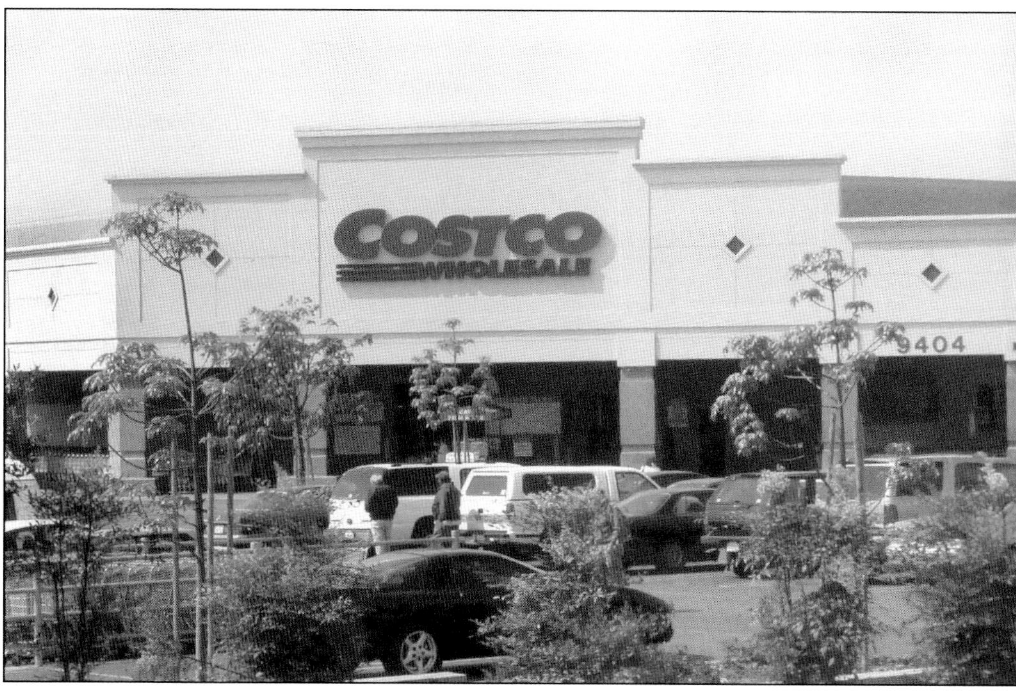

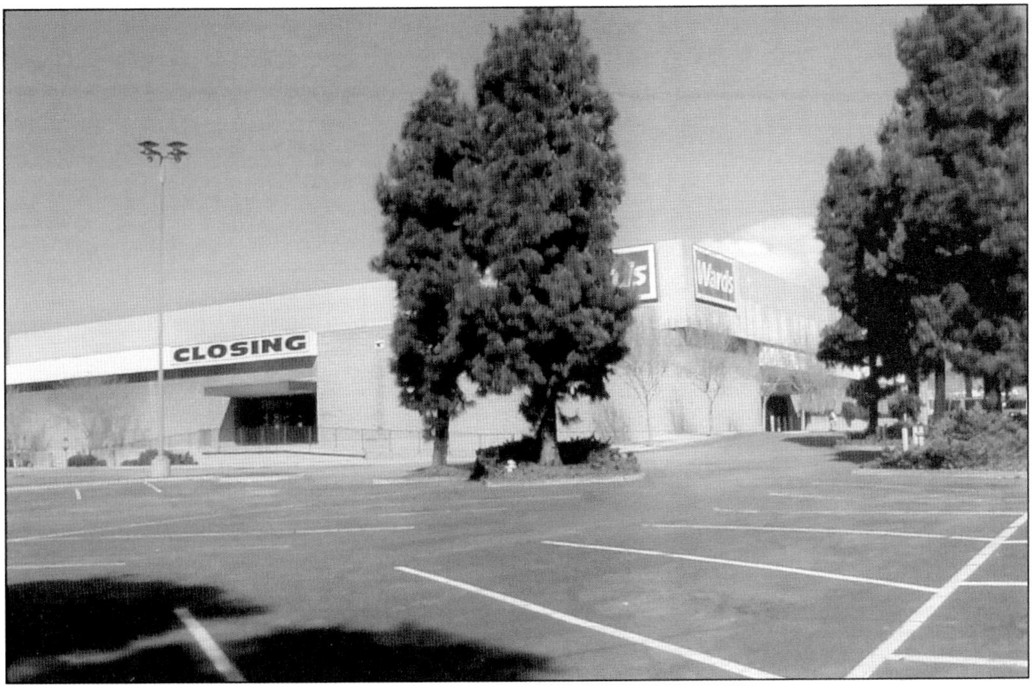

Out With the Old, in With the New, 2001. The Montgomery Ward building, located on Central Avenue, is shown above before its demolition. Once the demolition was complete, a new 136,000-square-foot Target store was put in its place (below).

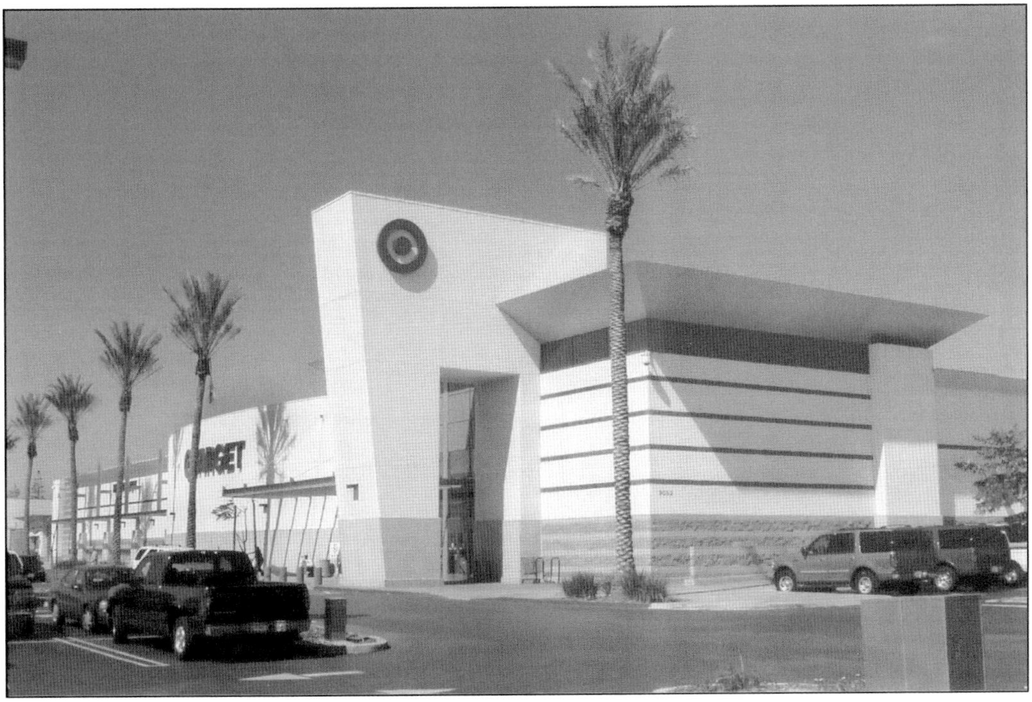

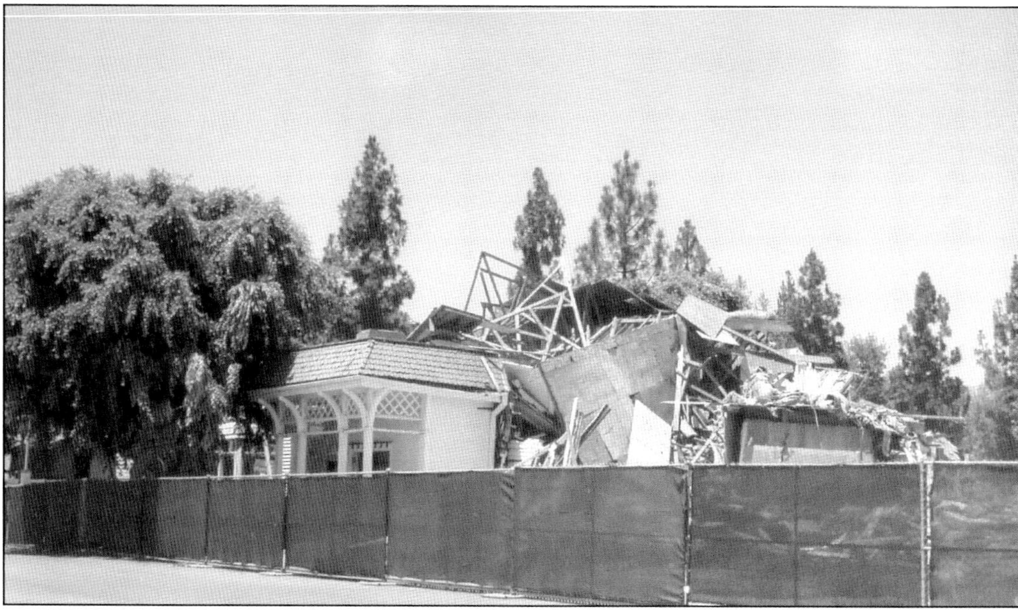

DEMOLITION OF CRESCENT CITY CREOLE RESTAURANT, 2004. This building was once home to the Big Yellow House restaurant. Because of the restaurant's architecture, many residents were concerned that a historic home was being demolished. All were pleased to find out that this landmark was actually built in 1980 by the Big Yellow House restaurant chain. Today Chili's Grill and Bar occupies the space.

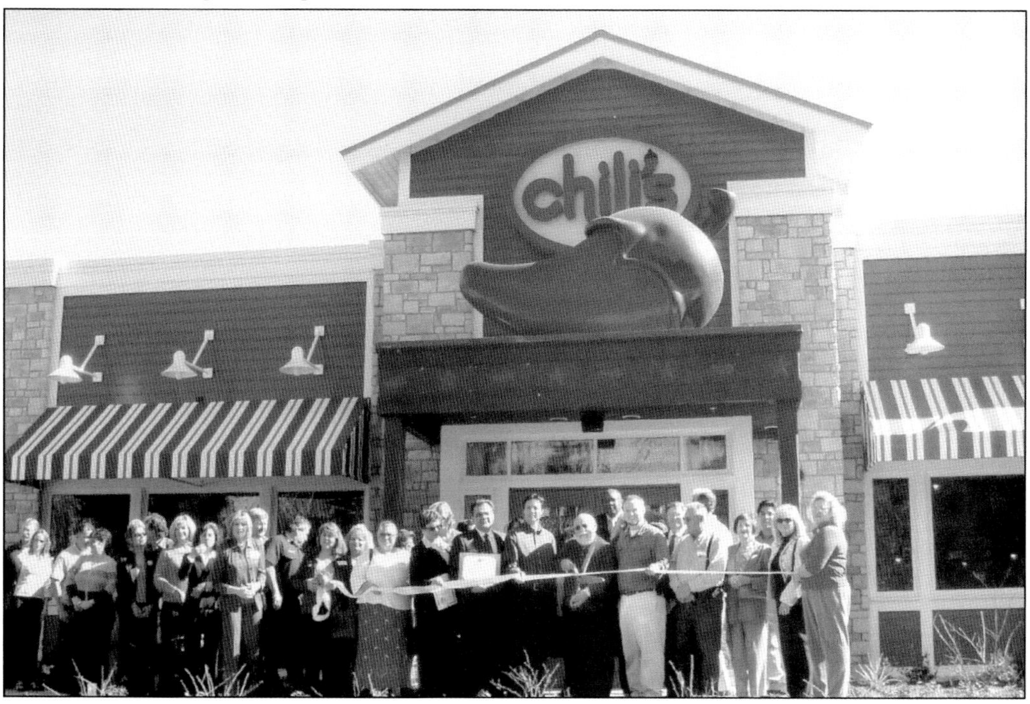

CHILI'S RIBBON CUTTING, 2005. Not too long after the demolition of Crescent City Creole (top), Chili's held its grand opening. Many local residents have already enjoyed the casual dining the restaurant has to offer.

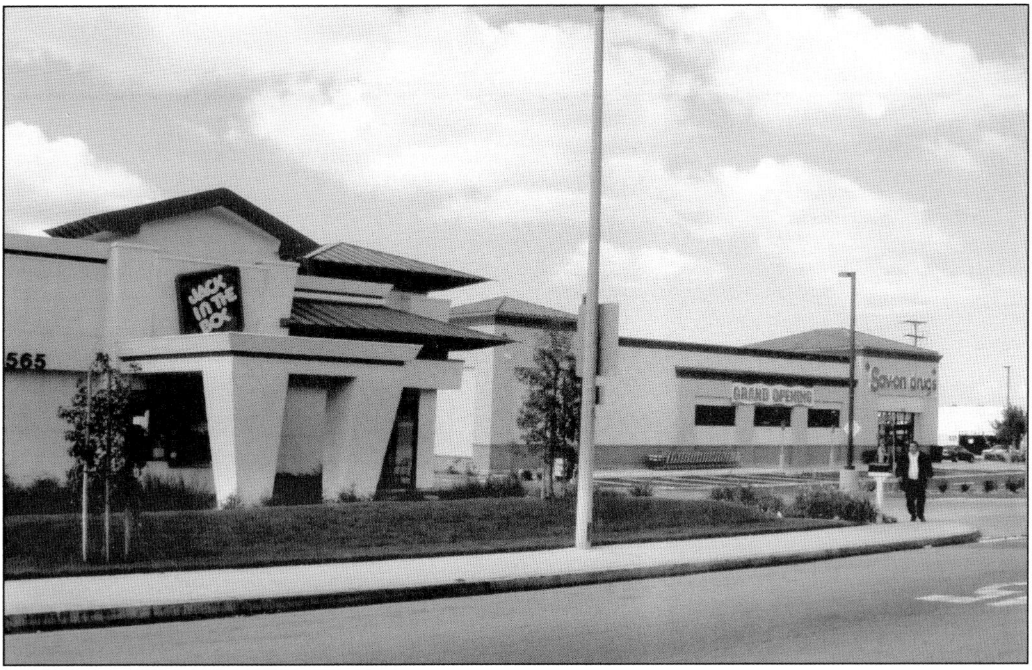

NEW BUSINESSES, 2004. In an effort to revitalize Holt Boulevard, many new businesses are being constructed along that route. Jack in the Box and Save-On Drugs are only two of many new companies coming to Montclair.

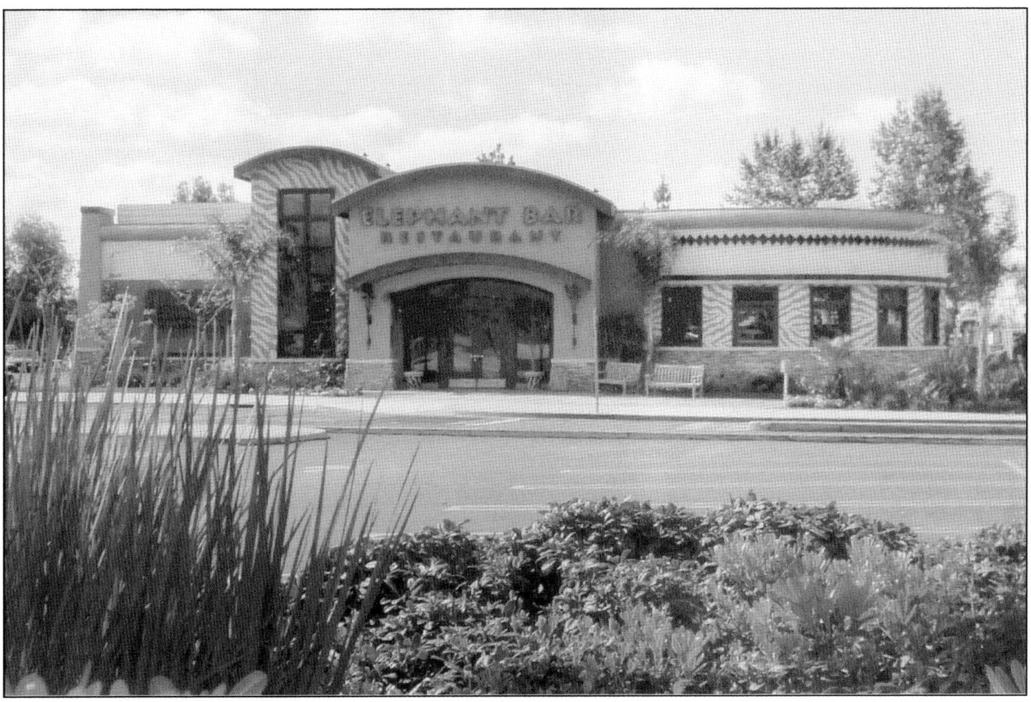

ELEPHANT BAR RESTAURANT, 2002. Opened in spring 2002, the Elephant Bar Restaurant has an exotic, fun, and festive menu featuring international cuisine.

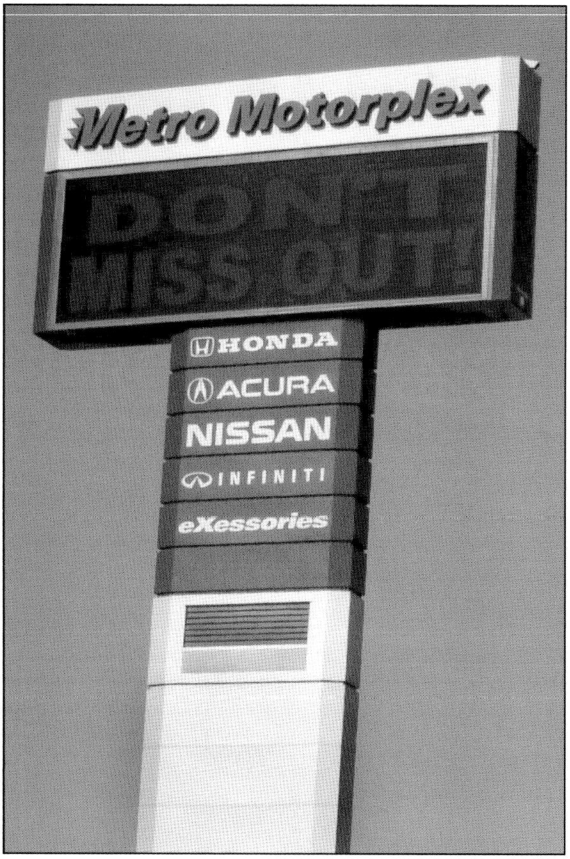

METRO MOTORPLEX, 2005. Montclair, being situated on the I-10 Freeway, is an ideal location for many businesses. Metro Motorplex is comprised of four car dealerships that take advantage of this prime location.

BORDERS, 2004. Borders Books and Music, located in Montclair's Entertainment Plaza, is surrounded by nine popular dining establishments and the Montclair Plaza regional mall. Other retailers in the immediate area include Ethan Allen, Linen's 'N Things, and Bally's Total Fitness.

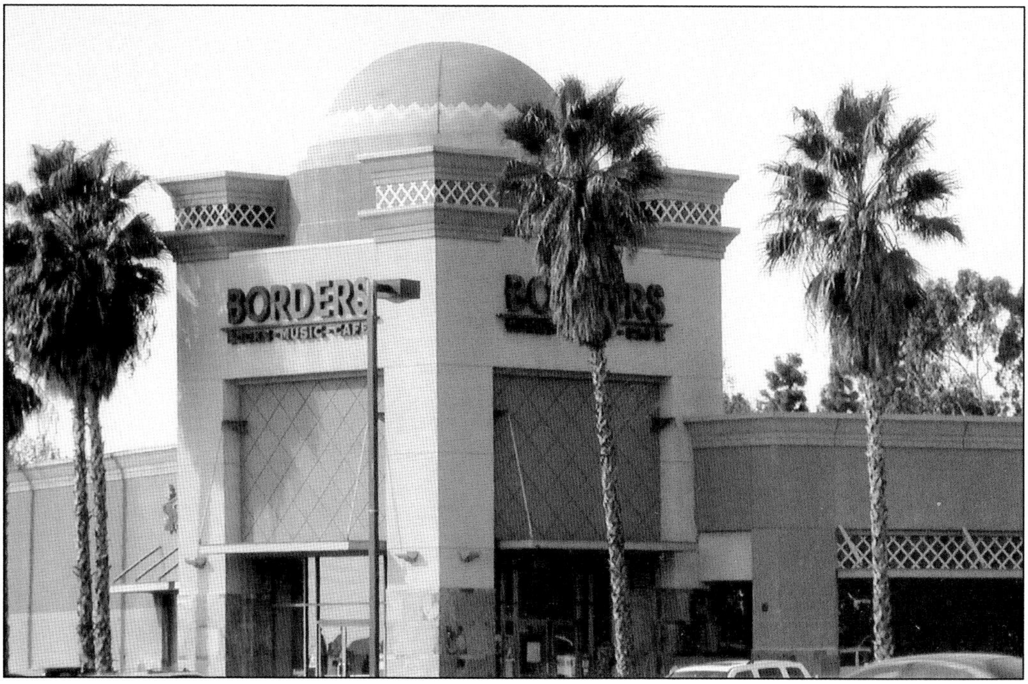

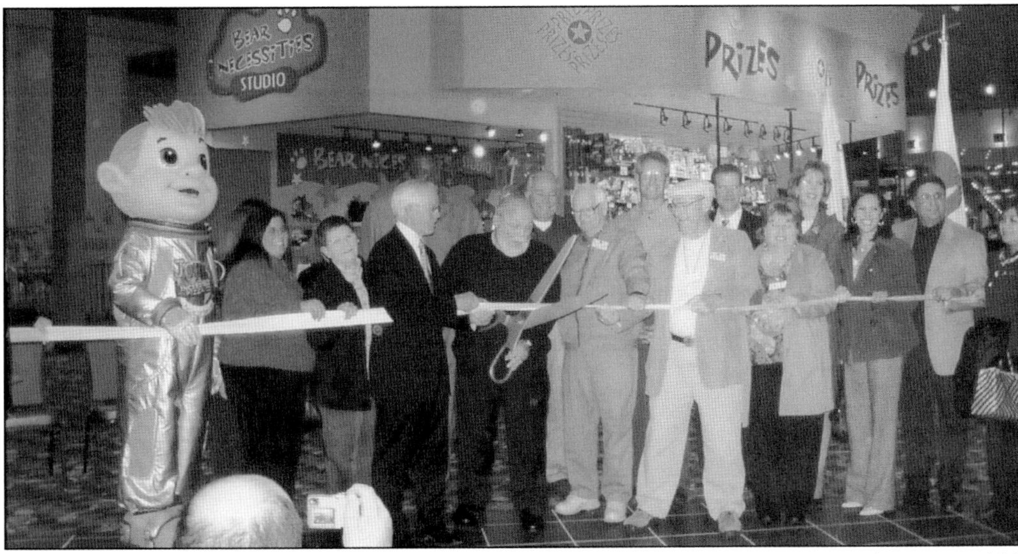

RIBBON CUTTING FOR JOHN'S INCREDIBLE PIZZA COMPANY, JANUARY 2005. John's Incredible Pizza Company offers a unique dining and entertainment experience, occupying 50,000 square feet of the former House2Home building located on the northwest corner of Moreno Street and Central Avenue. During its preview party, the 600 estimated guests enjoyed all-you-can-eat pizza, pasta, salads, and hours of entertainment in the arcade/gaming area. One hundred percent of the requested $15 donation per guest was split by the local Spanish Trails Girl Scouts Council and the Boy Scouts of America Old Baldy Council.

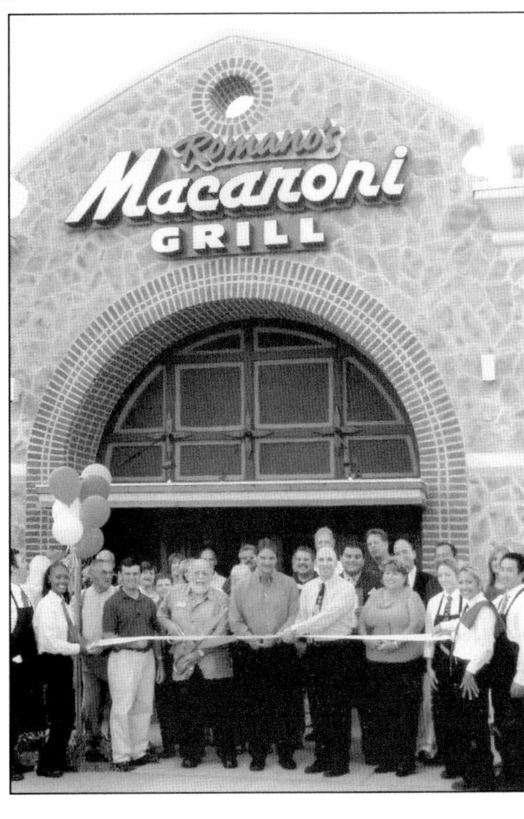

ROMANO'S MACARONI GRILL, 2004. Situated at the southern end of the Montclair Plaza, Romano's Macaroni Grill held its grand opening in 2004. The Macaroni Grill is neighbor to many other restaurants, including the Elephant Bar Restaurant, Acapulco Restaurant, Stuart Anderson's Black Angus, Chili's, Tony Roma's, Olive Garden, Red Lobster, and Applebee's.

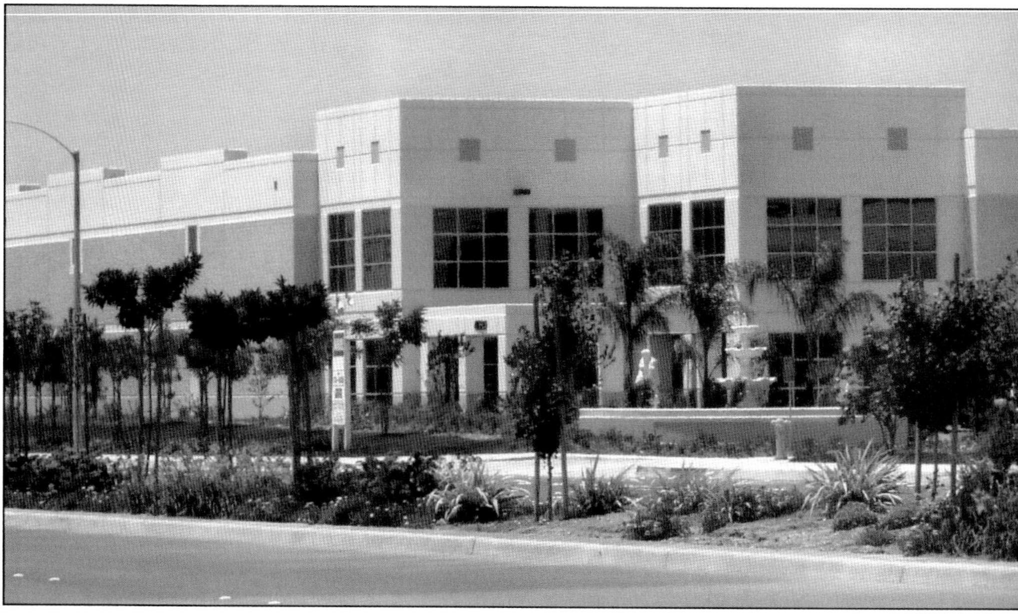

TOPLINE BUSINESS PARK, 2004. In June 2003, the Montclair Redevelopment Agency, together with the San Bernardino County Redevelopment Agency, adopted the Mission Boulevard Joint Redevelopment Project Area. This project area encompasses acreage in both jurisdictions along Mission Boulevard. The Topline Business Park was one of the businesses that opened as a result of this joint venture.

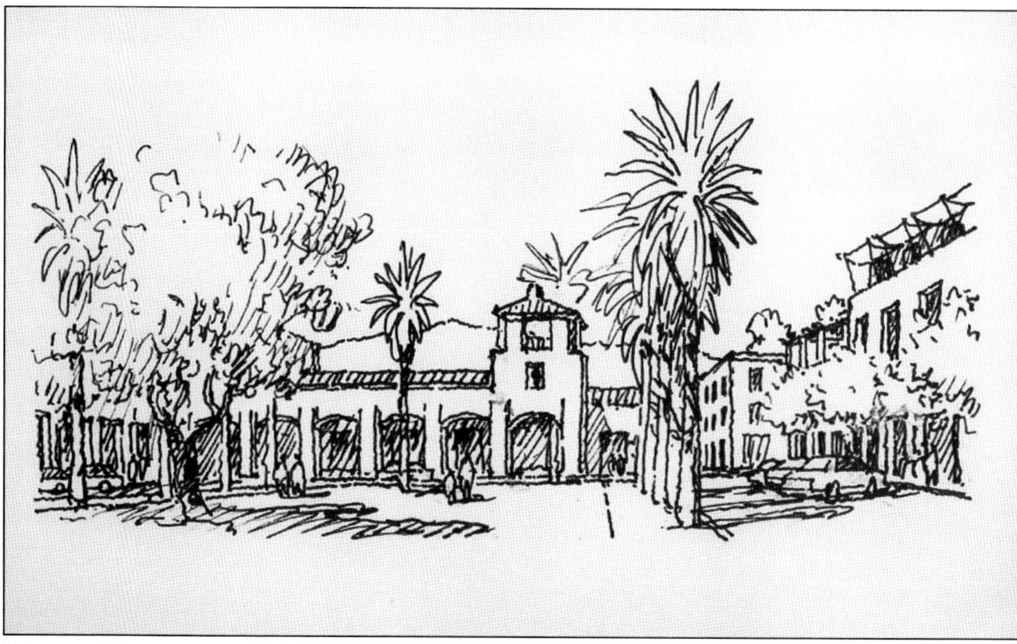

NORTH MONTCLAIR, 2005. Montclair continues expanding its business district. This is a conceptual drawing of a portion of the North Montclair Downtown Specific Plan. The proposed North Downtown Specific Plan is a major land-use plan under development. The plan will create new development opportunities for a mixed-use, transit-oriented, downtown district between the Metrolink station, the future Gold Line station, and the Montclair Plaza fashion mall.

Three

PROTECTING MONTCLAIR

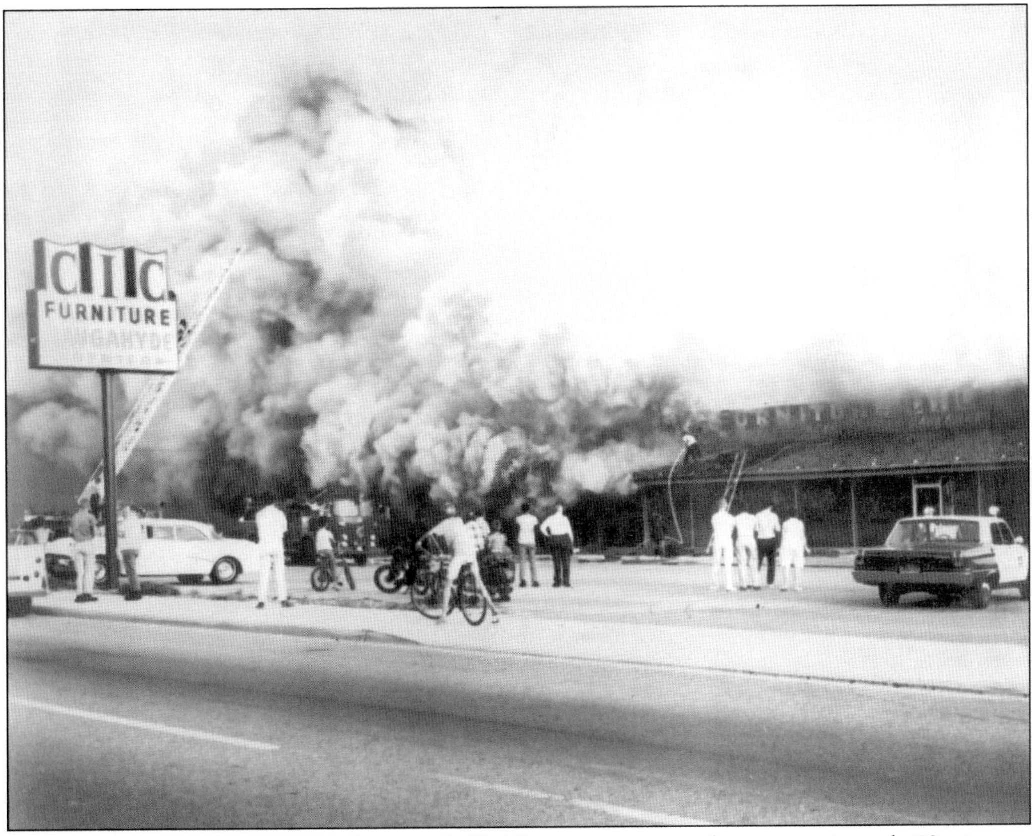

FIRE AT THE CIC FURNITURE STORE, 1965. This picture was taken approximately 10 minutes after emergency crews arrived at the scene.

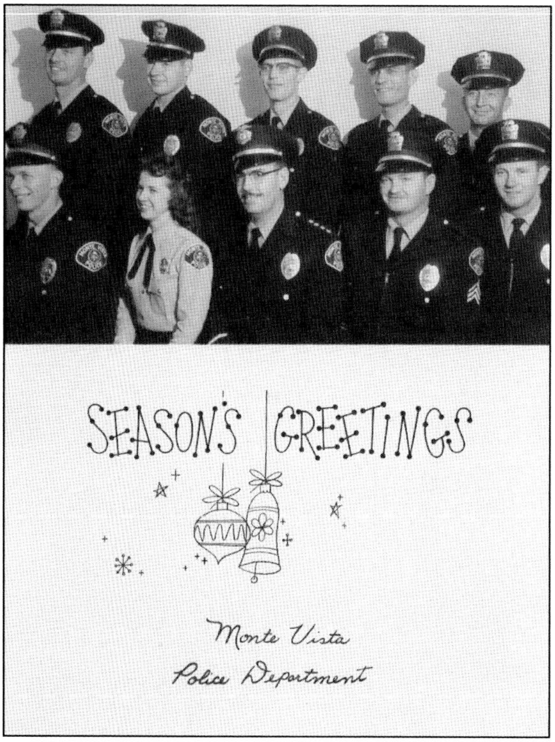

MONTE VISTA POLICE DEPARTMENT HOLIDAY POSTCARD, C. 1957. This holiday postcard was sent out by the Monte Vista Police Department.

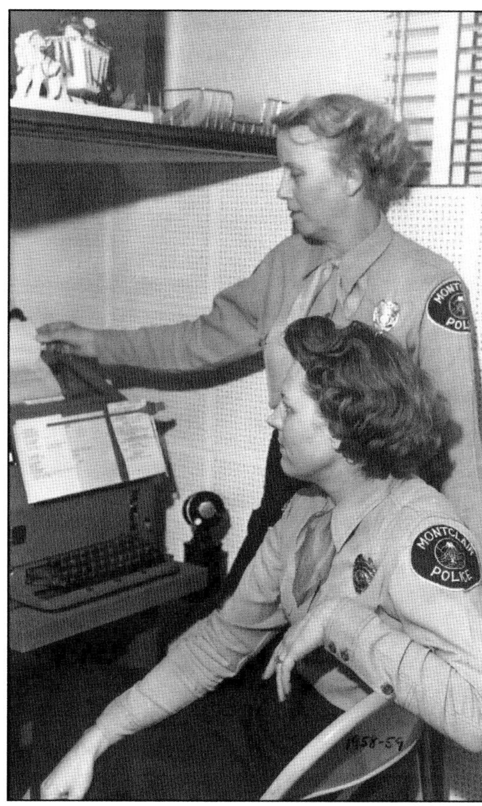

POLICE DISPATCHERS, C. 1958. Claudia Kirshnan is sitting; the other dispatcher is unidentified.

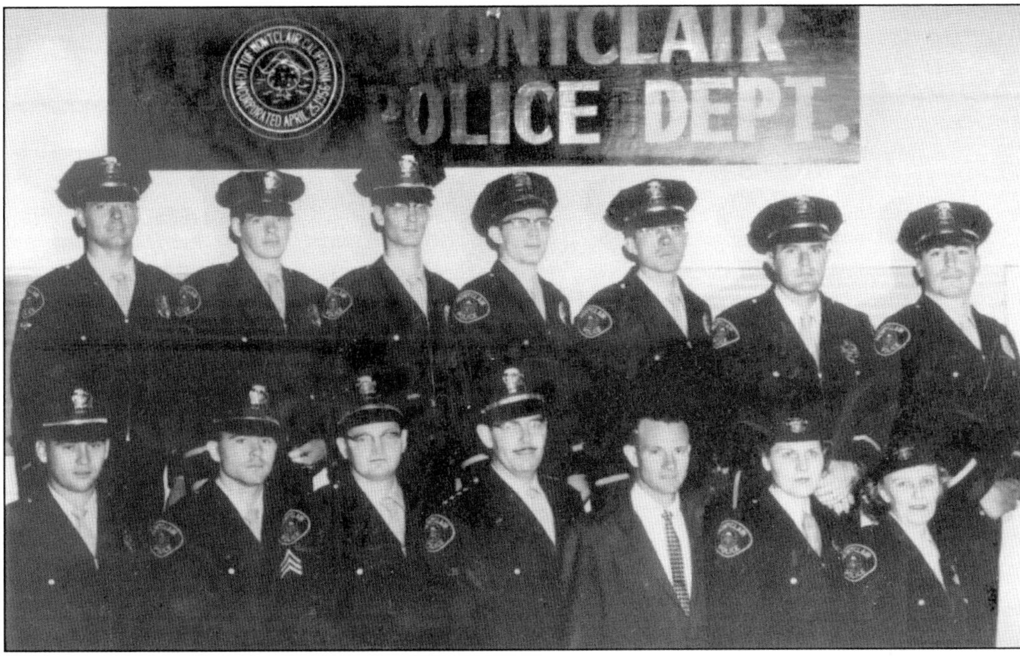

MONTCLAIR POLICE DEPARTMENT, *1958*. This photograph was used as the police department's annual Christmas postcard. Pictured, from left to right, are (first row) Don Sanders, Billy King, Louis Van Norman, Chief Benjamin Smith, Detective James Blacksher, Claudia Kirshnan, and Marjorie Bates; (second row) Walt Ryan, J. D. Miller, Andrew Farthing, Noel Whitman, Dave Martin, Richard Pettit, and Salomon Valdez Jr.

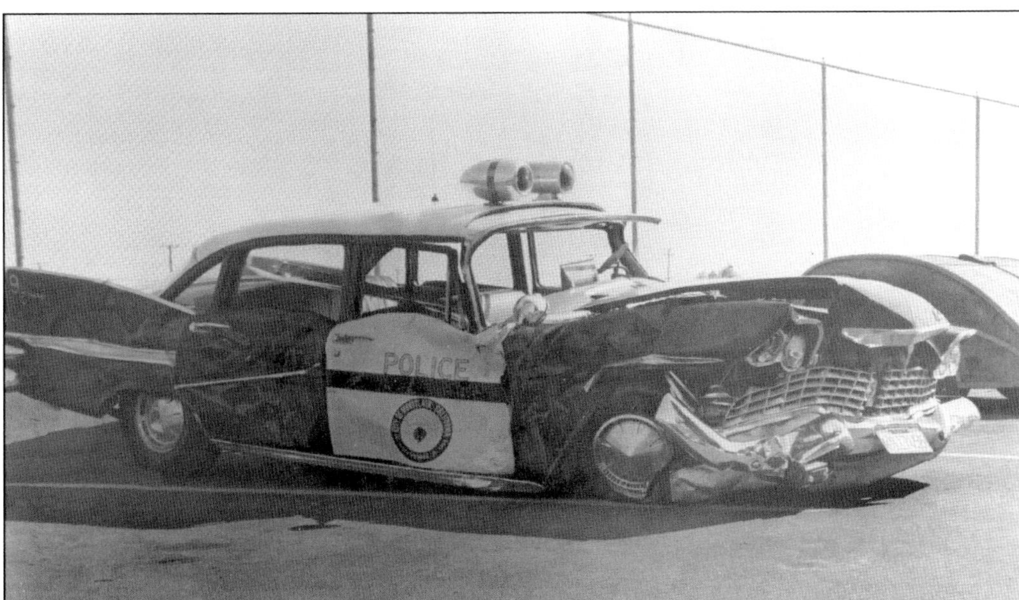

WRECKED POLICE CAR, JUNE 1959. Virtually demolished, this is the police car that Officer David Martin was driving when he was seriously injured in a serious automobile accident on Holt Boulevard. Although Martin was dazed and semiconscious, he managed to report the accident.

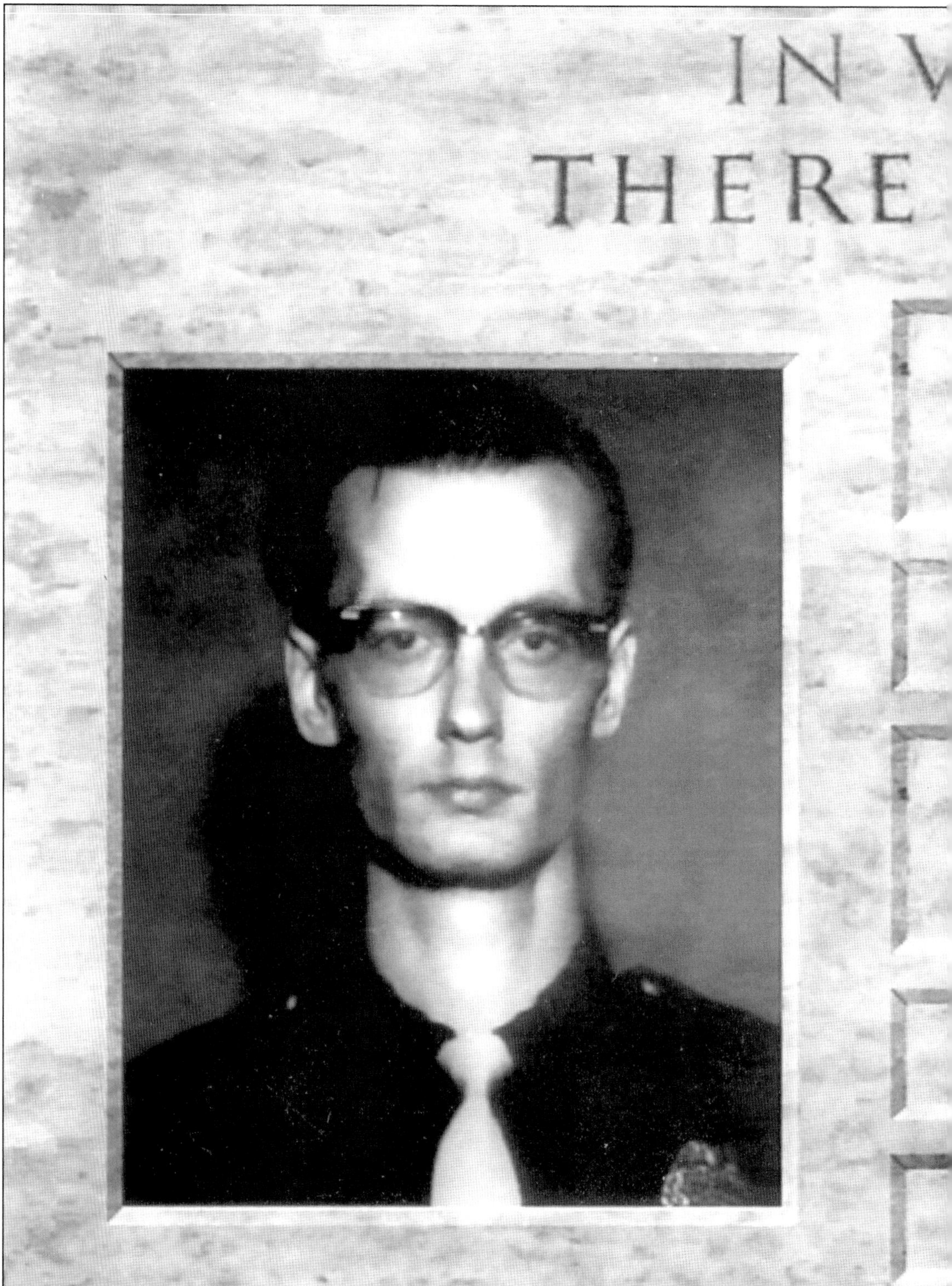

FALLEN MONTCLAIR POLICE OFFICER, 1961. On June 18, 1961, Andrew W. Farthing was killed

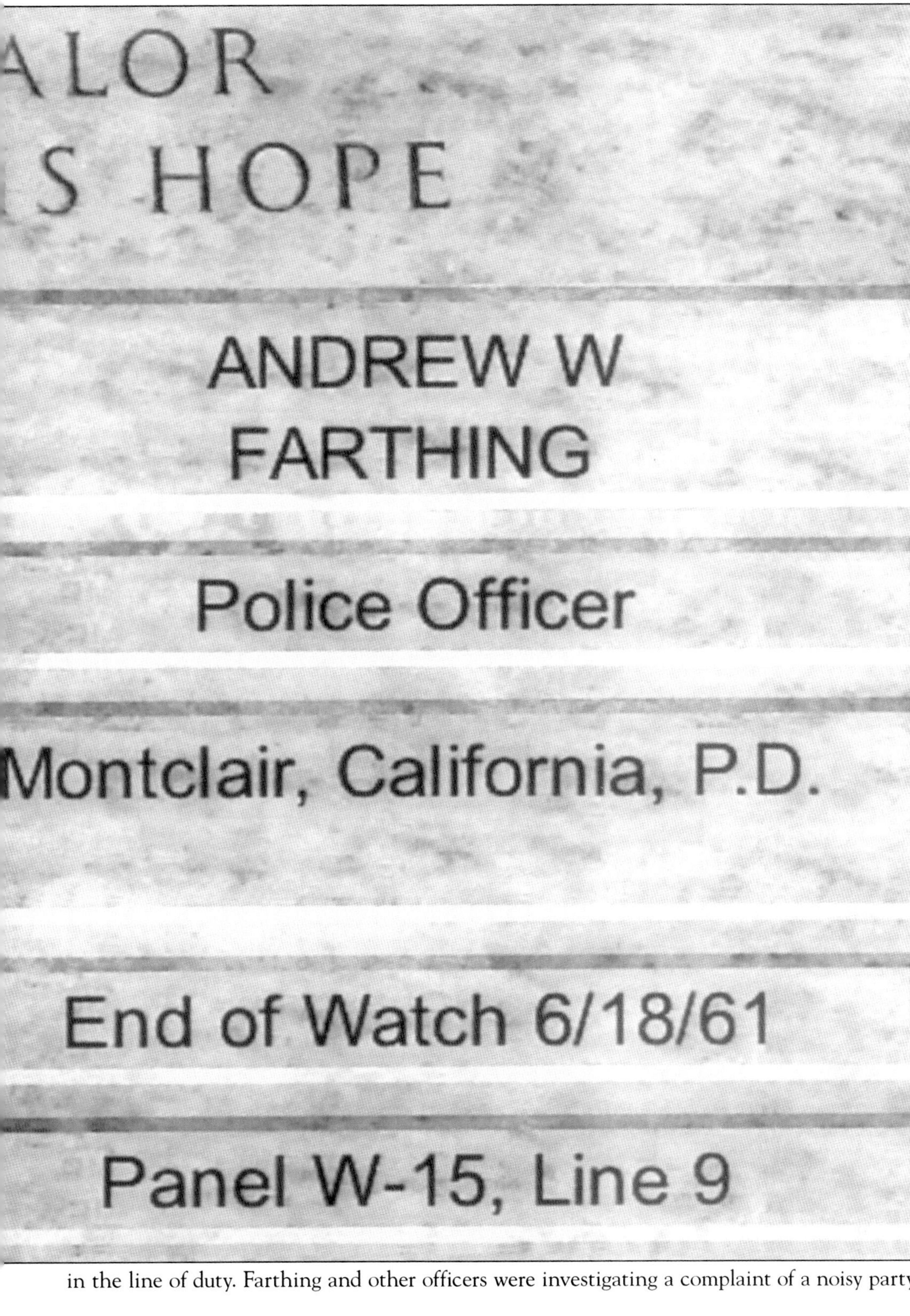

in the line of duty. Farthing and other officers were investigating a complaint of a noisy party.

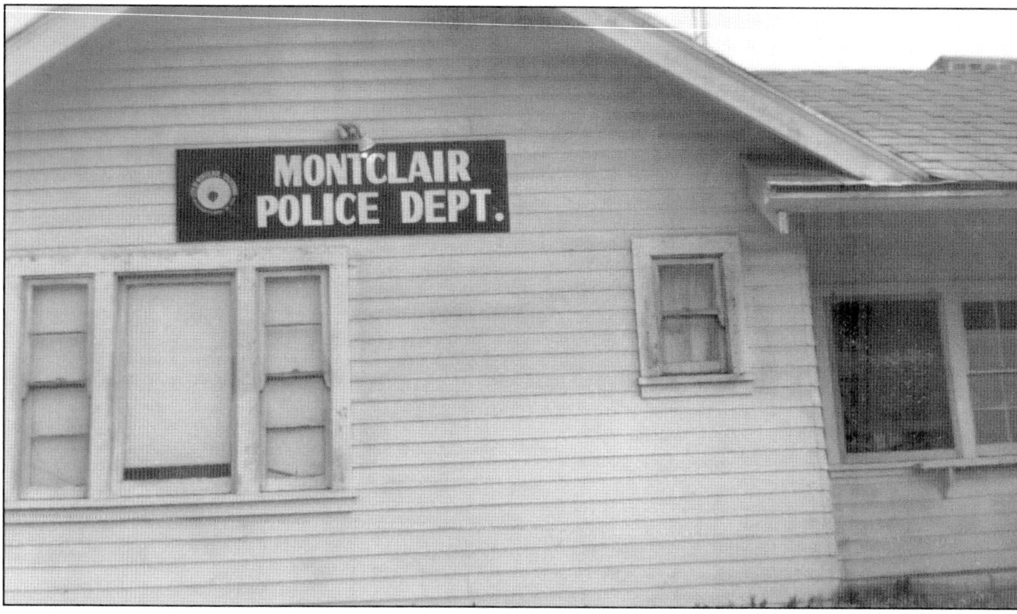

MONTCLAIR'S SECOND POLICE HEADQUARTERS, JULY 1961. The second police headquarters was located at 5396 San Bernardino Street at the corner of San Bernardino Street and Exeter Avenue. The police department stayed in this building until the completion of the civic center in 1963. (Courtesy of Mike Hance.)

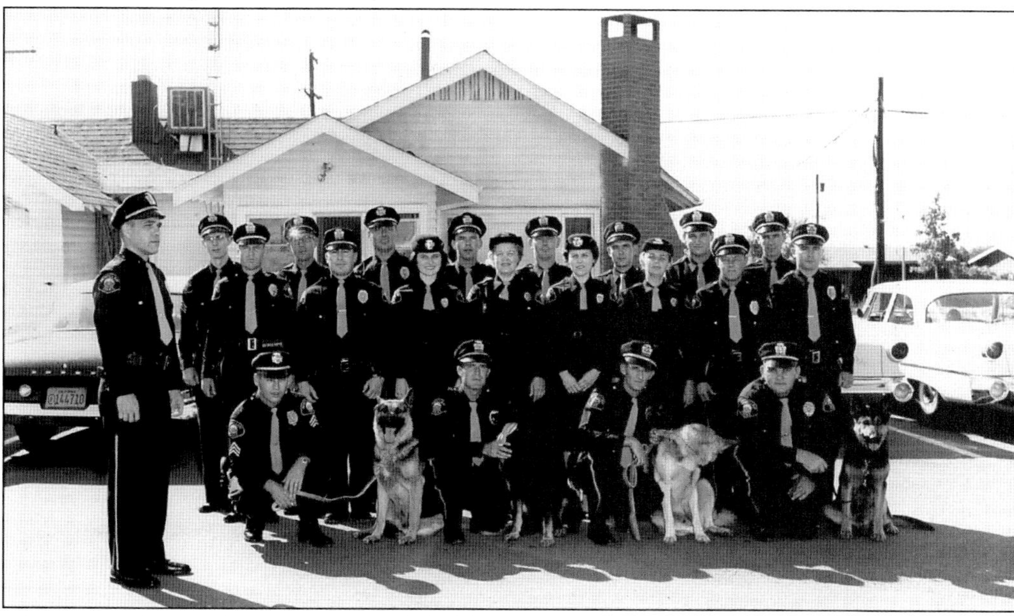

MONTCLAIR POLICE DEPARTMENT, 1961. Twenty-one personnel and four K-9 dogs are pictured as the Montclair Police Department observed its fifth anniversary. Pictured, from left to right, are (first row) Richard Pettit, Walt Ryan, Gil Baughman, and Donald Lawrence; (second row) Tommy Jordan, Salomon Valdez, Maxine McLain, Dora Nicholas, Claudia Kirshnan, Jeanne Swart, Bill Goff, and Don Sanders; (third row) Andrew Farthing, Dave Martin, James (J. D.) Miller, Bill Klink, Ed Duran, John Muskthel, Dave Hutchinson, and Eugene Combes. Standing in the forefront of the picture is Chief Ray McLean.

ROBBERY INVESTIGATION, 1961. John Muskthel, left, and Henry Wong gather evidence after a robbery at the Jade Palace.

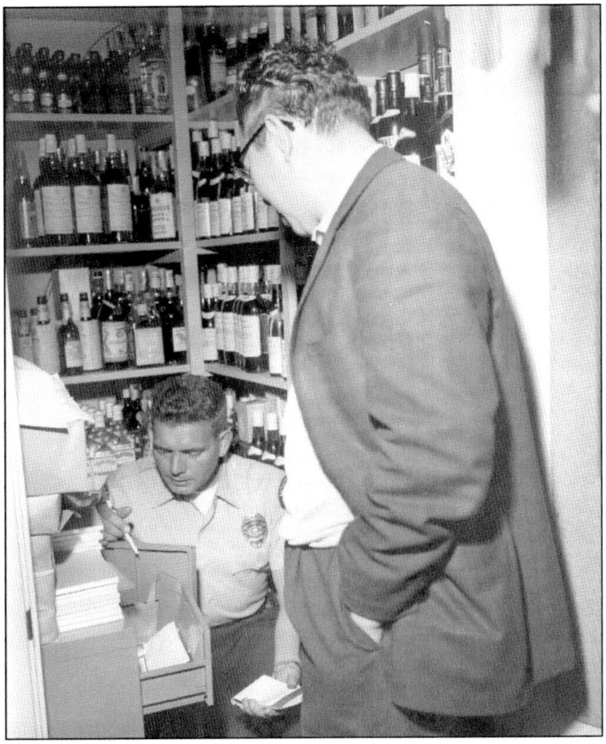

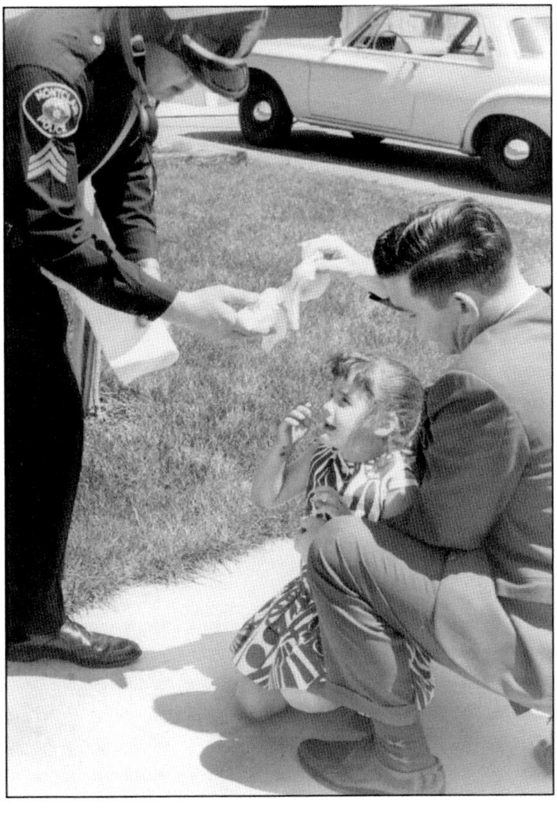

LENDING A HELPING HAND, C. 1962. A Montclair police officer lends a helping hand by giving a young girl tissues.

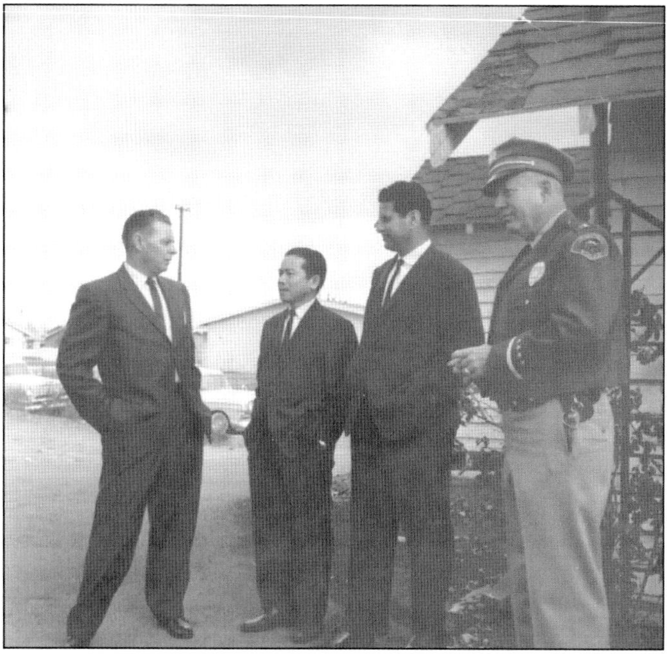

K-9 Demonstration, January 10, 1963. Pictured here, from left to right, are R. Lowe, Montclair Police Department; Colonel Saboor, National Police Iran; Inspector Ngan Bnan, Saigon Police Department; and Captain Butcher; Pomona Police Department.

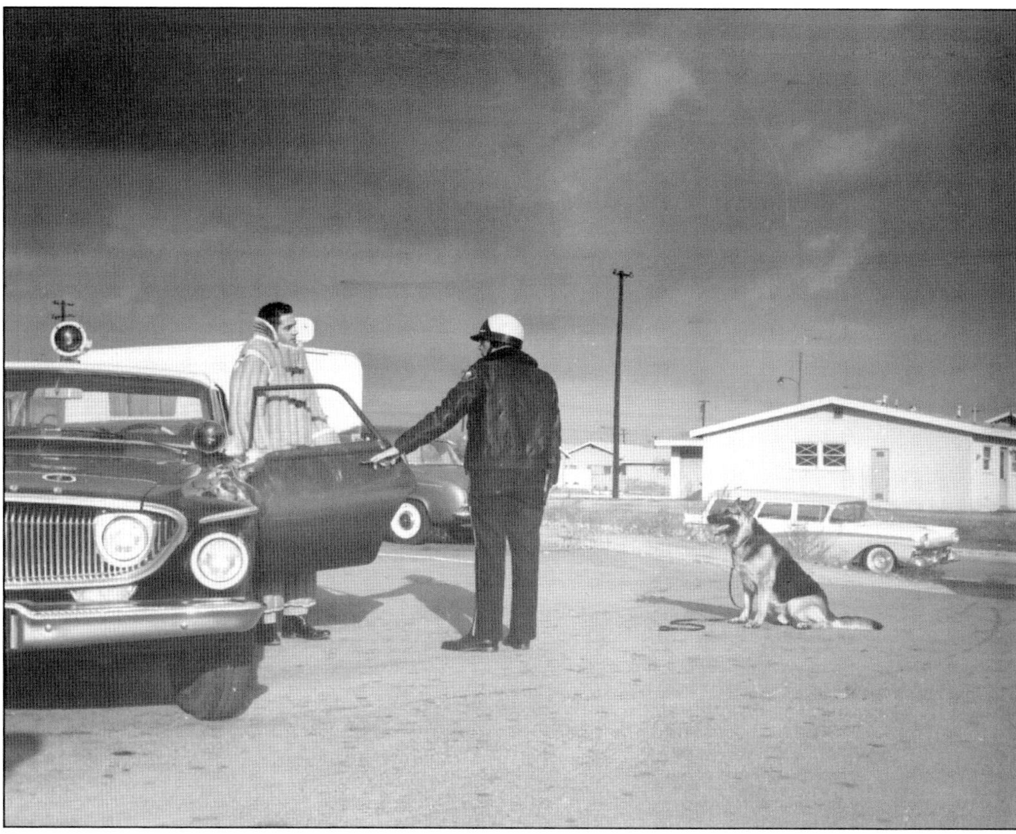

Ready for the Dogs, 1963. Leonard Mosley (in pads), Dave Martin, and Mace, sitting patiently, are ready for a canine demonstration.

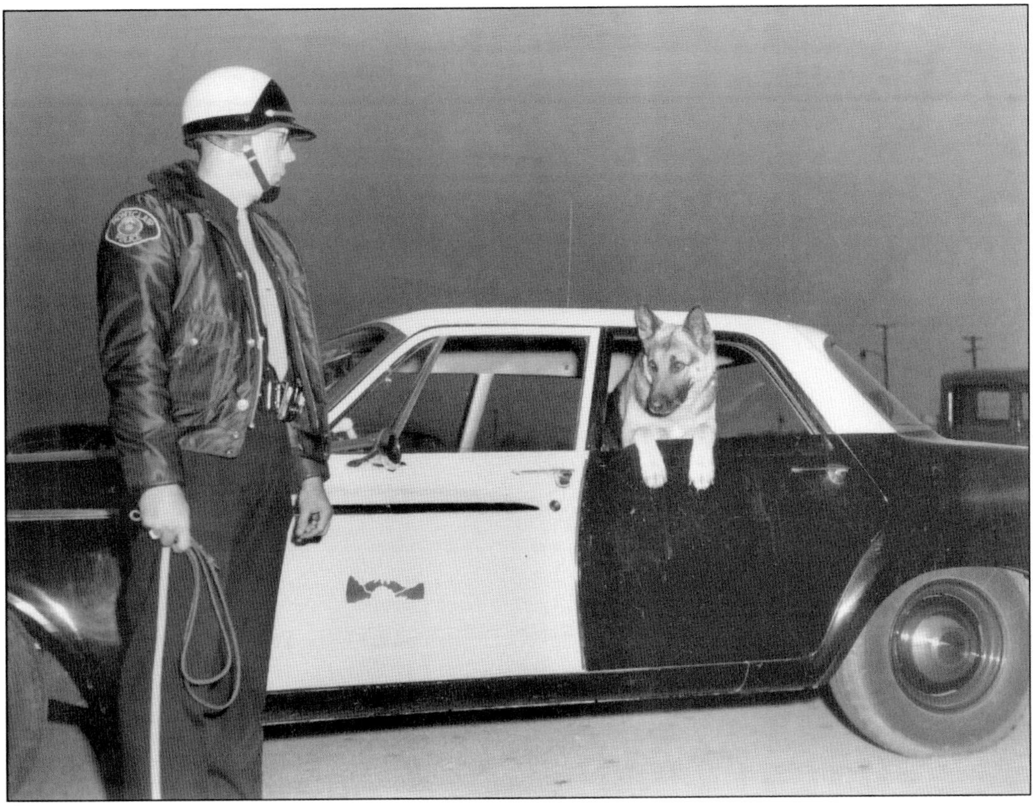

A Faithful Friend, 1963. Dave Martin and his canine Mace are pictured here during a demonstration.

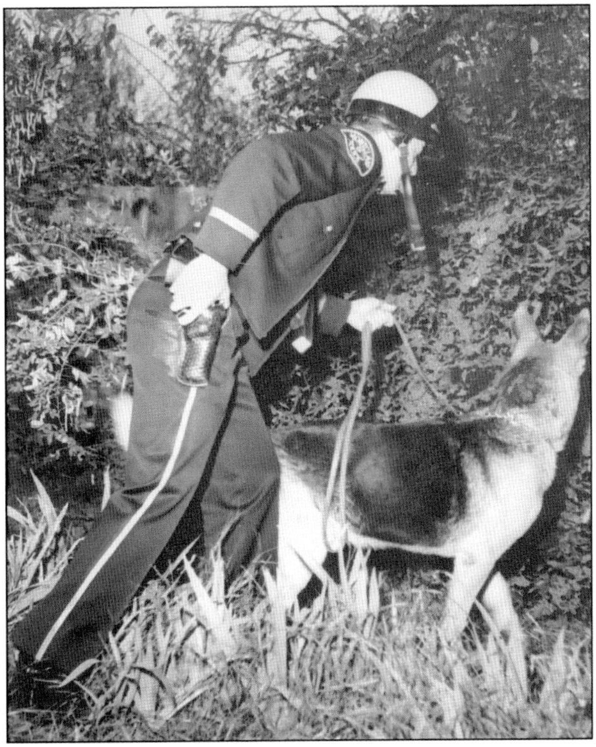

Montclair Canine Demonstration, 1963. A Montclair police officer and his canine demonstrate their crime fighting skills.

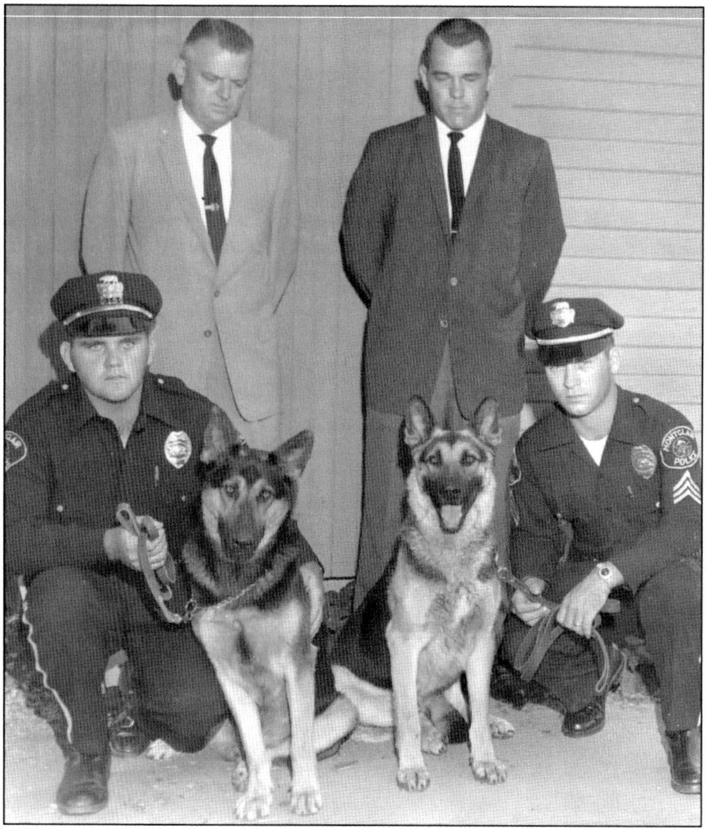

Montclair Police Department Canine Unit, c. 1963. This photograph of the canine unit includes Don Lawrence (left) with his canine Jet, and Mace with his unidentified handler.

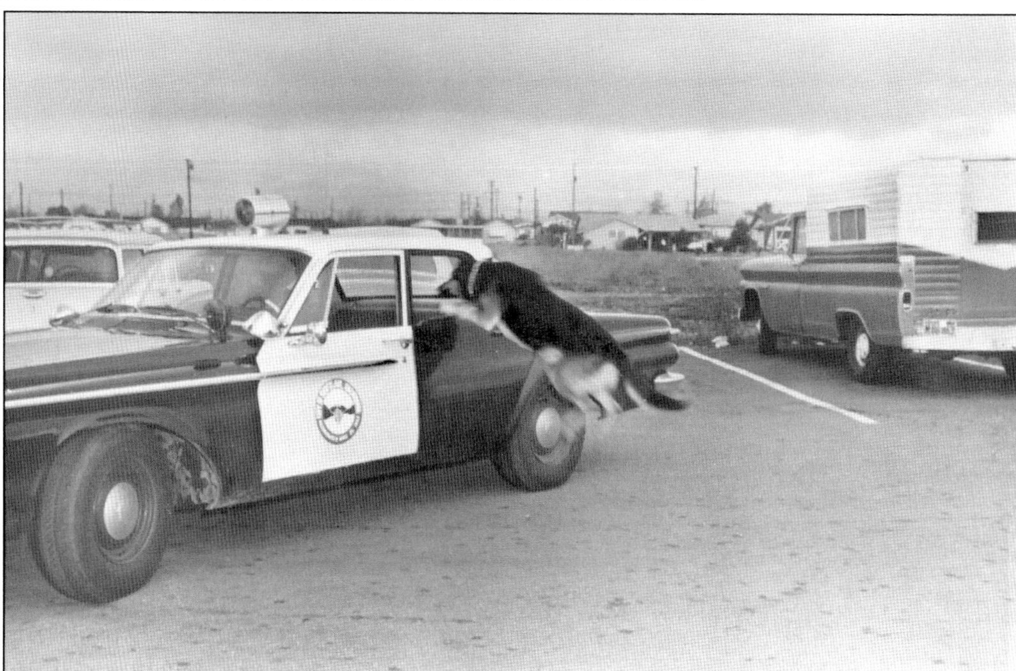

Canine Demonstration, c. 1963. Jet shows off his capabilities during a demonstration.

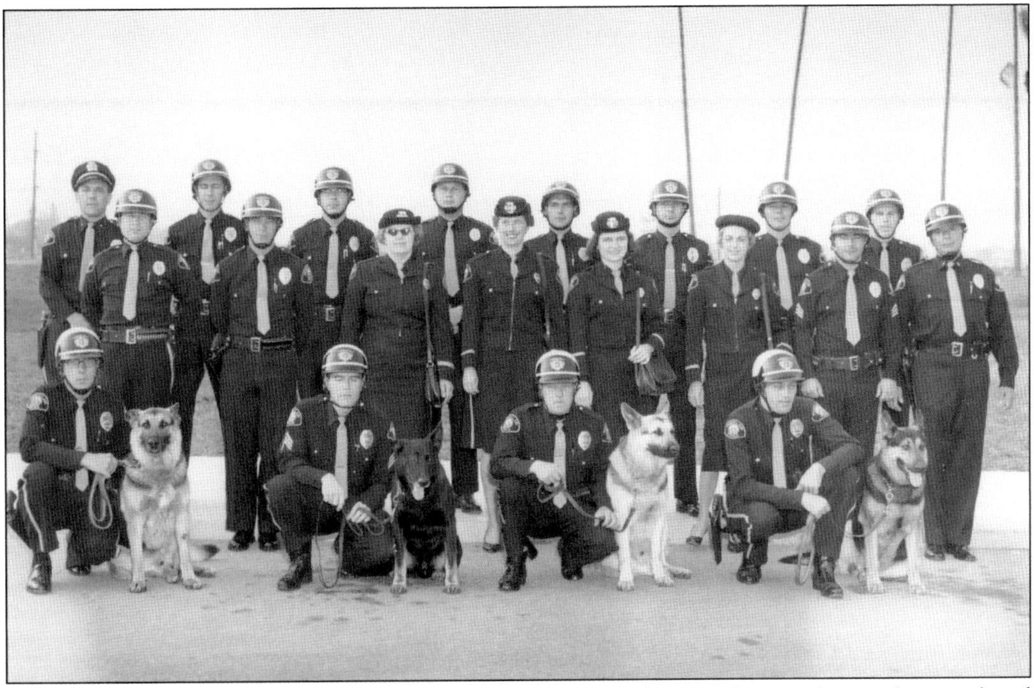

MONTCLAIR POLICE DEPARTMENT, 1963. This photograph was taken at the newly completed civic center.

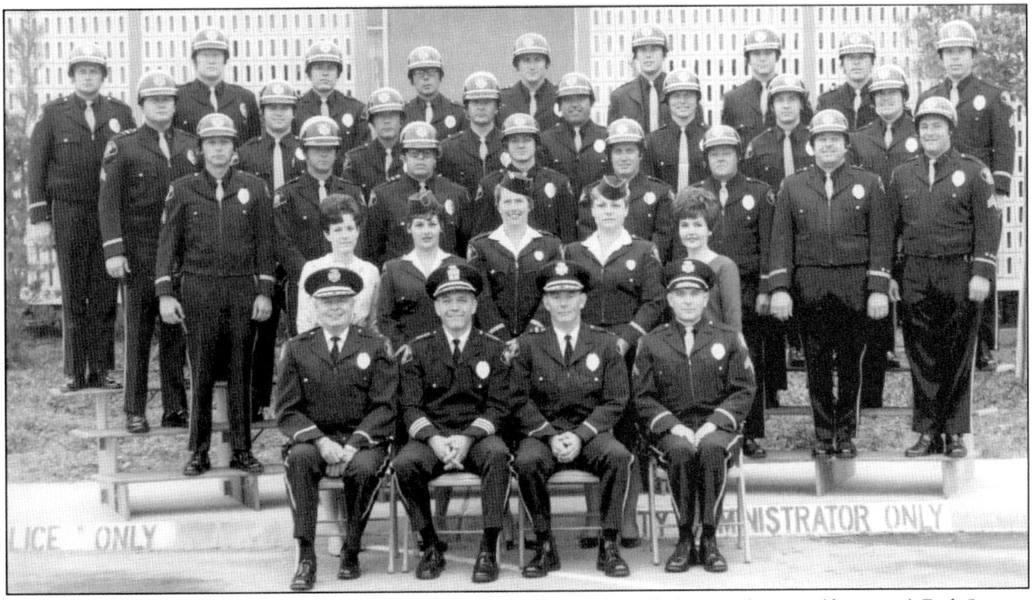

MONTCLAIR POLICE DEPARTMENT, 1969. Pictured here, from left to right, are (first row) Bob Lowe, Ray McLean, Ed Duran, and John Musketelle; (second row) unidentified, Toby Gann, Barbara Wilson, Cheryl Mulligan, and Carol Angel; (third row) Dave Spalding, Andy Allison, Carlos Pena, Bob Greenhaulh, Floyd Yates, Bill Borr, Bob Abshire, and Don Whipp; (fourth row) Jerry Frusher, Dennis Sedler, Walt Ryan, Art Gunchel, Bob Metzger, Terry Belland, unidentified, and John Nelson; (fifth row) Jim Berg, Jim Bailey, Dennis Tedder, Dave Martin, Dave Hutchinson, Russ Smith, Greg Caldwell, Larry Smith, and Clyde Graham.

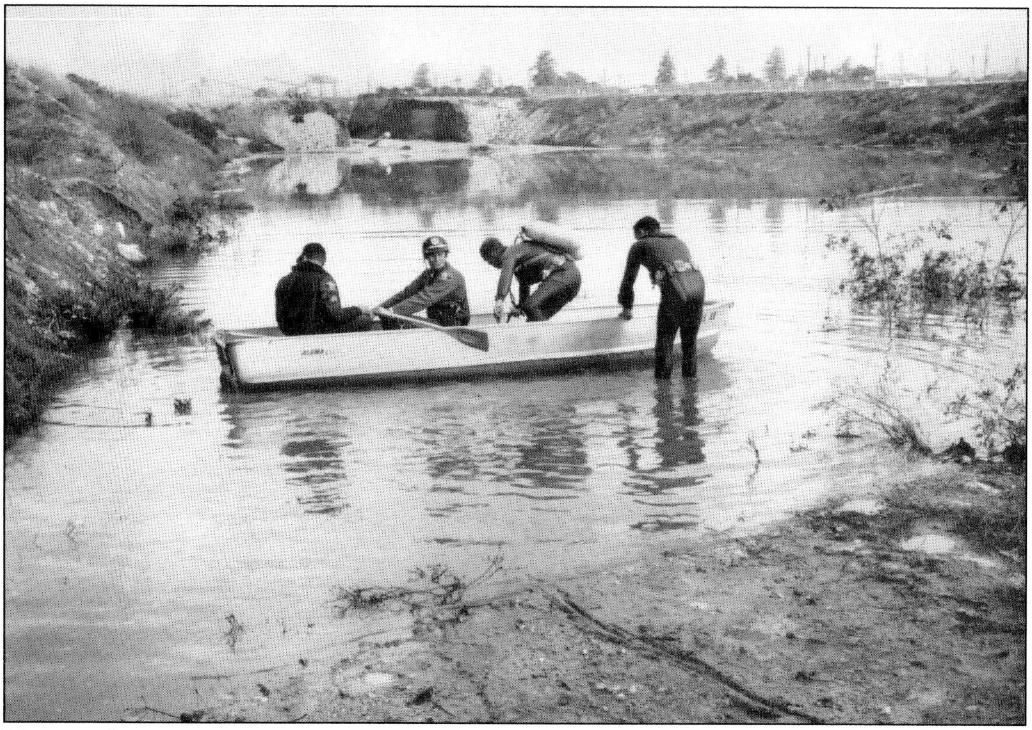

MORENO STREET FLOOD C. 1968. A Montclair police officer takes search and rescue crews by boat during a flood on Moreno Street. Eyewitnesses saw at least one car get caught in the current.

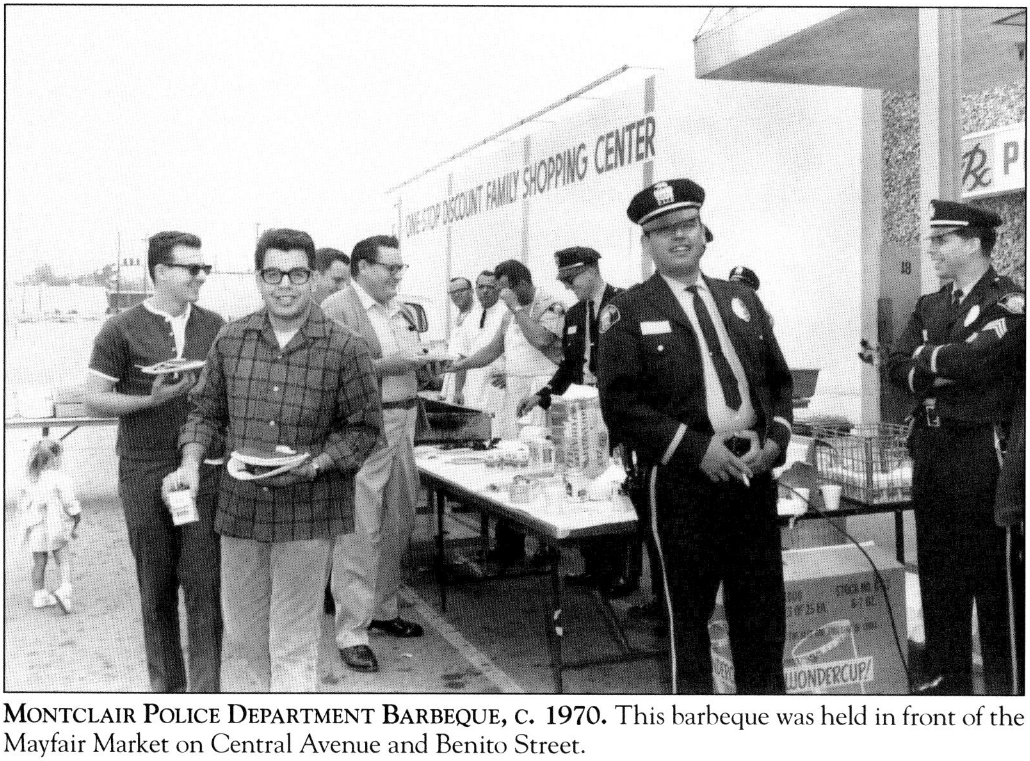

MONTCLAIR POLICE DEPARTMENT BARBEQUE, C. 1970. This barbeque was held in front of the Mayfair Market on Central Avenue and Benito Street.

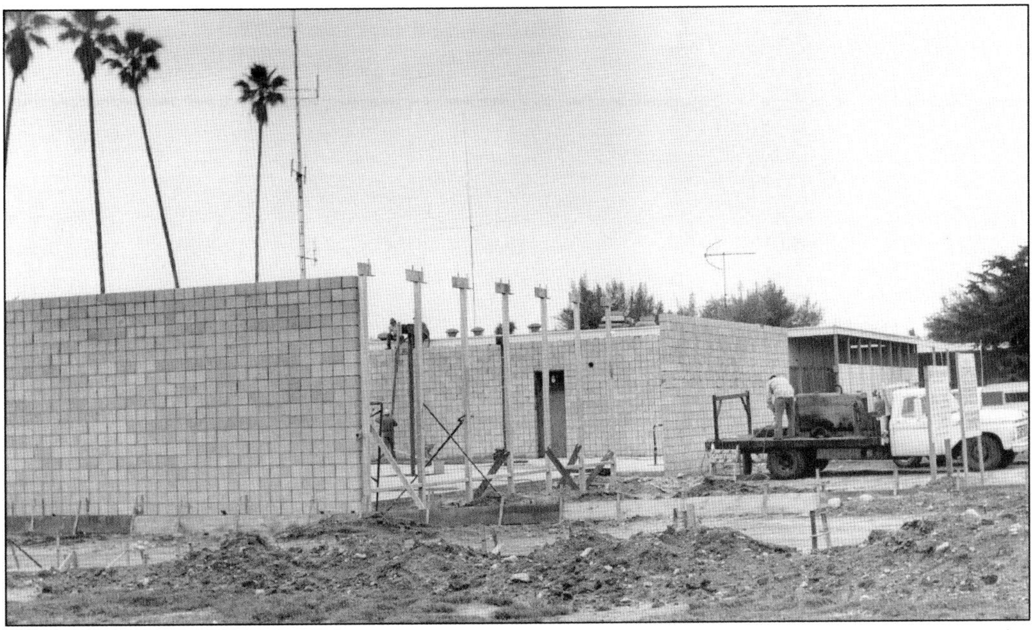

POLICE BUILDING ADDITION, C. 1972. Construction is taking place on the expansion of the police department located at the civic center.

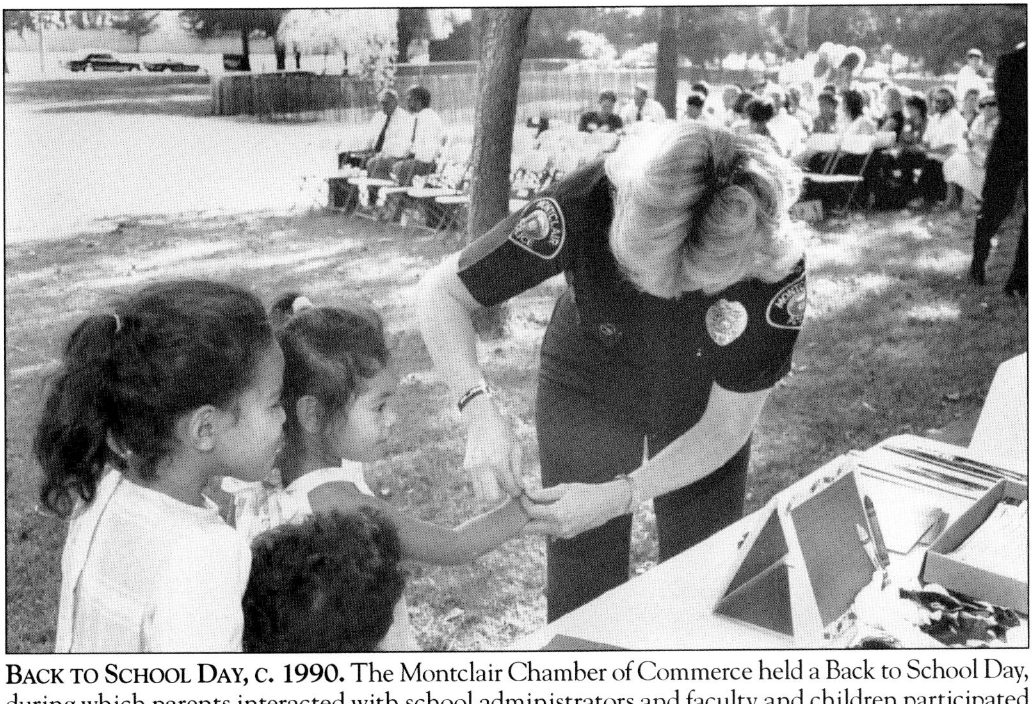

BACK TO SCHOOL DAY, C. 1990. The Montclair Chamber of Commerce held a Back to School Day, during which parents interacted with school administrators and faculty and children participated in various activities throughout the day. (Courtesy of the Montclair Chamber of Commerce.)

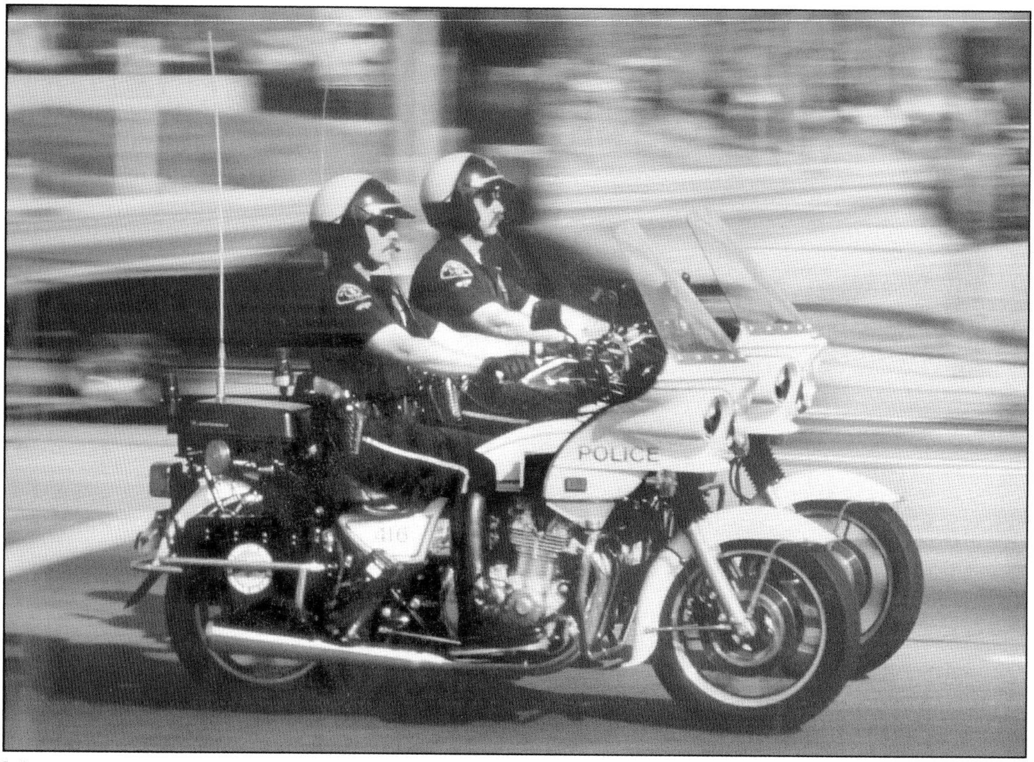

MONTCLAIR MOTOR OFFICERS, C. 1986. Montclair's motor patrol was created in 1980, starting with only two officers.

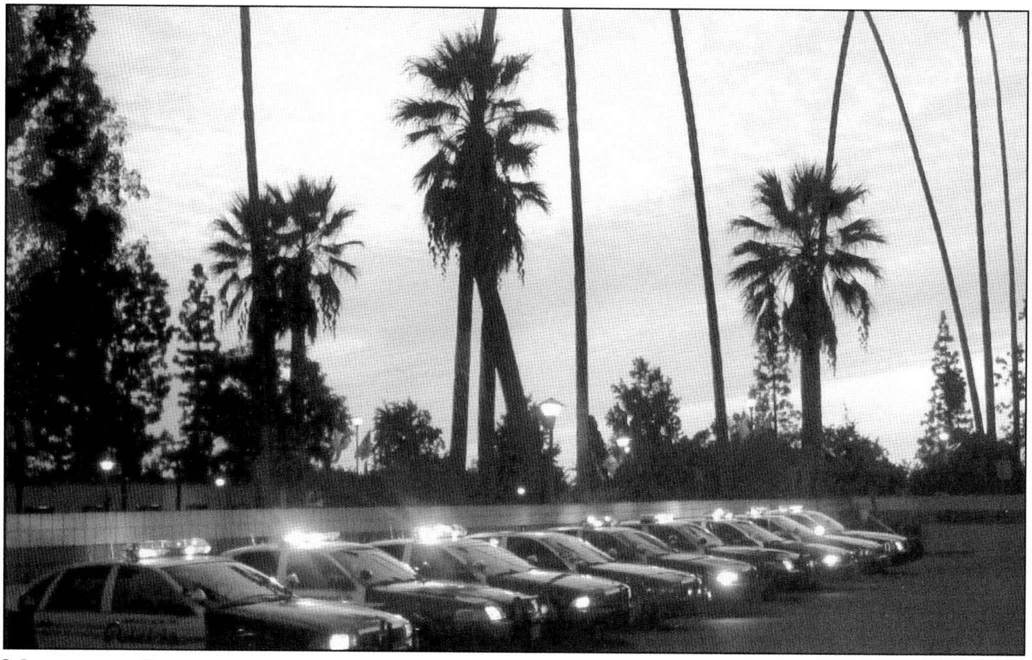

MONTCLAIR POLICE UNITS, C. 2002. In this photograph taken at the Montclair Police Station, lights on the squad cars complement a picturesque sunset.

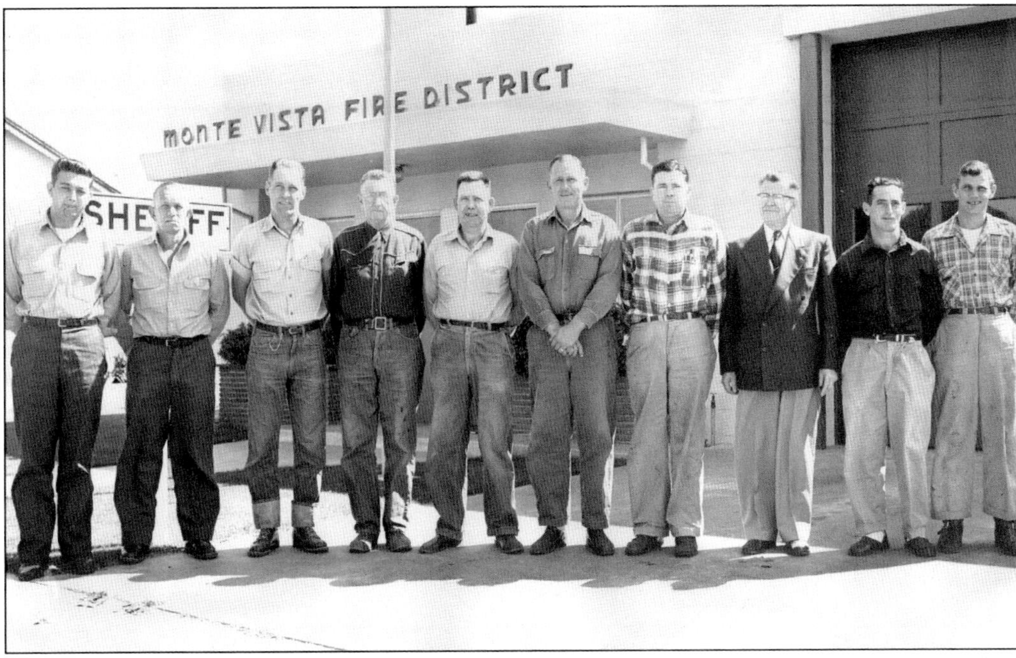

MONTE VISTA FIRE DISTRICT, 1953. Pictured here, from left to right, are Harold Duncan, chief; Elmer Snyder, captain; and volunteer firemen G. S. Brown, H. B. Jones, Marion Cantrell, Lyle Keiser, Hugh Guinn, L. E. Jones, Max Ernst, and Art Pantazin. This station was located at 10585 Central Avenue.

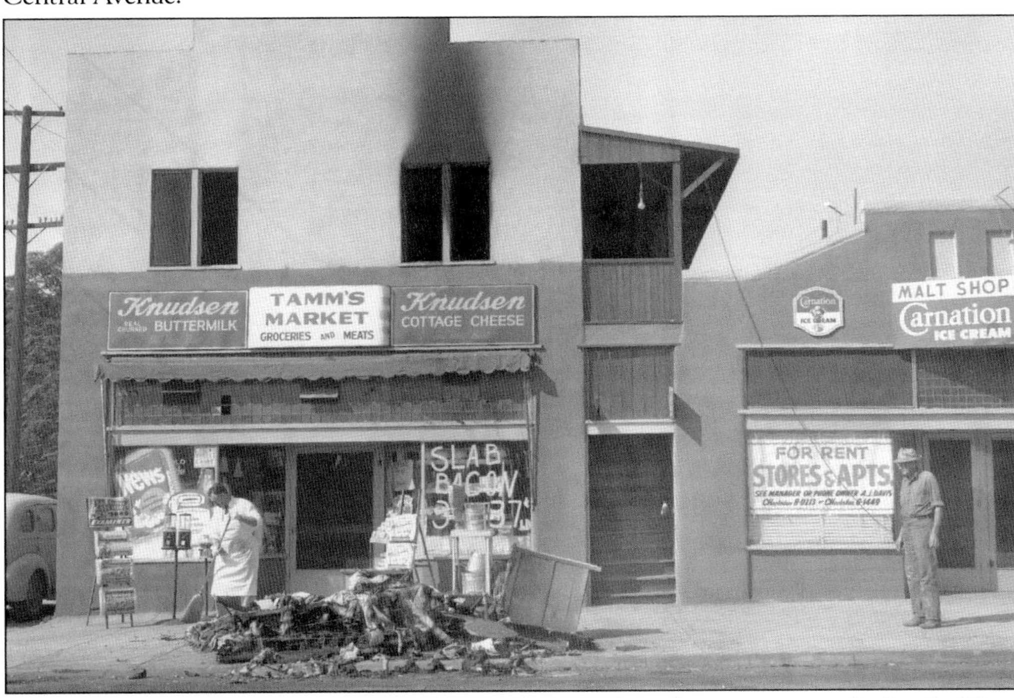

CLEANUP BEGINS, OCTOBER 19, 1951. Cleanup begins after a fire was extinguished at the Narod Apartments on Central Avenue and State Street. Pictured here are Mr. Tamm (left), store owner, and H. B. Jones, Monte Vista fire volunteer.

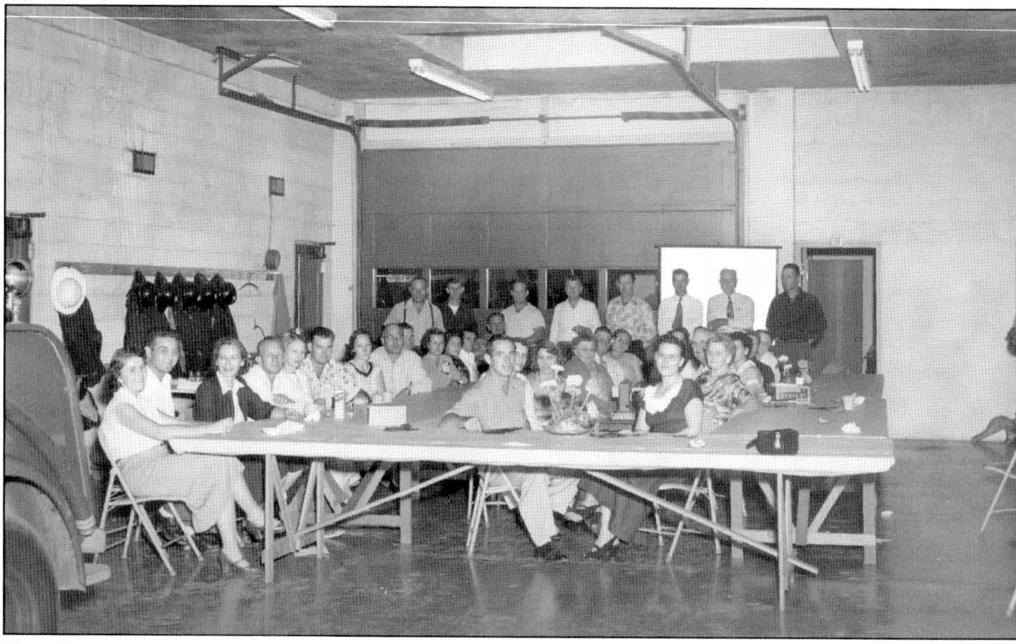

FIRE DEPARTMENT ANNUAL DINNER, NOVEMBER 1953. This annual event was held in the bay of the fire station.

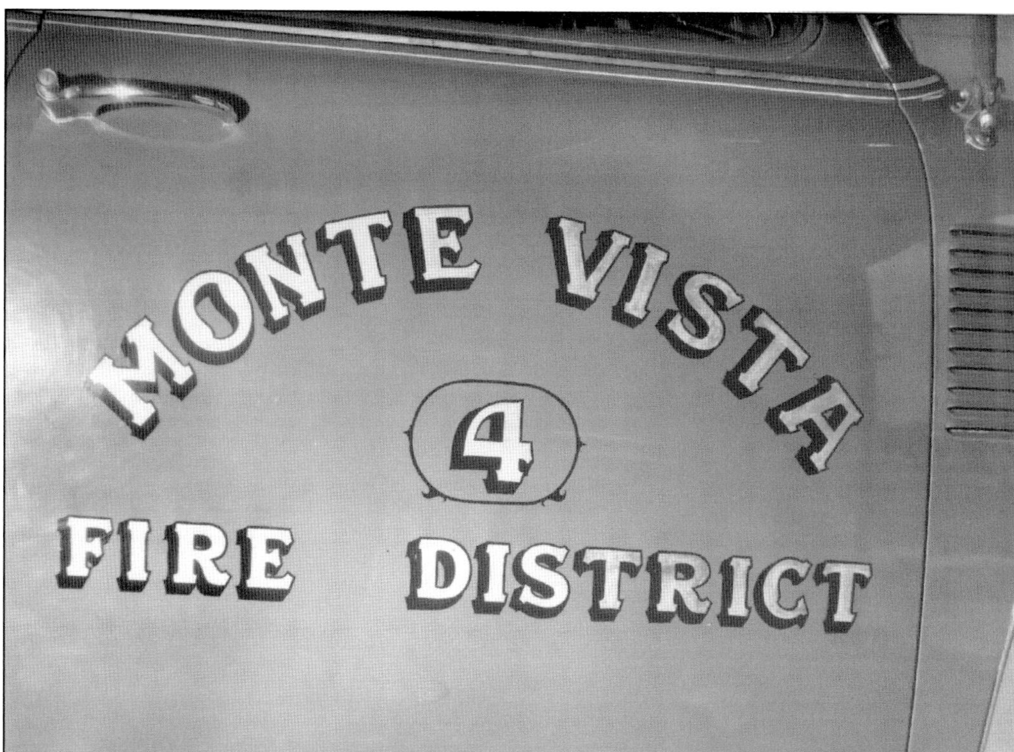

NEW MONTE VISTA FIRE TRUCK, 1954. The fire truck purchased by the Monte Vista County Fire Protection District cost a total of $15,661.80.

MONTE VISTA FIRE DISTRICT ENGINE NO. 1, C. 1956. Pictured here, from left to right, are firefighters Harold Duncan, Darrel Pennington, Ernie Tindall, and Ron Mathis.

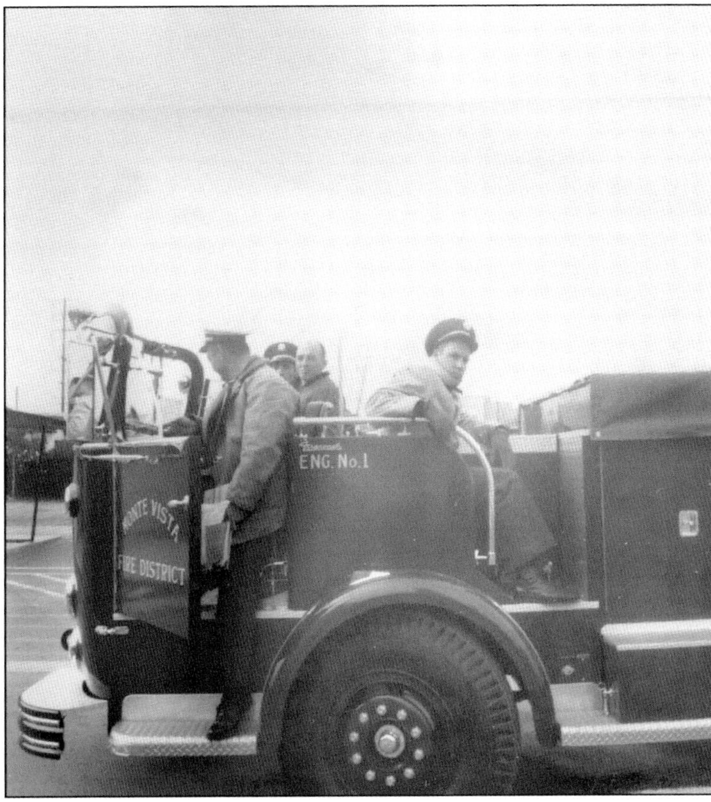

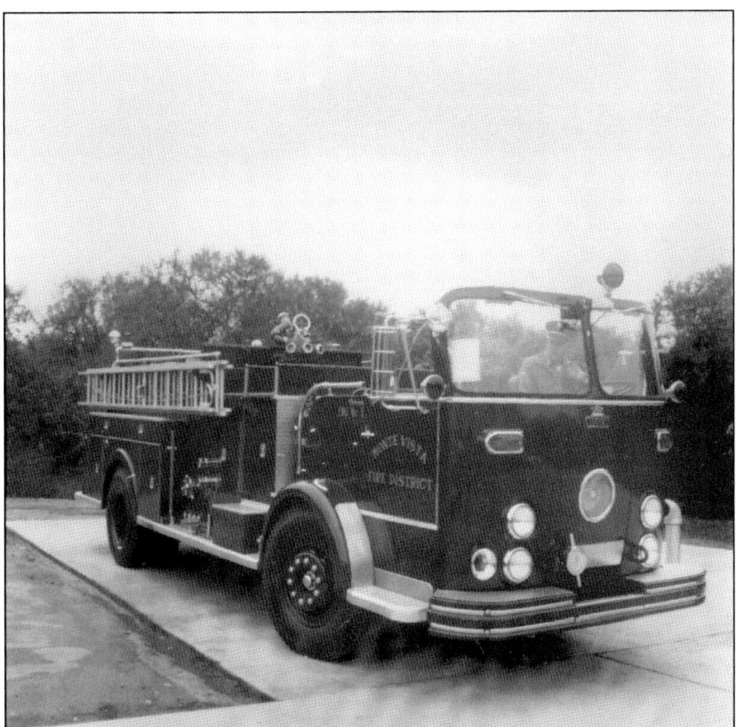

MONTE VISTA FIRE DISTRICT ENGINE NO. 1, 1956. Engineer Ron Mathis is driving.

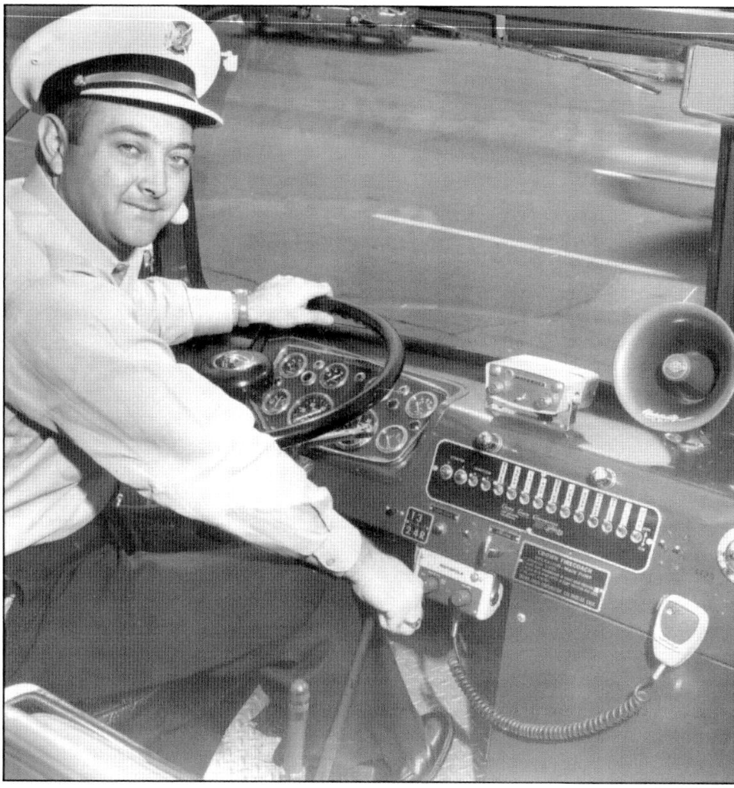

Fire Chief Harold Duncan, c. 1961. Chief Harold Duncan tests the new Crown Firecoach delivered to the Monte Vista Fire District.

Monte Vista Fire District, c. 1961. Assistant fire chief Mellinger, left, and Chief Duncan examine the fire truck.

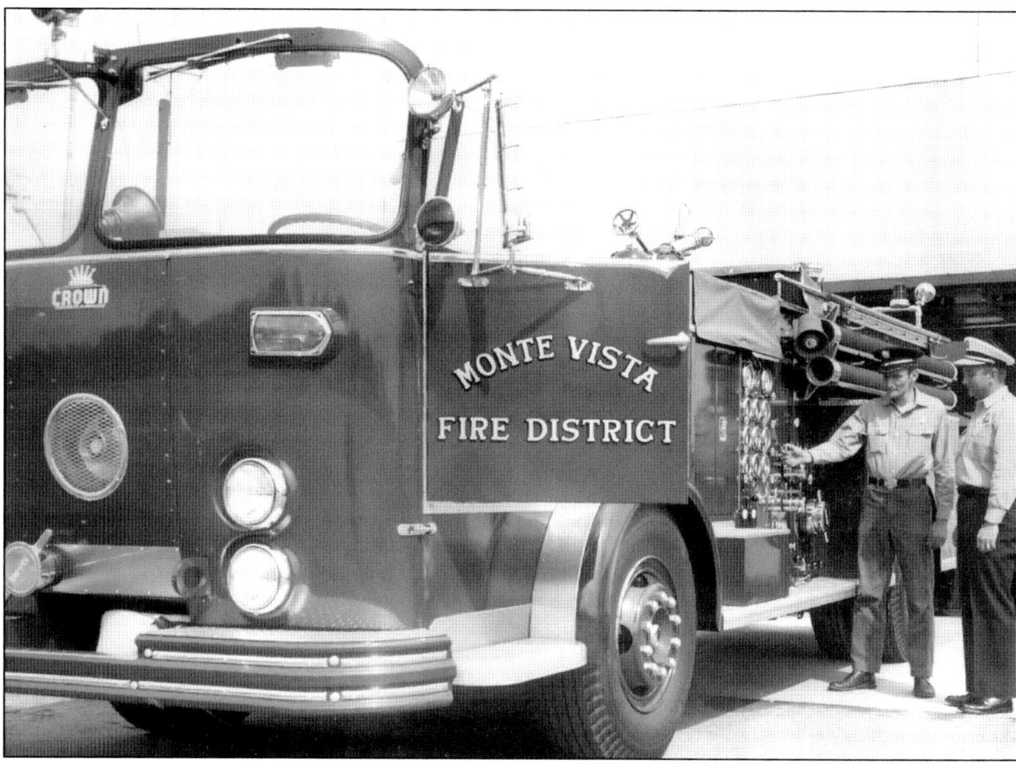

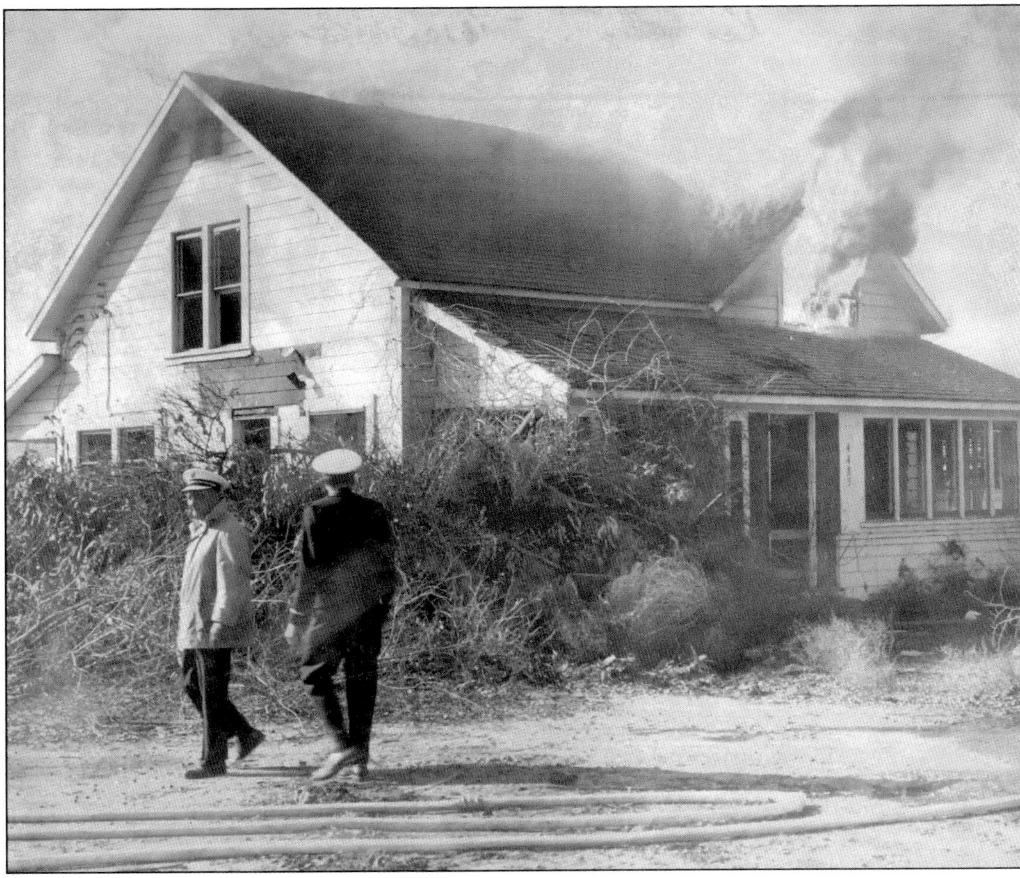

FIRE AT RAMONA AVENUE AND KINGSLEY STREET, JANUARY 7, 1965. Surveying the situation are Chief Harold Duncan, left, and assistant chief Duane Mellinger.

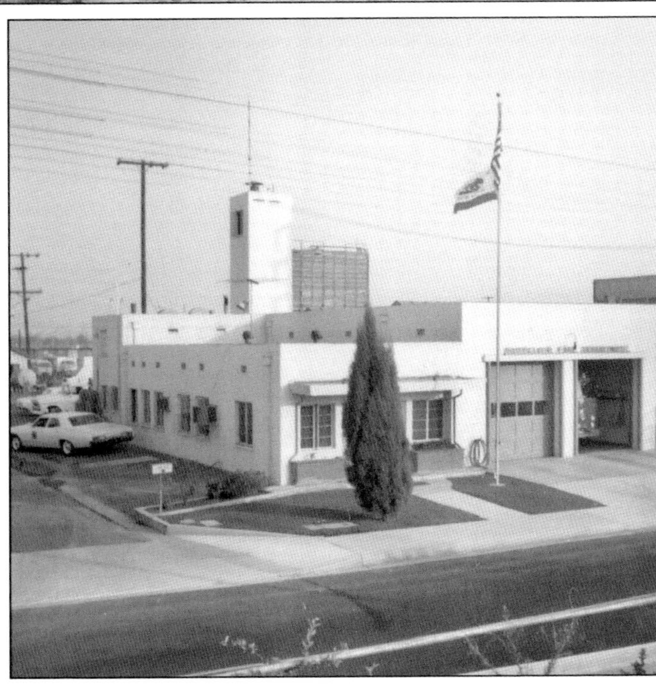

ORIGINAL FIRE STATION, NOVEMBER 20, 1967. The original Montclair Fire Department station headquarters was located at 10585 Central Avenue.

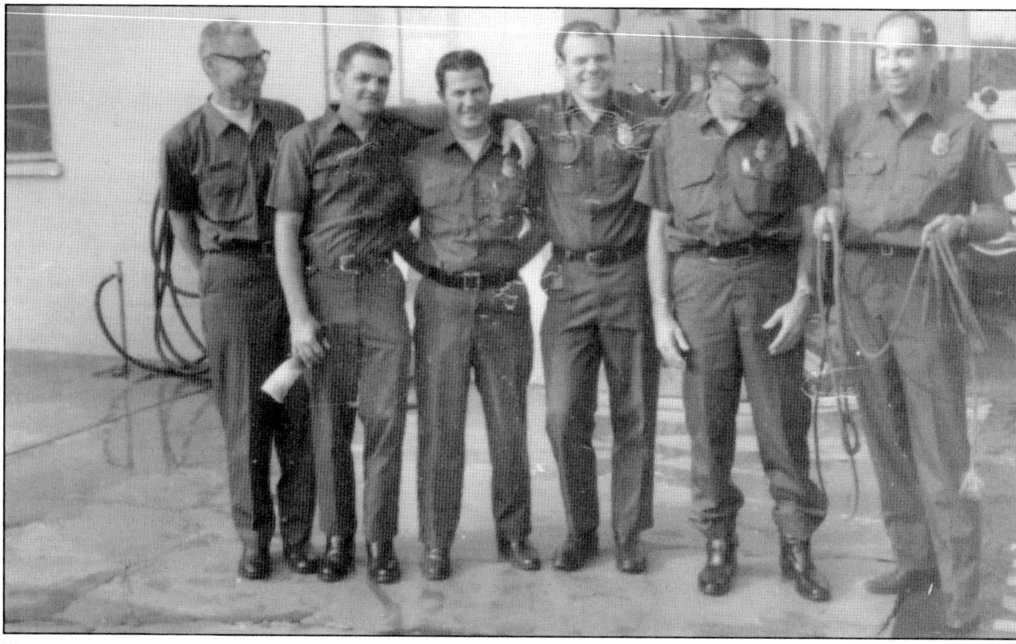

FIREFIGHTERS, NOVEMBER 1968. Pictured, from left to right, are firefighters Fred Haueter, Jerry Hall, Rich Warmouth, Geery Hughes, Joe Schonert, and Lloyd Kear.

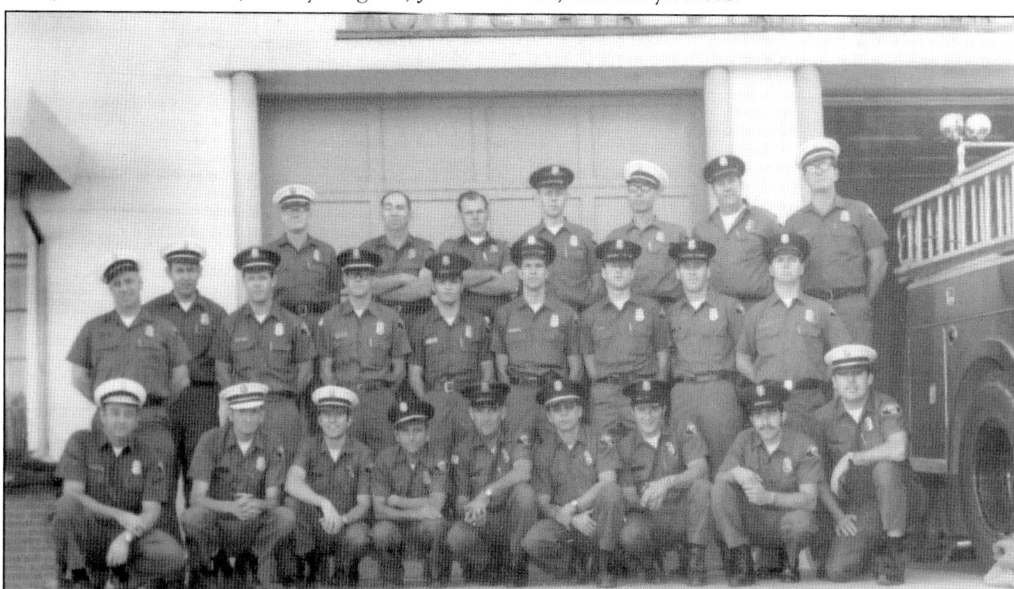

MONTCLAIR FIRE DEPARTMENT, C. 1969. This photograph was taken at the station headquarters located at 10585 Central Avenue. Pictured, from left to right, are (first row) Chief Harold Duncan, assistant chief Duane Mellinger, Capt. Jim Rankin, engineer Ernie Tindall, fireman Bill Ketchum, engineer Corey Silves, fireman Rich Warmuth, fireman Ted LaRue, and Capt. Moe Fitch; (second row) Capt. John Pruiksma, unidentified, engineer Bill Boock, engineer Bob Parker, fireman Jerry Hall, fireman Mike Harden, fireman Donnie Moore, fireman Larey Smith, and fireman Joe Nietz; (third row) Capt. Joe Schonert, mechanic Loyd Kear, engineer David Geery Hughes, fireman Loren Pettis, Capt. Fred Haueter, fireman Bob Anderson, and Capt. Eddie Smith.

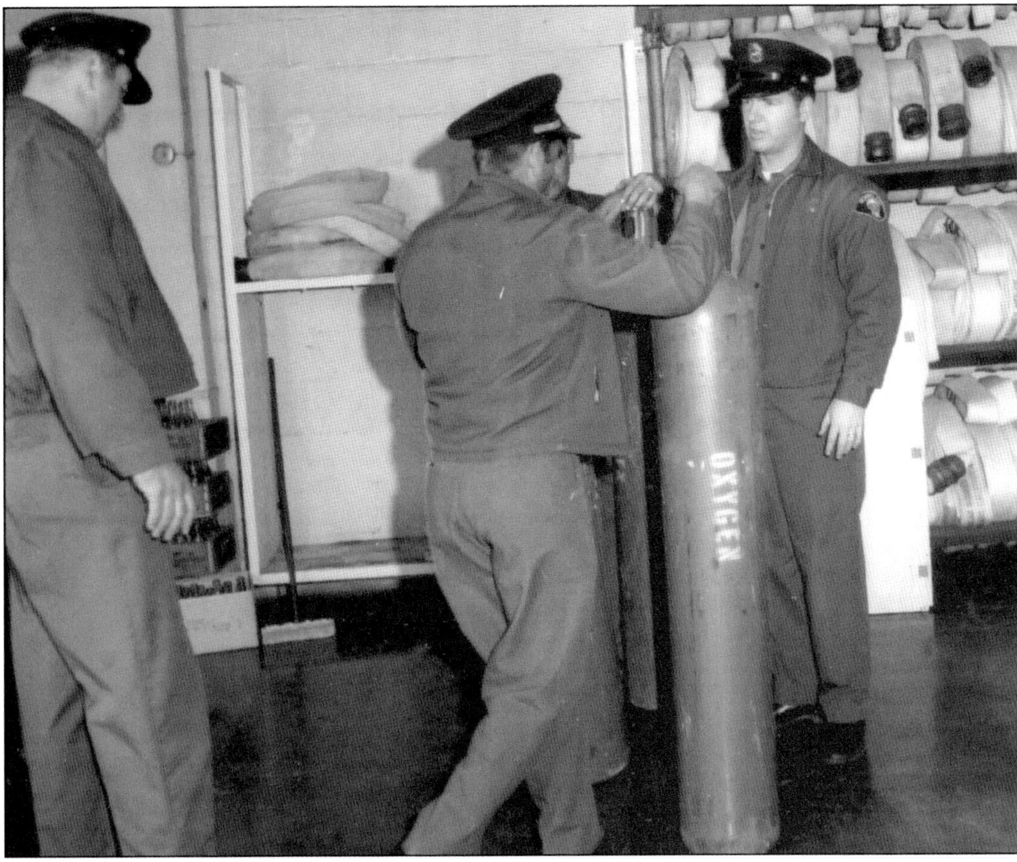

Making Preparations, c. 1969. Montclair firemen prepare and inspect their equipment.

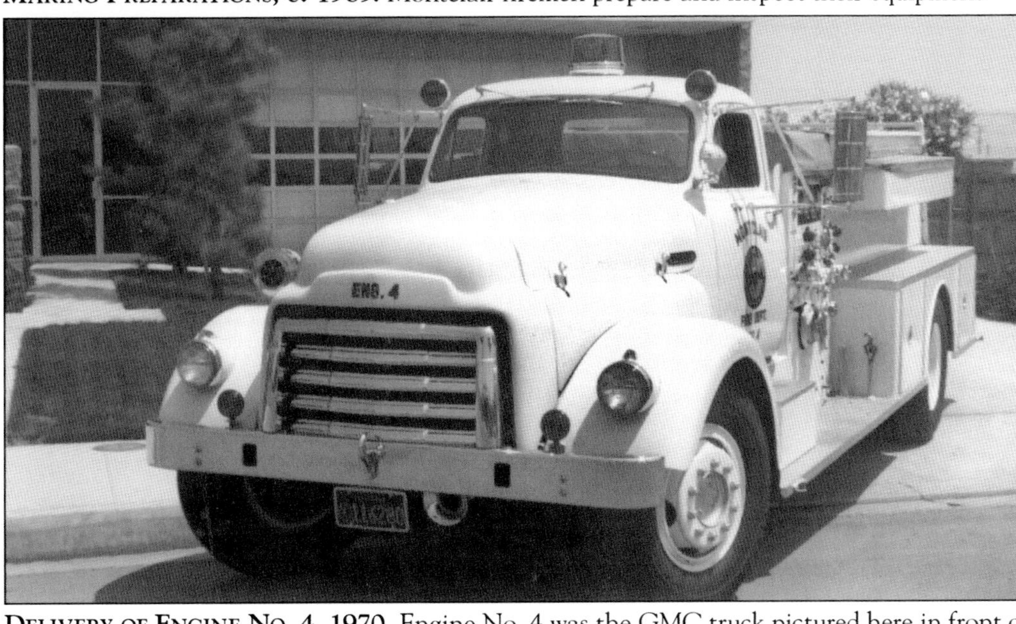

Delivery of Engine No. 4, 1970. Engine No. 4 was the GMC truck pictured here in front of Station No. 2.

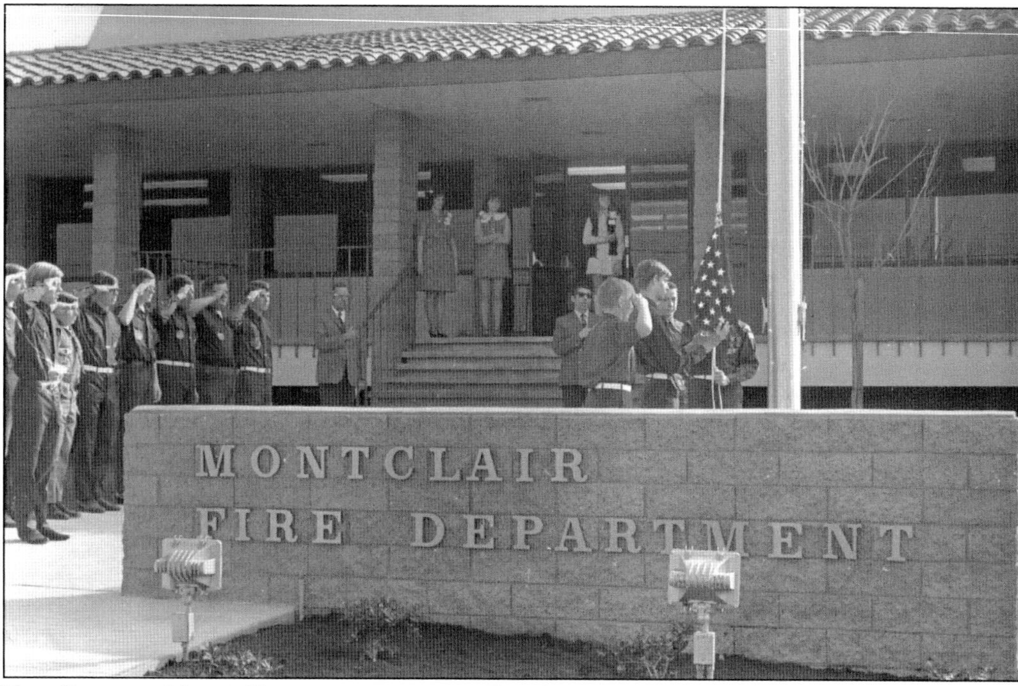

FIRE STATION NO. 1, FEBRUARY 19, 1970. Fire Station No. 1 was dedicated on February 19, 1970, and is home to fire department headquarters.

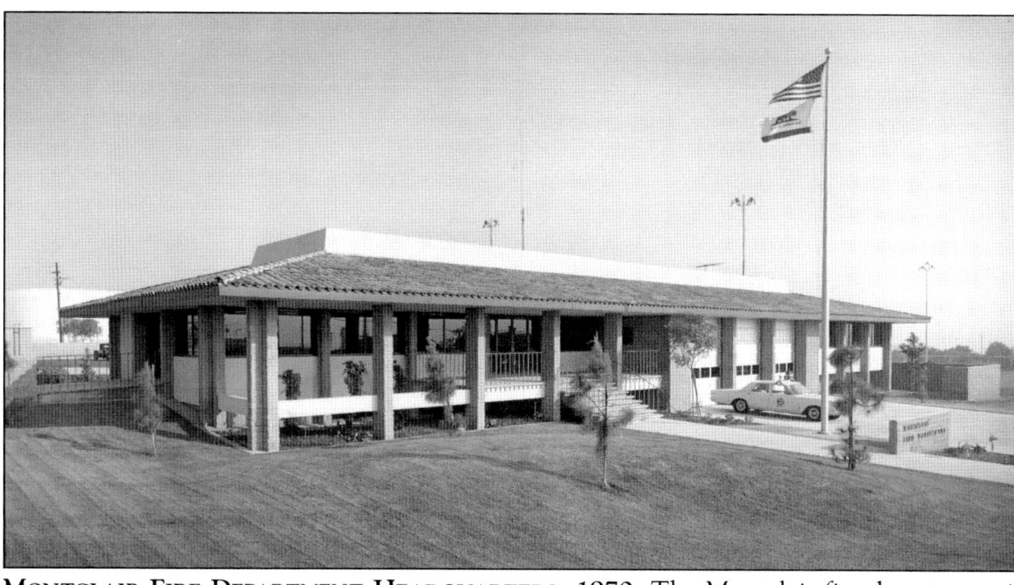

MONTCLAIR FIRE DEPARTMENT HEADQUARTERS, 1970. The Montclair fire department is located at 8901 Monte Vista Avenue.

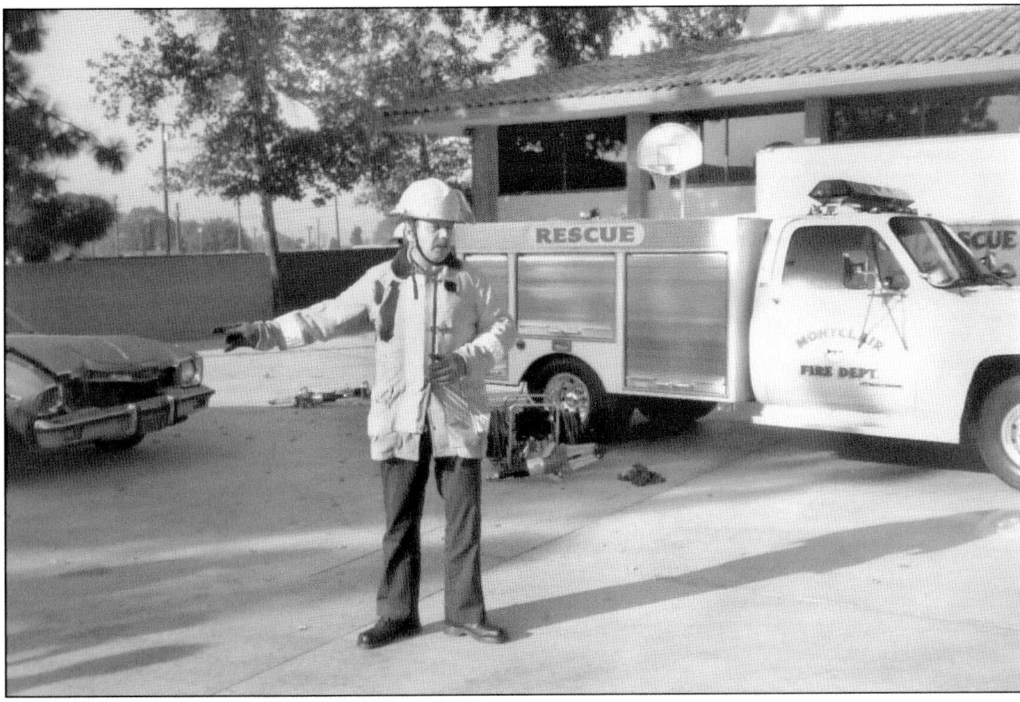

FIREFIGHTERS BREAKFAST, OCTOBER 12, 1990. A rescue demonstration is shown at the annual firefighters breakfast. (Courtesy of the Montclair Chamber of Commerce)

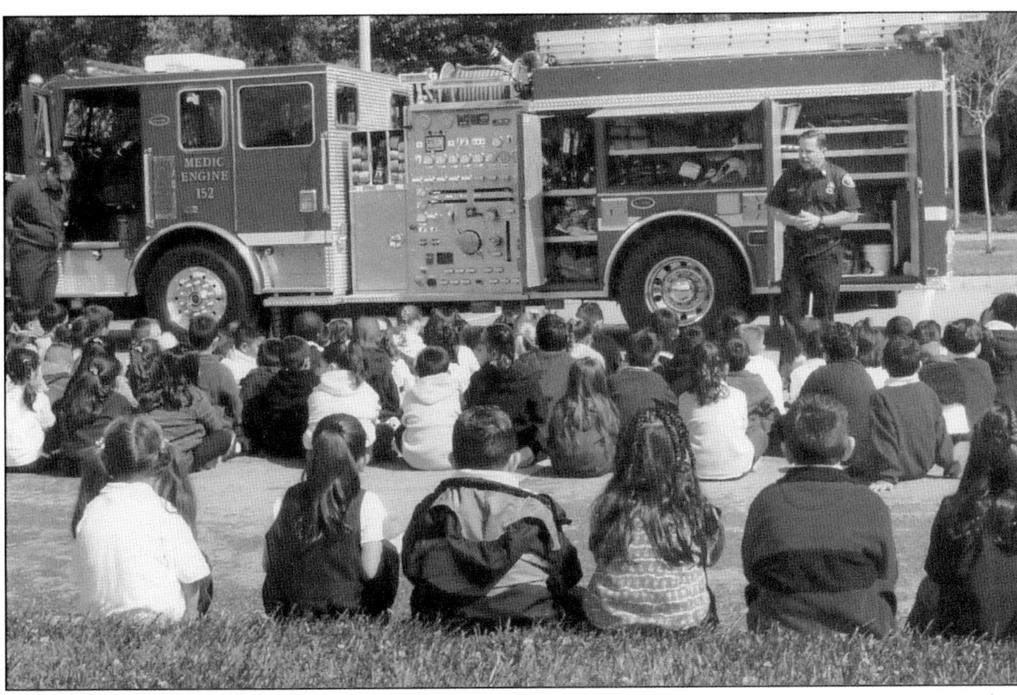

FIRE DEMONSTRATION, C. 2002. Today the fire department goes into the community to explain the services it provides to Montclair residents and the region. This was a demonstration at one of Montclair's local schools.

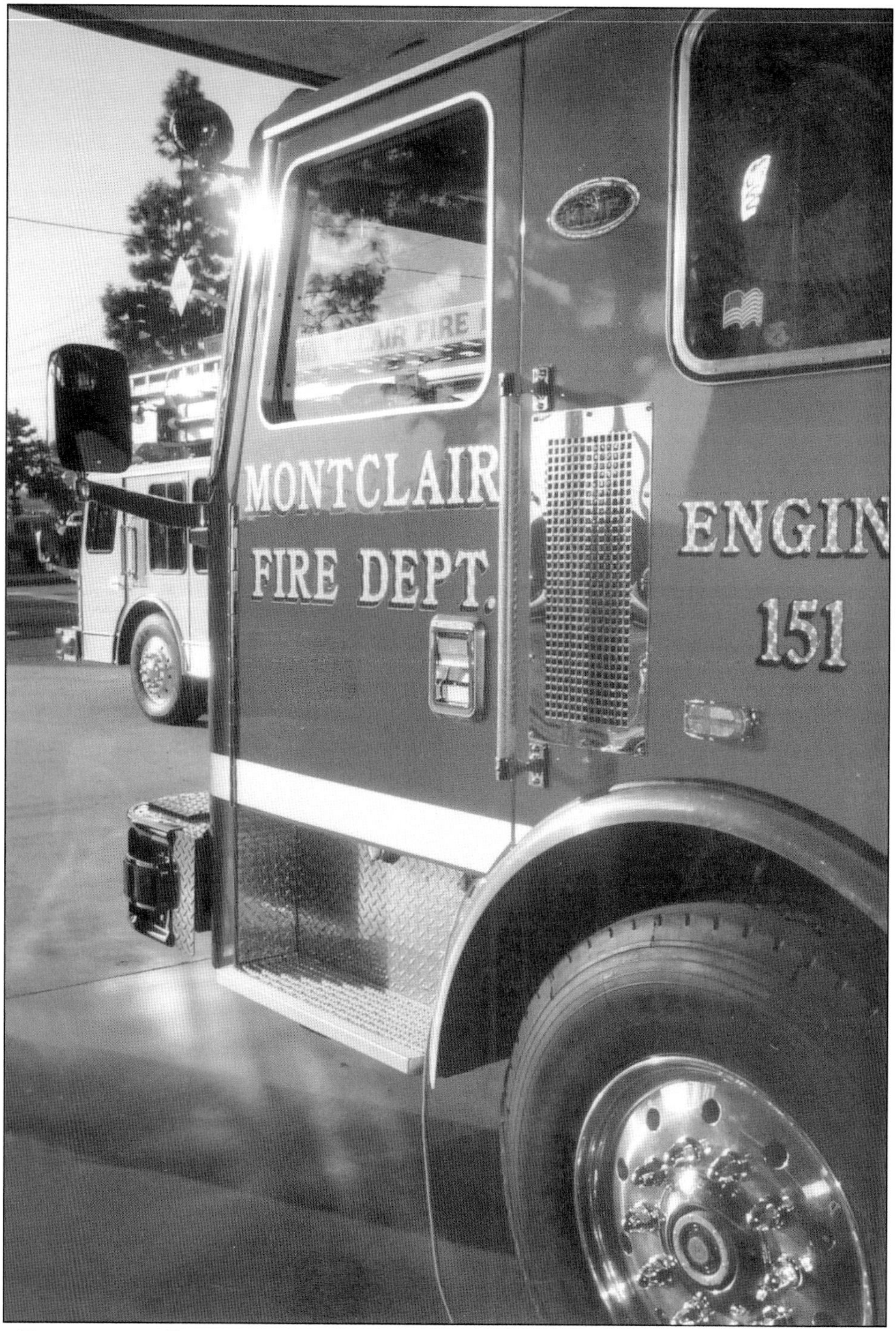

FIRE DEPARTMENT ENGINE 151, 2004. Pictured is one of Montclair's current fire engines. This photograph was taken from the bay of Fire Station No. 1.

Four

Do You Remember?

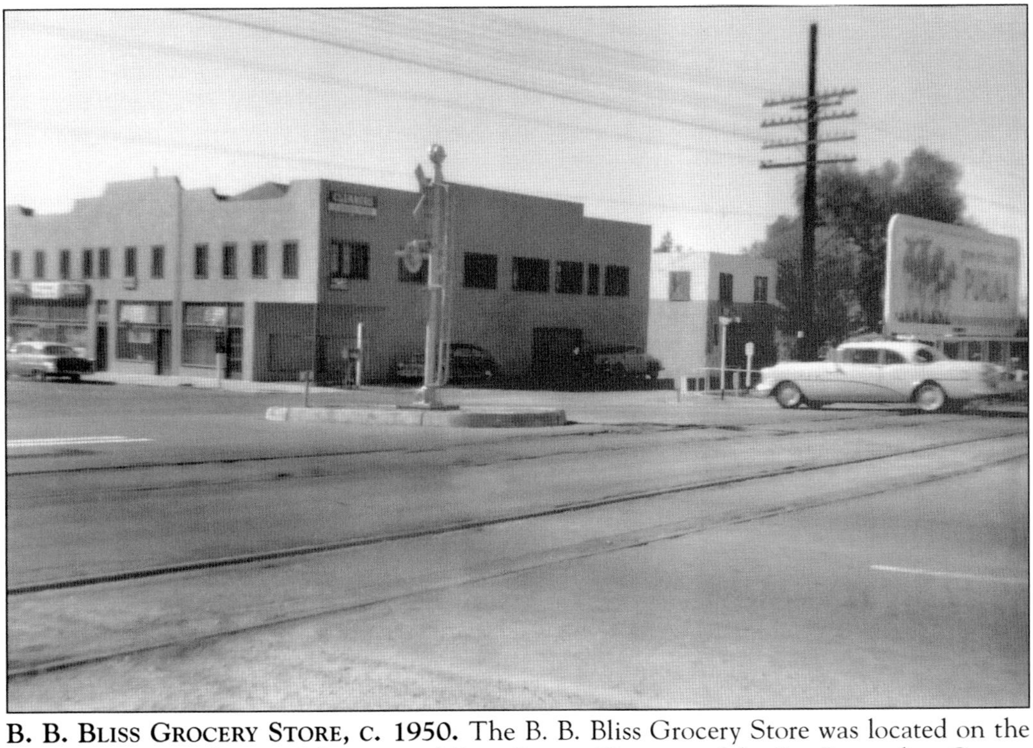

B. B. Bliss Grocery Store, c. 1950. The B. B. Bliss Grocery Store was located on the southwest corner of Central Avenue and State Street. (Courtesy of the San Bernardino County Museum Archives.)

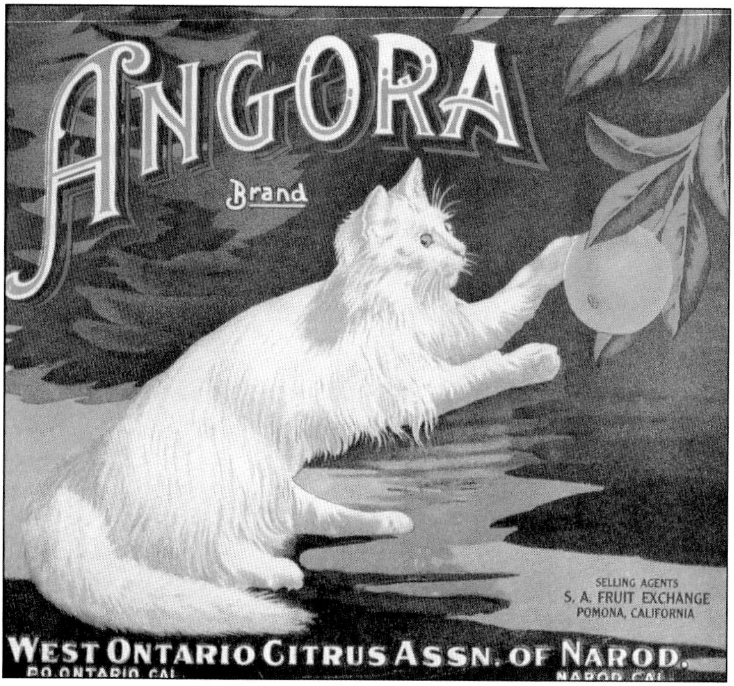

ORANGE CRATE LABEL. This orange crate label was the brand label of the West Ontario Citrus Association of Narod, California, located at the Southern Pacific Railroad tracks on the east side of Central Avenue in what is now Montclair. The association donated the land for the first fire station in Monte Vista. Ironically, the packing house burned down.

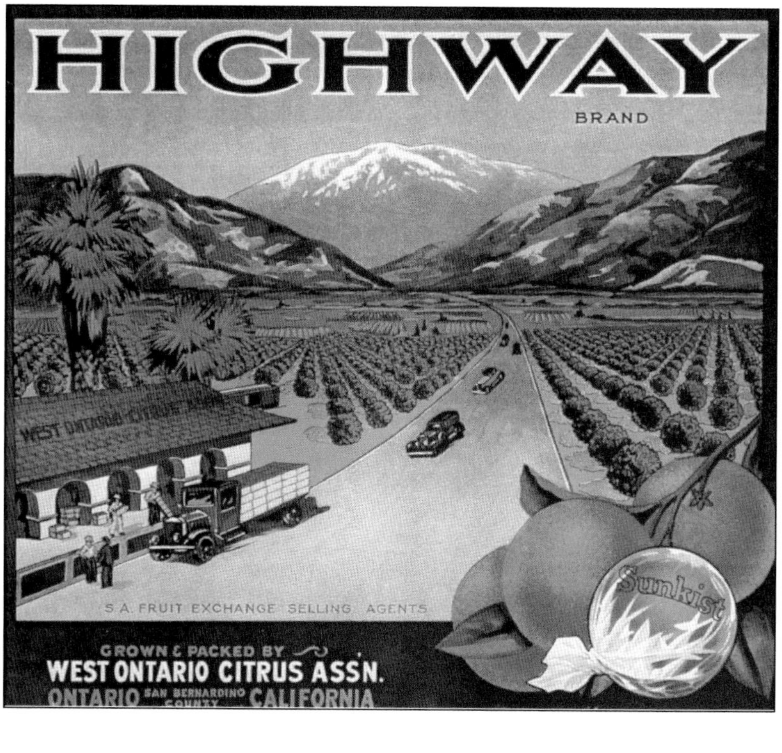

THE WEST ONTARIO CITRUS ASSOCIATION. This packing house was located on Central Avenue in what is now Montclair. The artist's "vision" of the citrus groves laying at the foot of Mount Baldy with its blanket of snow was not an exaggerated one.

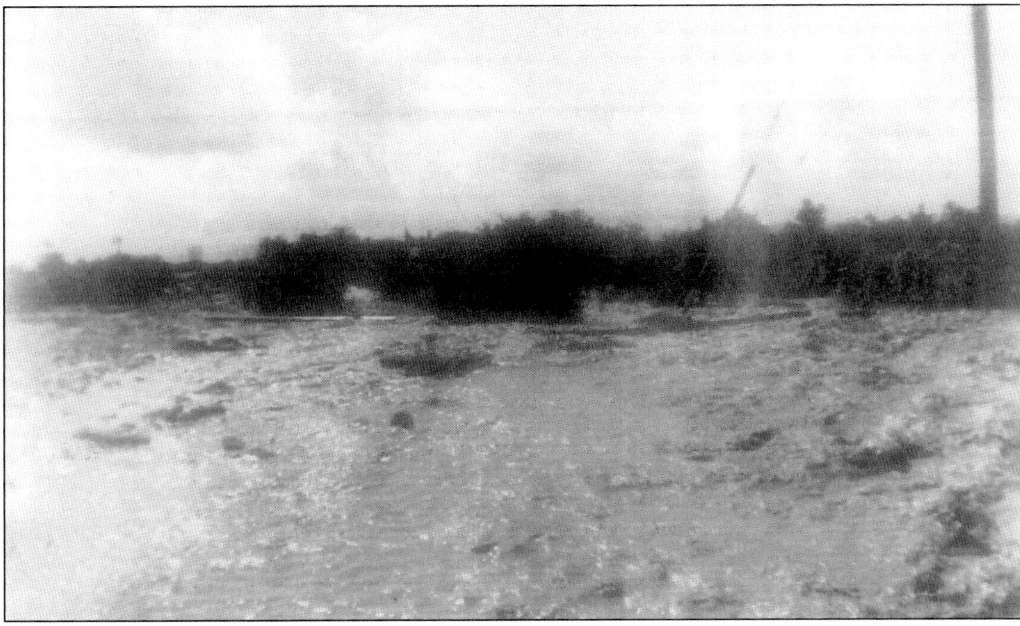

SAN ANTONIO WASH FLOOD, MARCH 2, 1938. These photographs were taken from the Murrays' front yard on Benito Street. The photograph above shows the rushing flood waters, and the photograph below shows the Murrays' yard once the water receded. (Courtesy of Janet Taylor.)

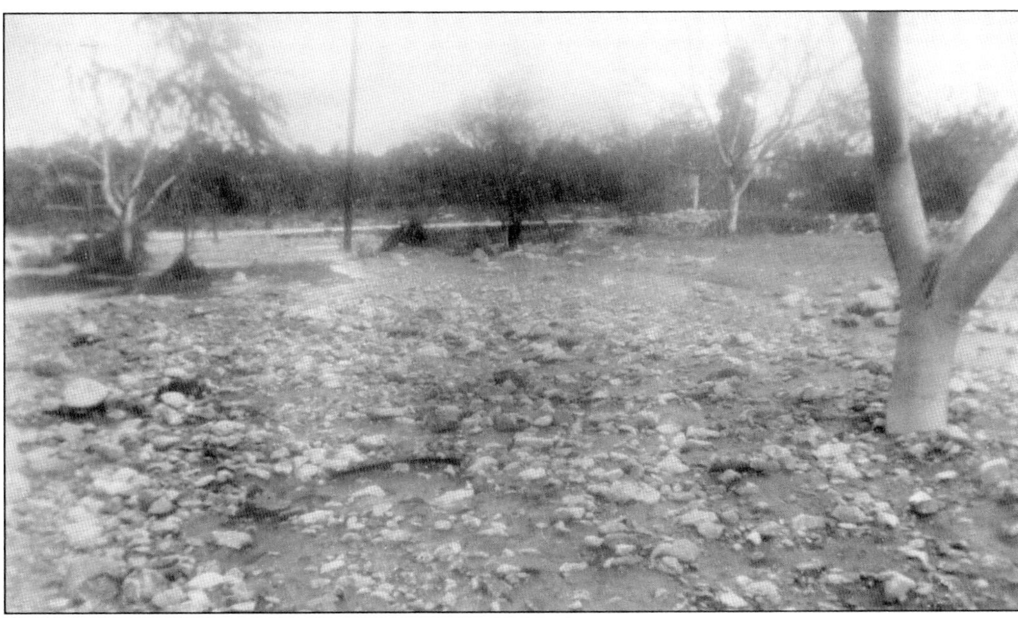

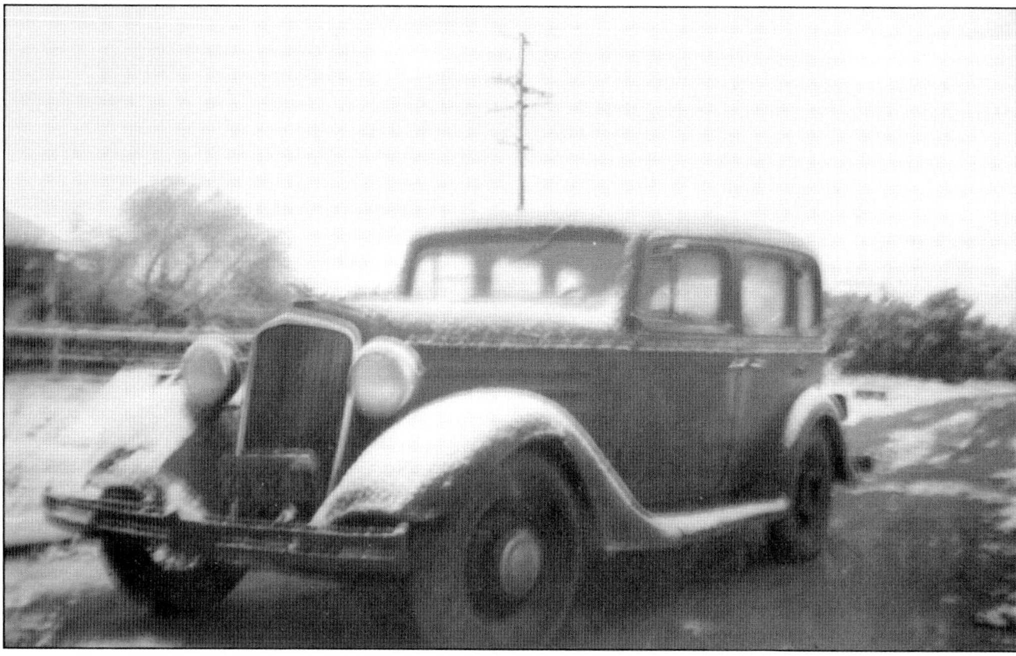

SNOW IN MONTCLAIR, 1949. In the winter of 1949, a freak snow storm visited Montclair. These photographs show snow in the yard of a home located on Orchard Street and ice hanging from a palm tree. (Courtesy of Sylvia Martens.)

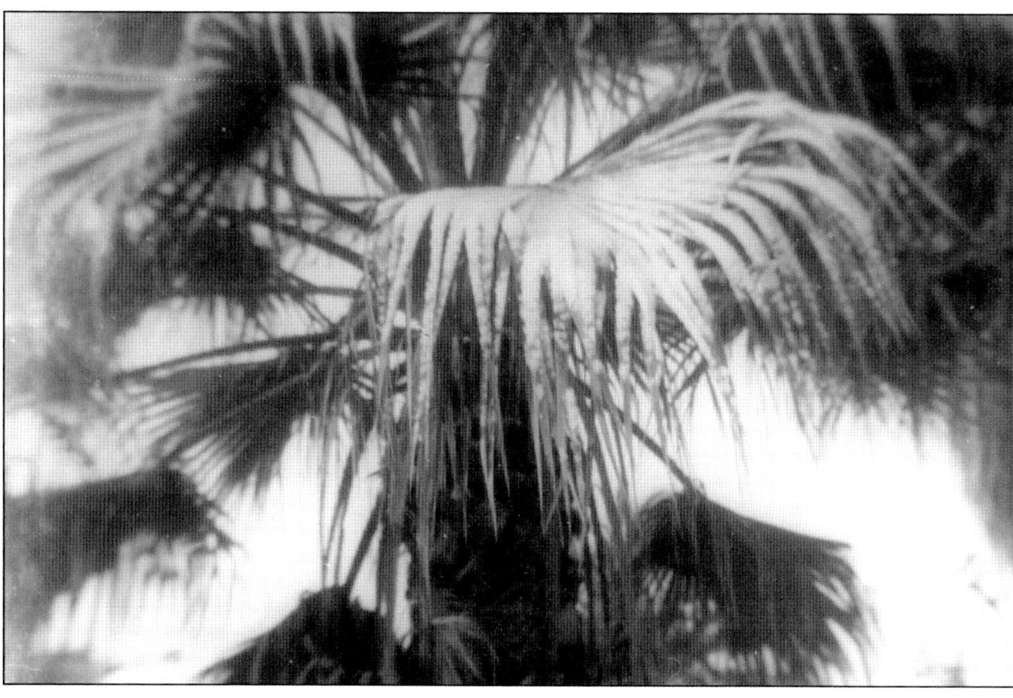

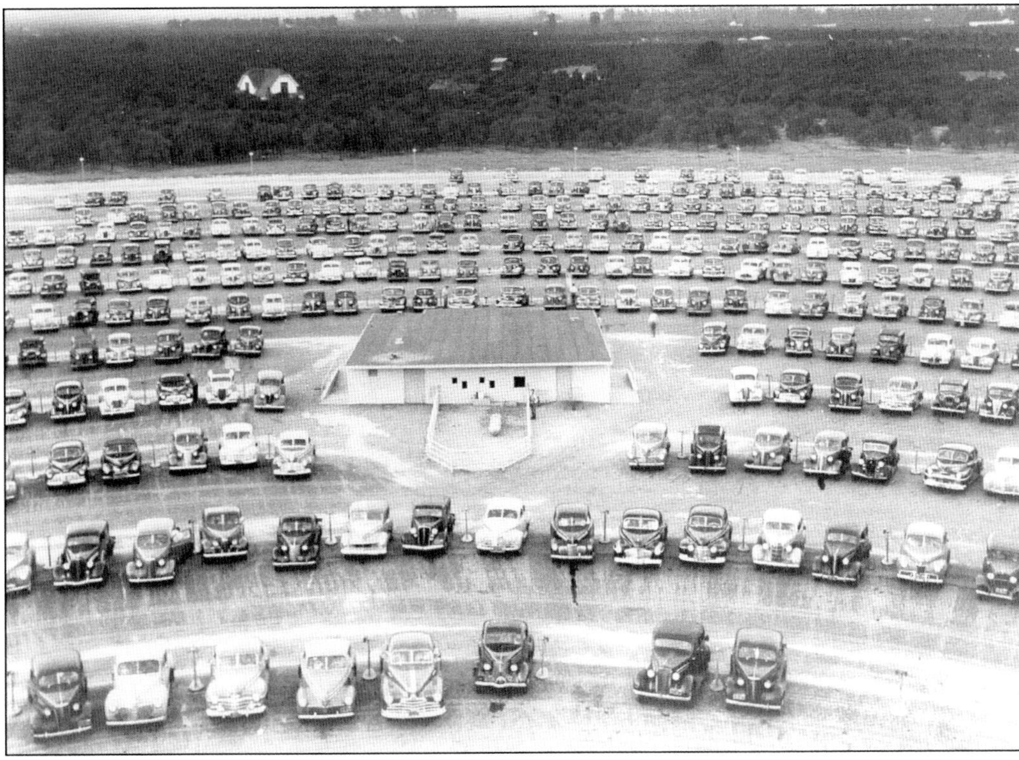

VALLEY DRIVE-IN, C. 1948. The Valley Drive-In was located at Central Avenue and Holt Boulevard. Local automobile dealers displayed new 1948 models for the above photograph.

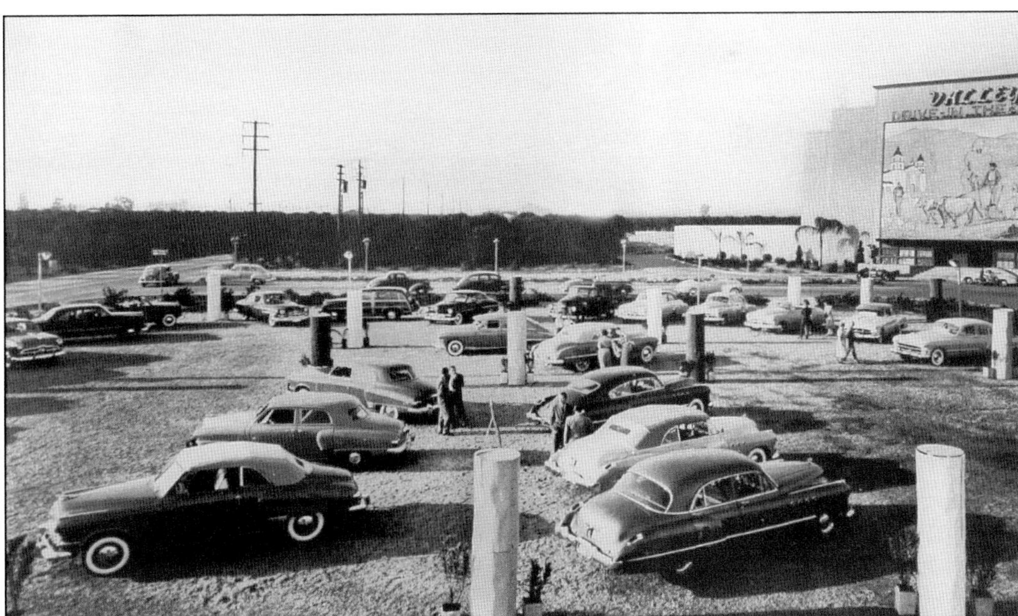

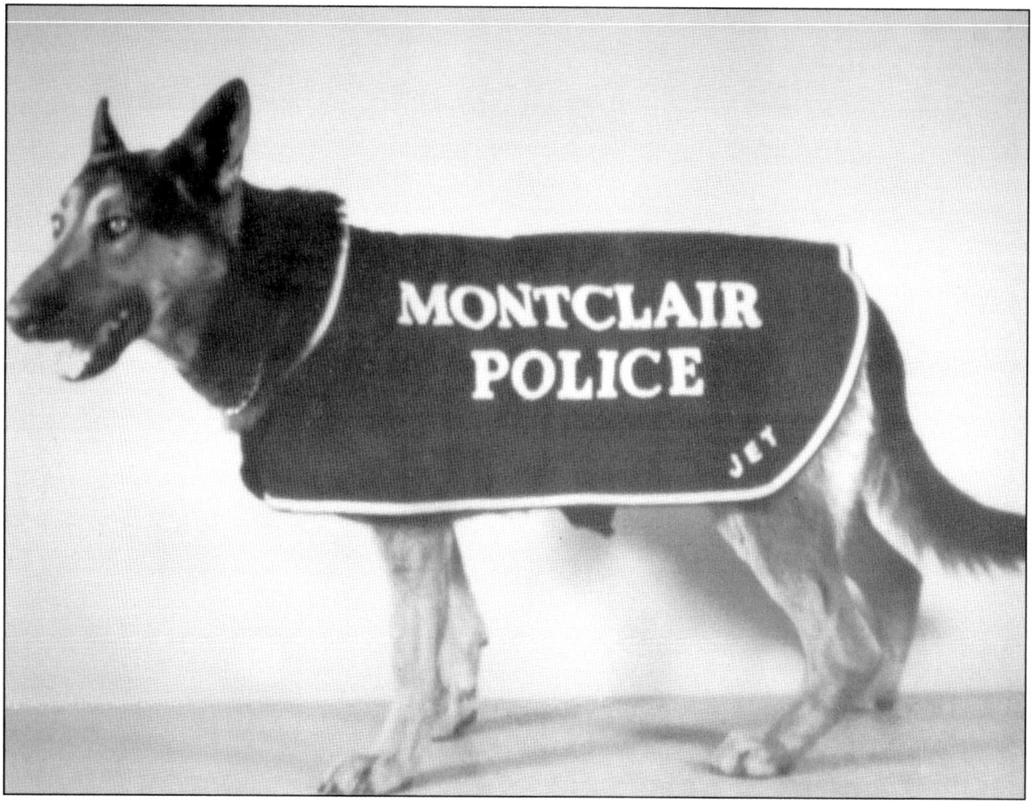

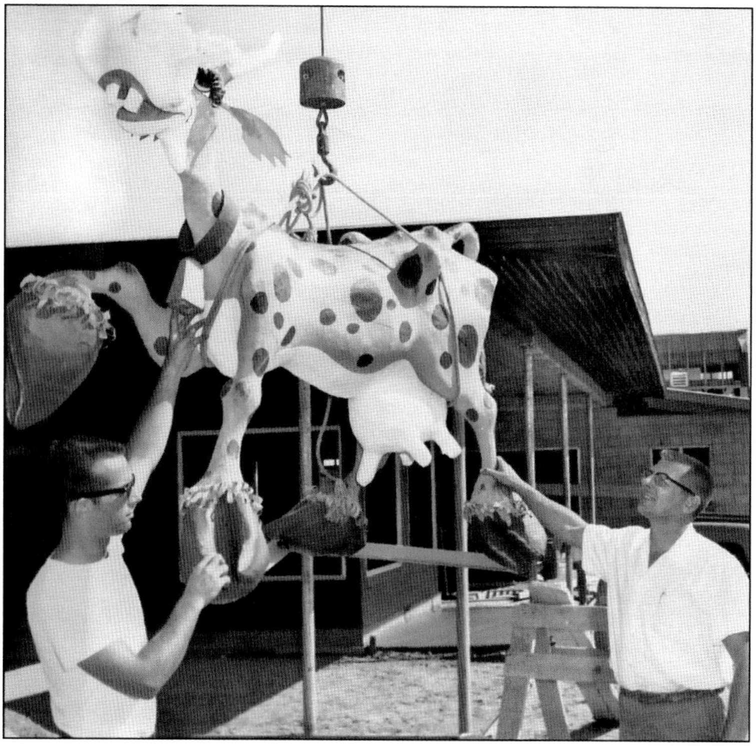

MONTCLAIR POLICE DOG. This is a photograph of Jet, one of the Montclair Police Department's canine recruits.

JERRY'S PURPLE SPOTTED COW, C. 1961. Jerry Van Andel (right) hoists the cow that stood in front of his dairy situated on the south side of San Bernardino Street just west of Central Avenue. He was not only a dairyman and businessman, he also served on the Montclair City Council.

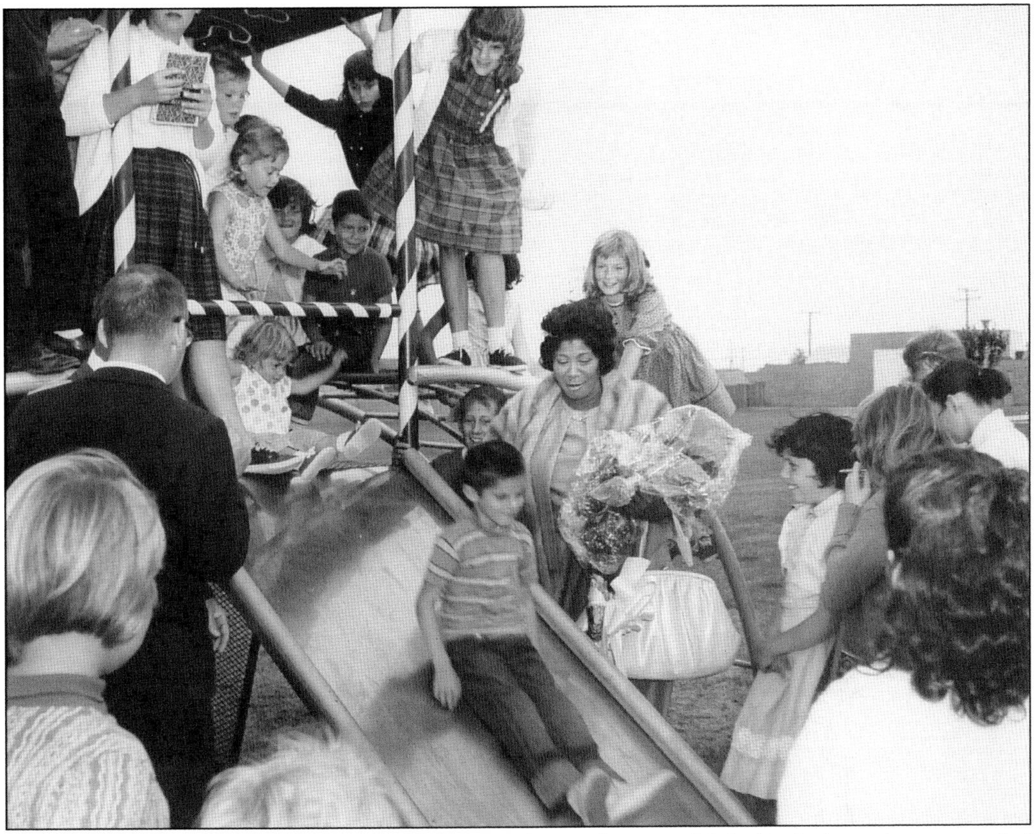

MAHALIA JACKSON, JUNE 3, 1963. Renowned gospel singer Mahalia Jackson is surrounded by children in the play area of Alma Hoffman Park, adjacent to the civic center complex. Miss Jackson gave three performances for the Montclair Kiwanis Club, which donated funds for park amenities, including the sand-filled pond and shark. (Courtesy of the Montclair Chamber of Commerce.)

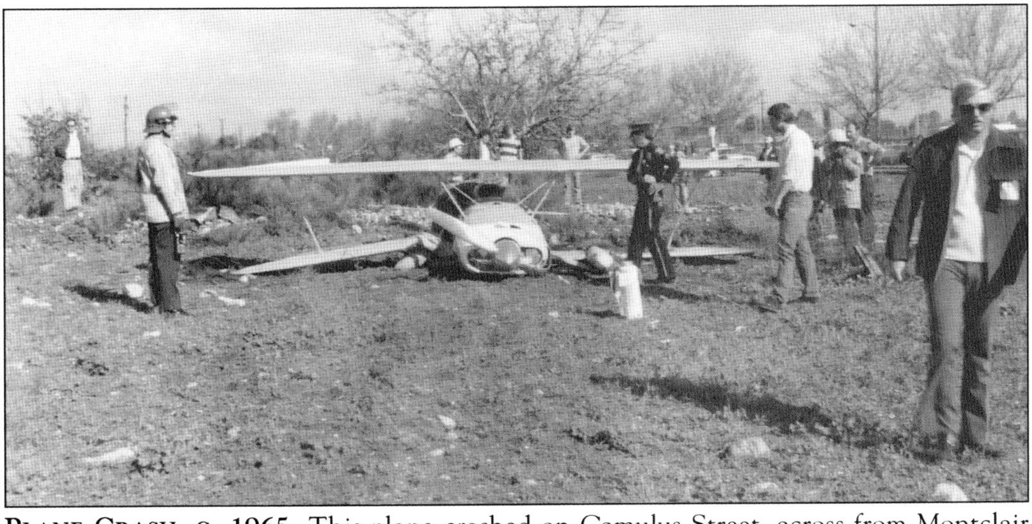

PLANE CRASH, C. 1965. This plane crashed on Camulus Street, across from Montclair High School.

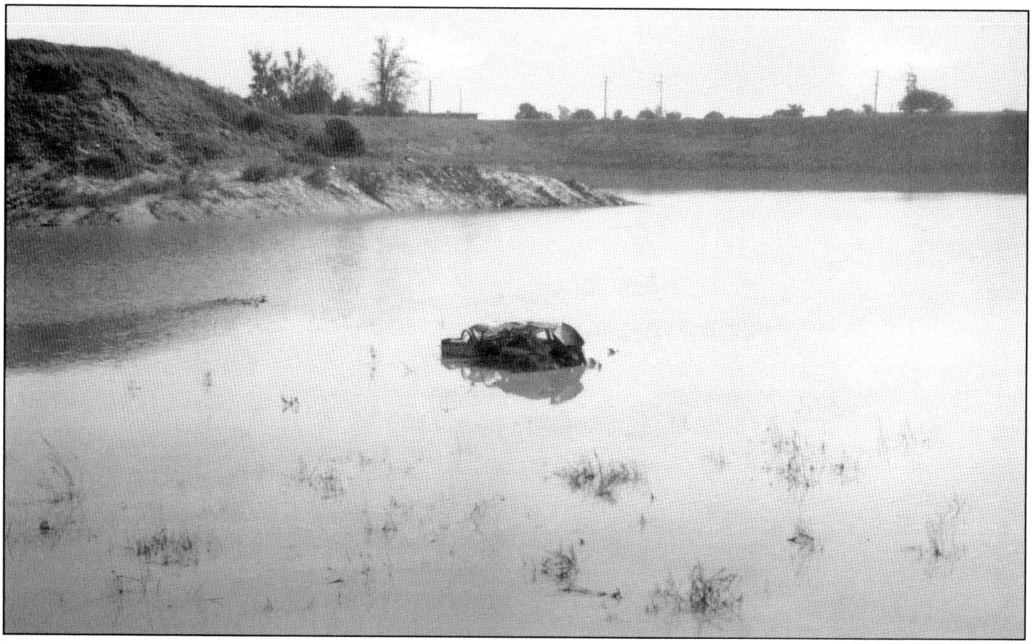

Moreno Street Flood, c. 1968. This car was caught when flood waters destroyed Moreno Street. Rescue workers were called to the scene to search for survivors.

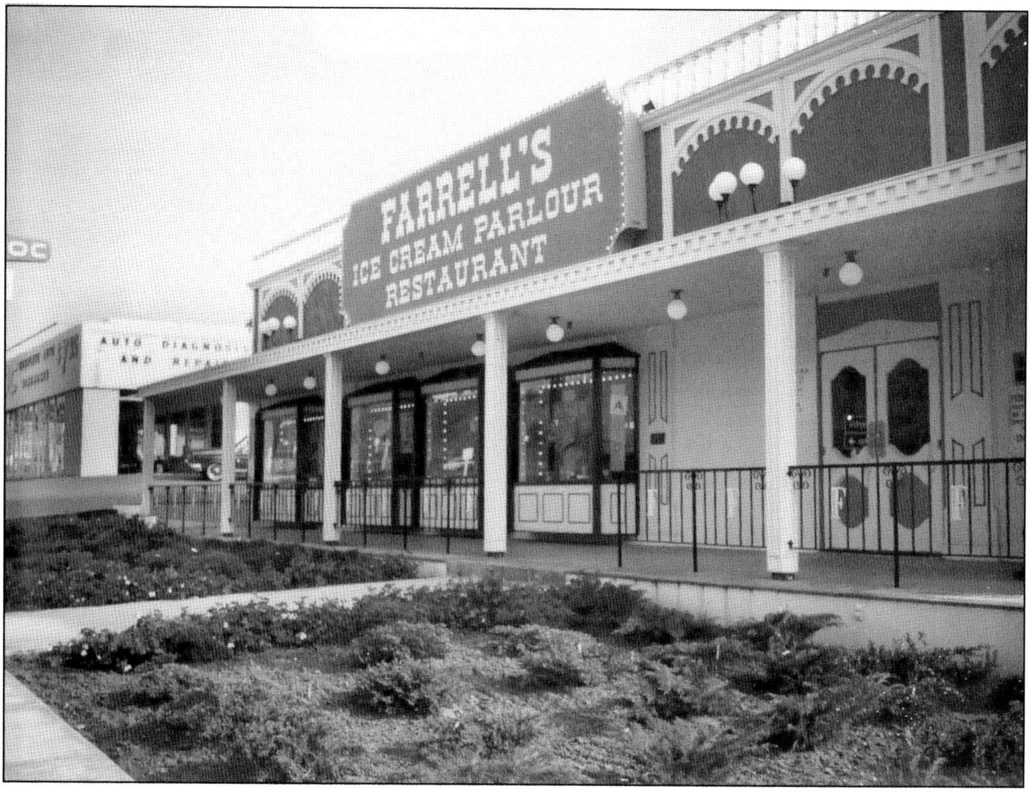

Farrell's Ice Cream Parlour Restaurant, 1967. Farrell's was located at the northwest corner of the Montclair Plaza parking lot.

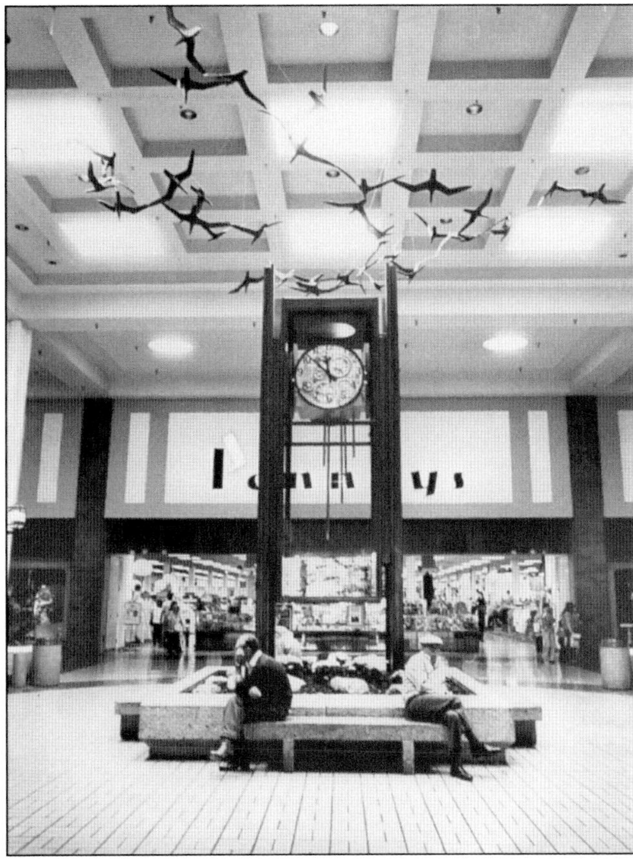

The Clock Tower and the Birds. For decades, the giant clock tower—above which hovered seagulls in flight, sculpted by artist John Svenson—was located in the center portico of the Montclair Plaza and served as a primary meeting place for shoppers.

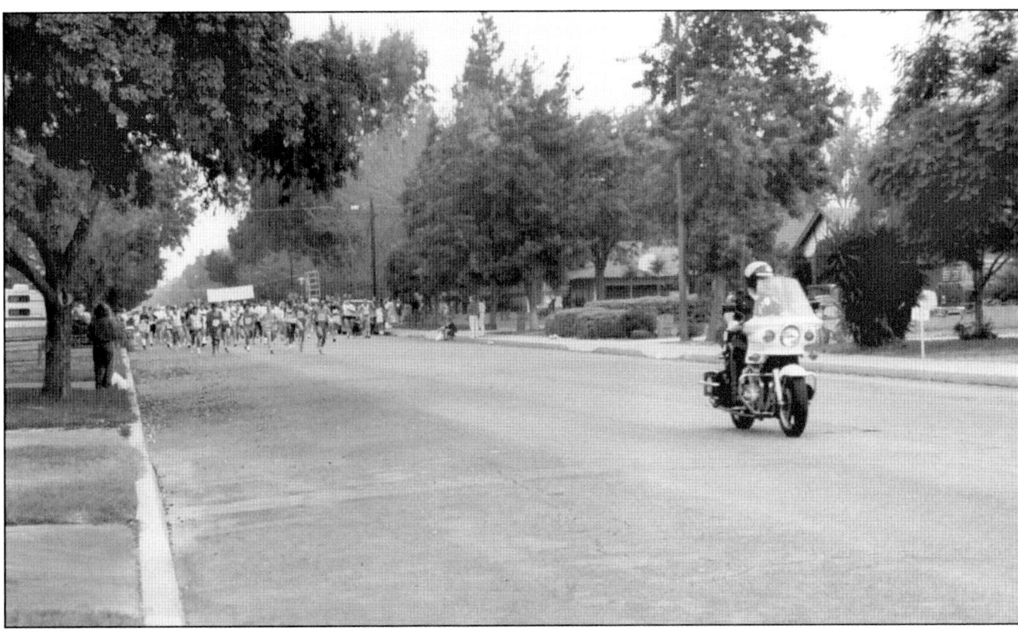

Montclair Run, c. 1980. Each year, the City of Montclair Human Services Department would hold a fun run in which many residents enjoyed participating.

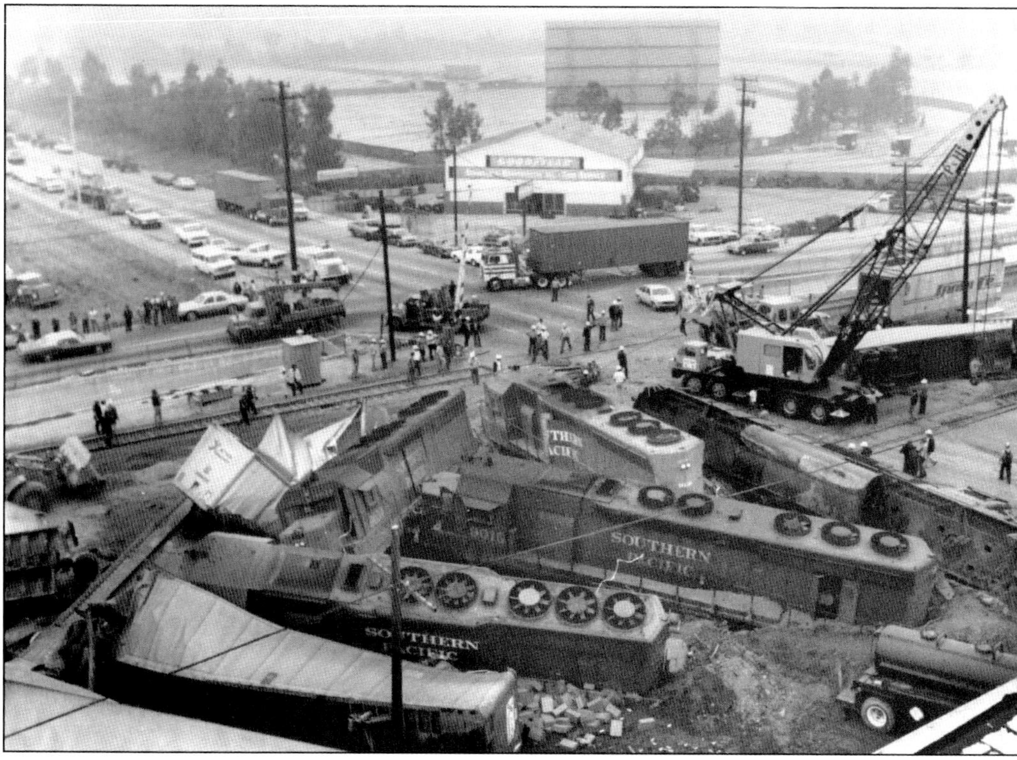

TRAIN WRECK, C. 1982. This crash happened on the southern tracks at Ramona Avenue, the street towards the center of the photograph, looking north. The Montclair Fire Department was on the scene cleaning up the debris for weeks after the wreck.

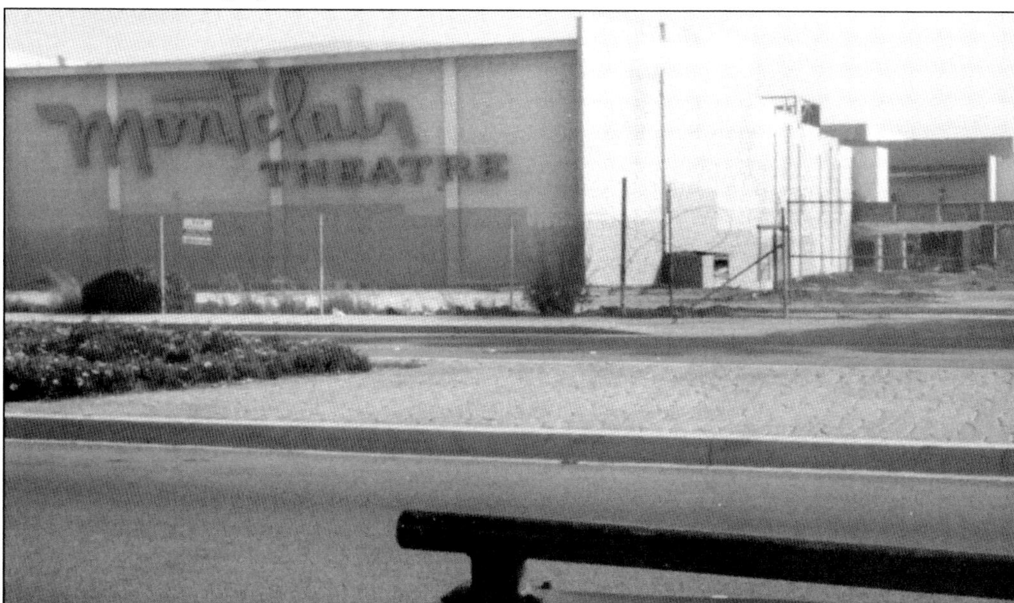

MONTCLAIR THEATRE, 1999. This theatre was located at 4377 Holt Boulevard. It was demolished in 1999 to make way for a new housing tract.

Five

BIRD'S-EYE VIEWS

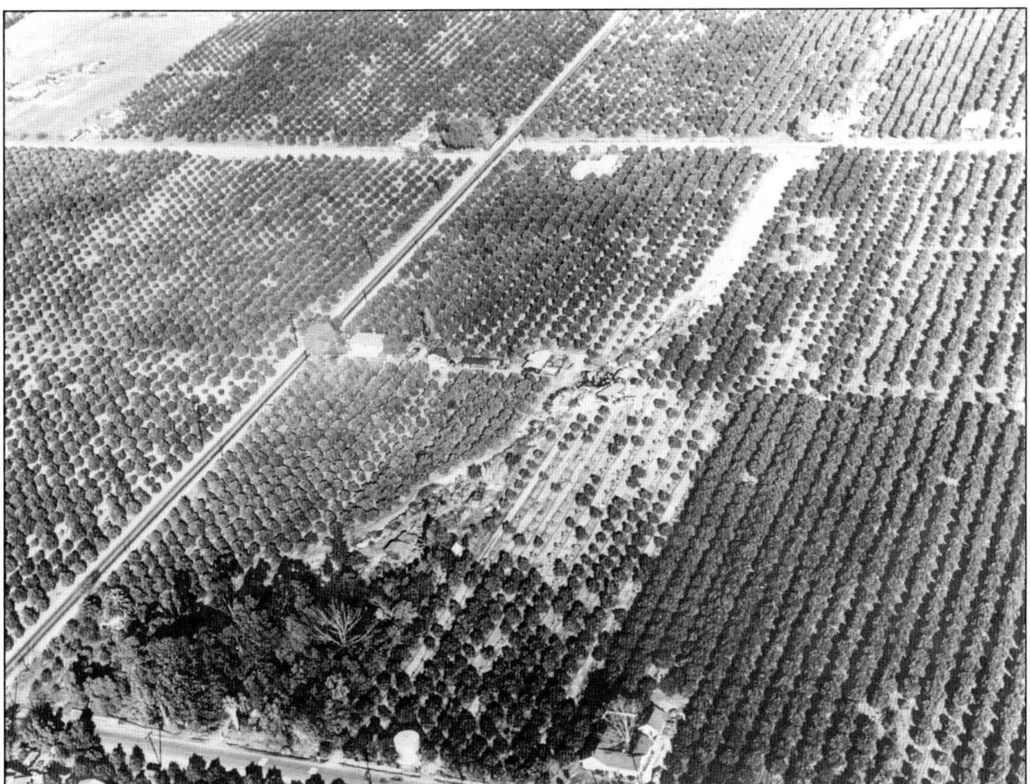

AERIAL SHOT OF MONTCLAIR. Central Avenue is on the left running north and south. The streets going across the page are San Jose Street, Palo Verde Street, and San Bernardino Street.

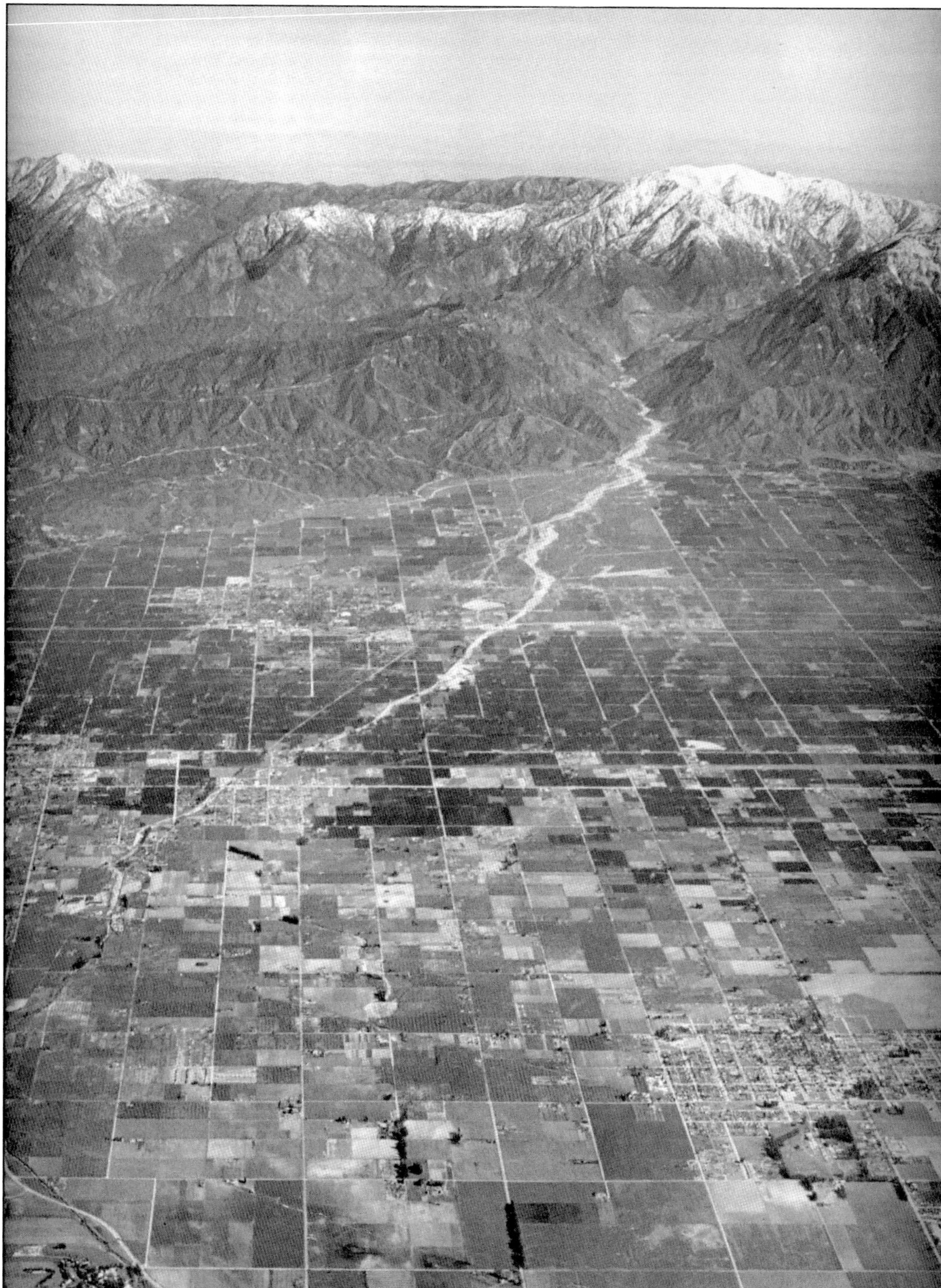

AERIAL VIEW OF THE MONTCLAIR VISTA TRACT, 1948. Note the abundance of orange groves covering the landscape of what was, in 1948, the Montclair Vista Tract and is now Montclair. The Valley Drive-In can be seen towards the middle of the photograph.

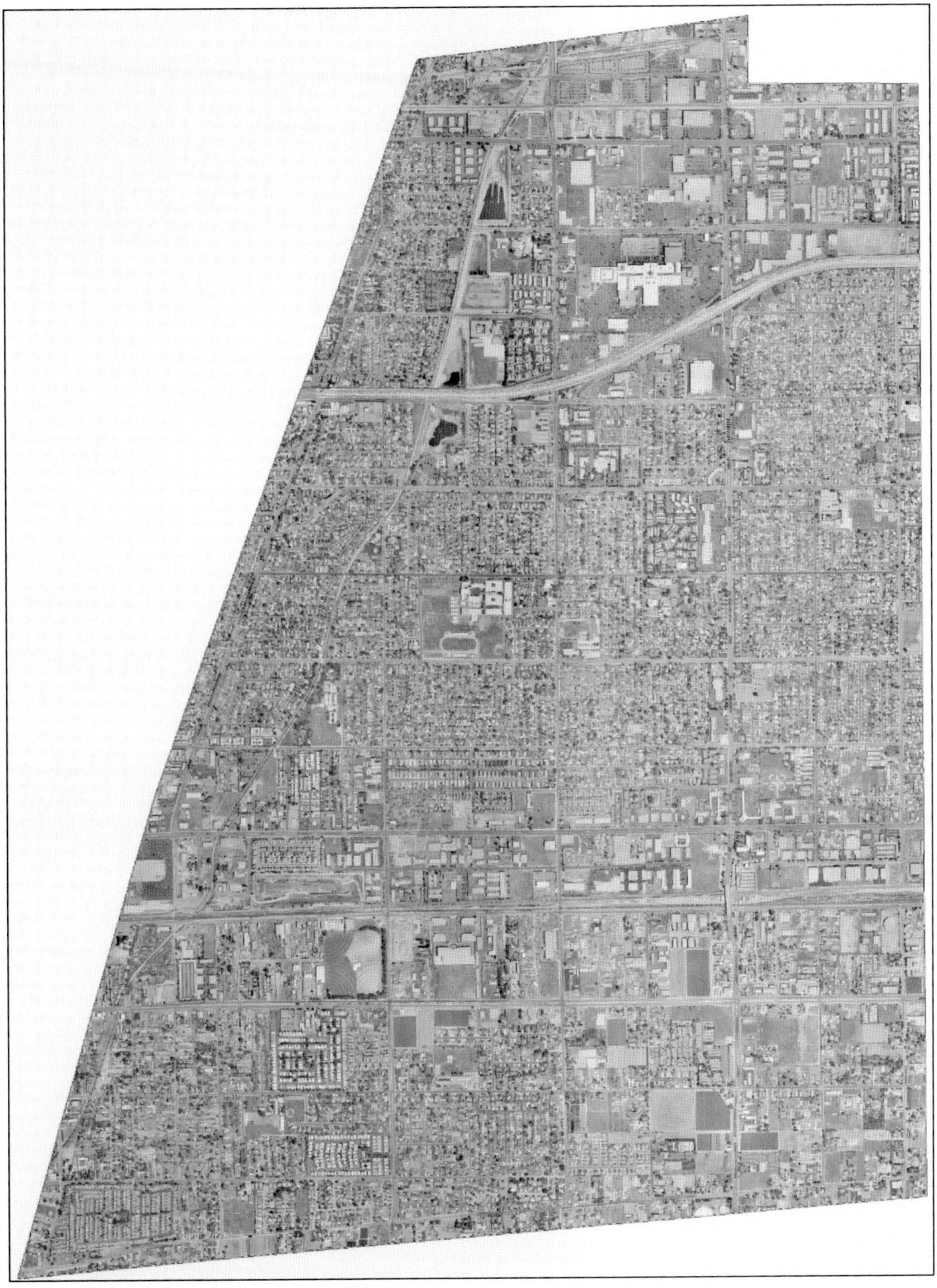

AERIAL VIEW OF MONTCLAIR, 2002.

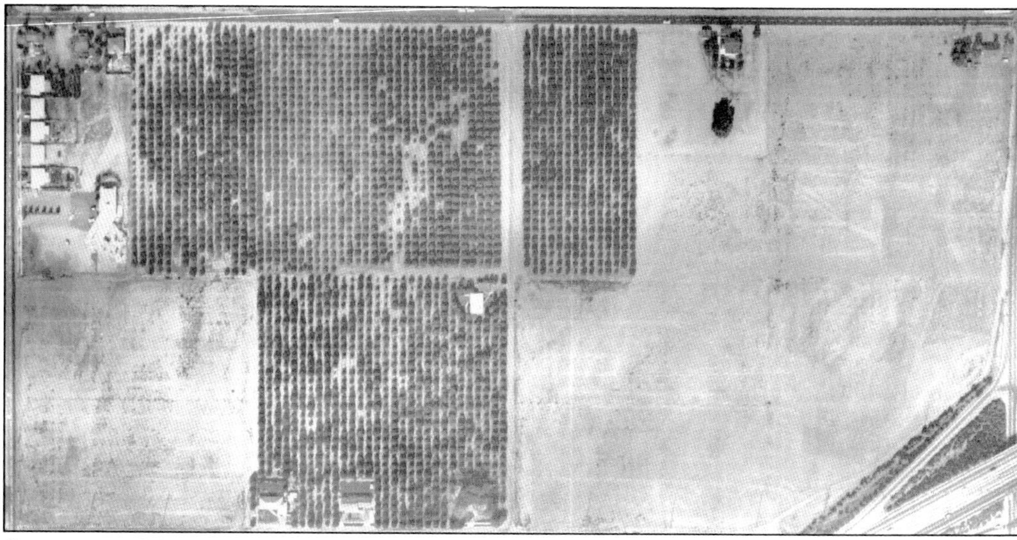

Site of the Montclair Plaza, 1962. This photograph shows the land currently occupied by the Montclair Plaza. The I-10 Freeway intersects Central Avenue in the lower right corner.

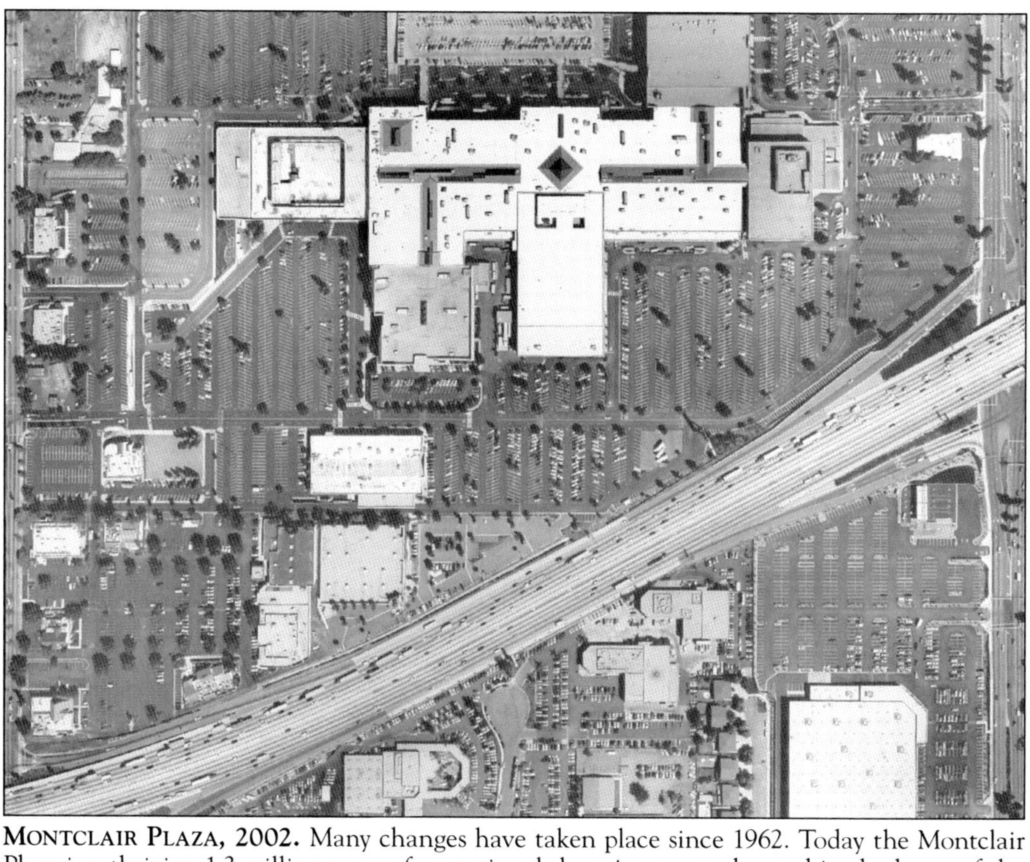

Montclair Plaza, 2002. Many changes have taken place since 1962. Today the Montclair Plaza is a thriving 1.3-million-square-foot regional shopping center located in the heart of the city, just off I-10.

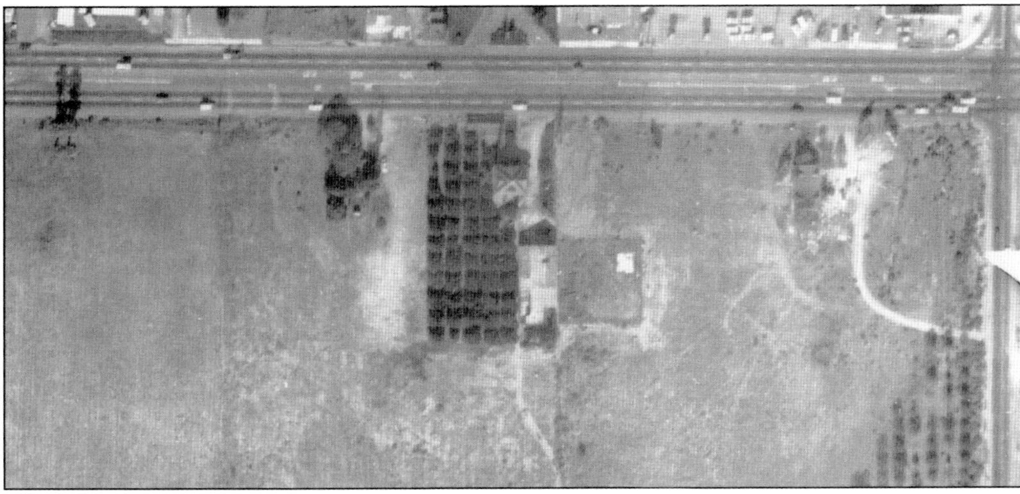

REEDER HOME, 1962. At the top of this photograph is the Reeder home, located on Holt Boulevard. The Reeder family moved the building was moved to this location in 1901, and it has remained in the family ever since. The Reeders were orange growers and were active in the Montclair community.

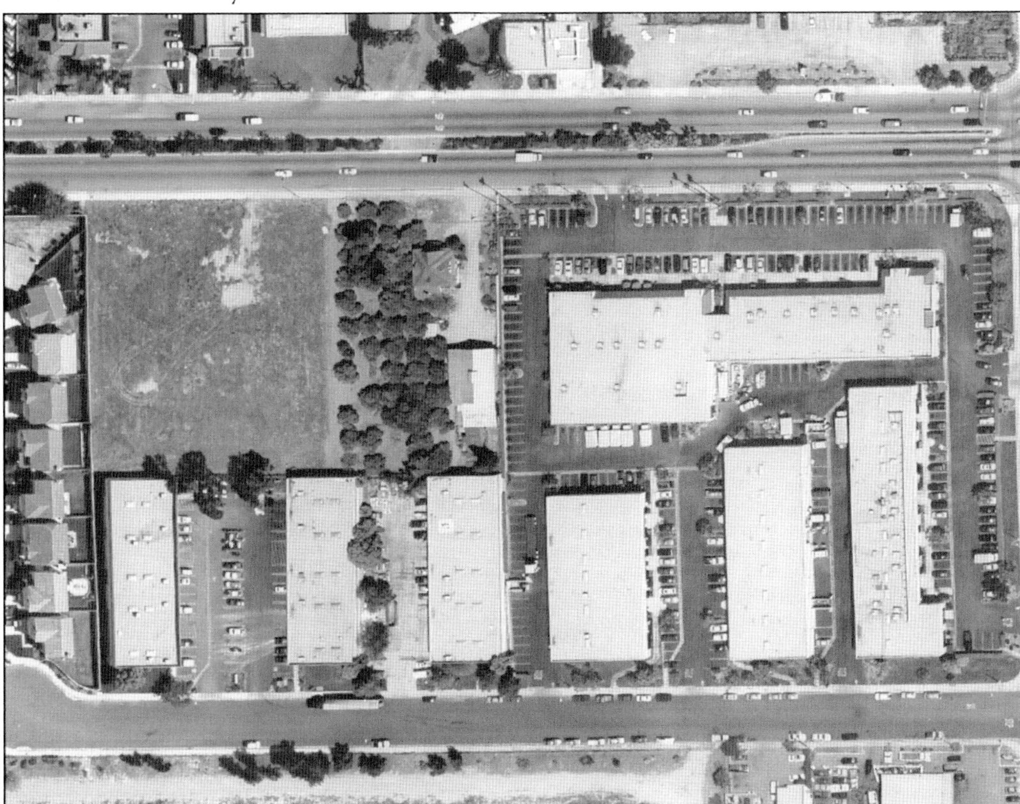

REEDER HOME, 2002. Much growth has taken place around the Reeder homestead. The city is working with the Reeder family to preserve the home as a historic site and local museum. The orange groves that remain on the property are over 100 years old and still produce an abundance of delicious fruit.

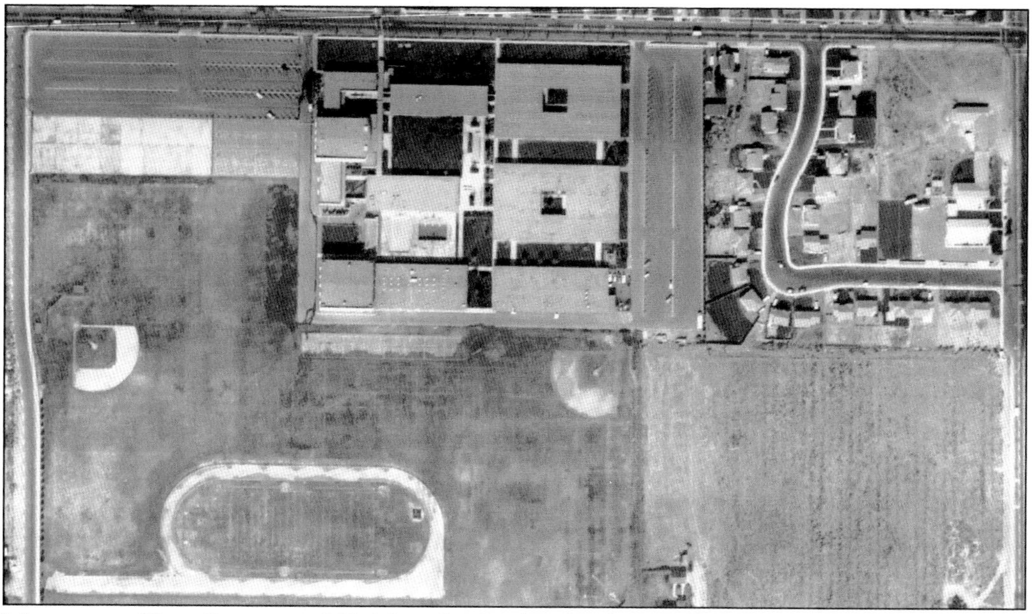

MONTCLAIR HIGH SCHOOL, 1962. Montclair High School opened it doors on Monday, September 14, 1959. When this photograph was taken in 1962, MHS was home to 1,585 students, 72 teachers, and 9 administrators.

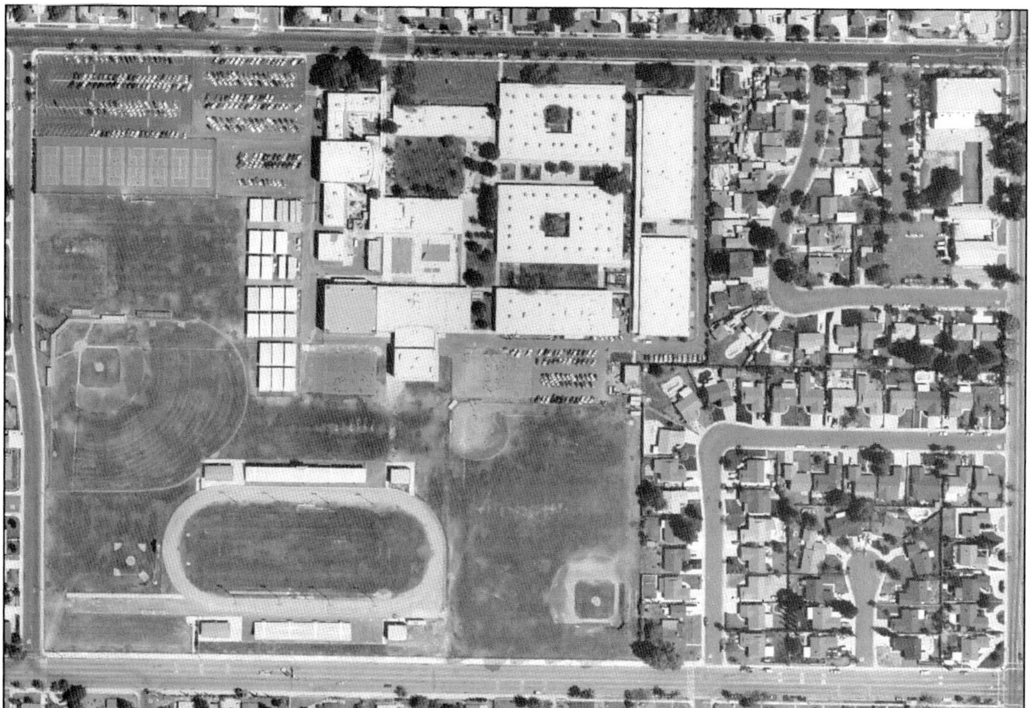

MONTCLAIR HIGH SCHOOL, 2002. Today MHS is one of six comprehensive high schools in the Chaffey Joint Union High School District, with more than 3,300 students enrolled in grades 9–12. This campus has served the community since 1959 and features a stadium, two gymnasiums, an auditorium, and the electronic media center.

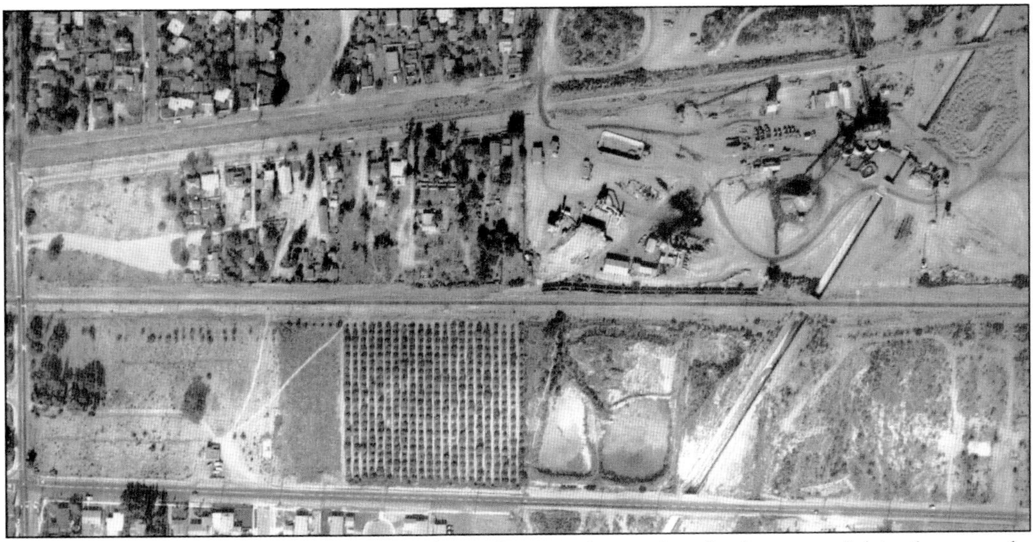

MONTCLAIR TRANSCENTER, 1962. Richton Street is located at the bottom of this photograph. The home and orange groves depicted in the center are situated where the upper parking lot is now located (see photograph below).

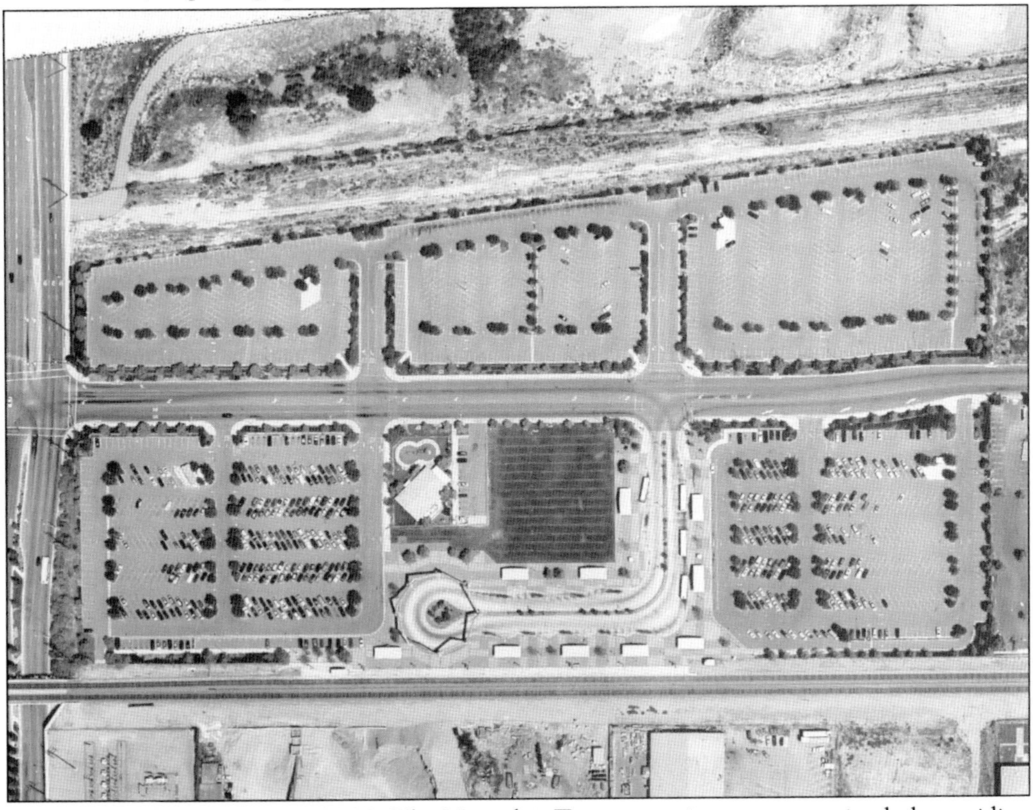

MONTCLAIR TRANSCENTER, 2002. The Montclair Transcenter is a transportation hub providing commuters with transit connections served by Metrolink, Onmitrans, and Foothill Transit bus services, and a park-and-ride facility. The Transcenter is the future home of a Metro Gold Line light rail system to take commuters from Montclair to Los Angeles.

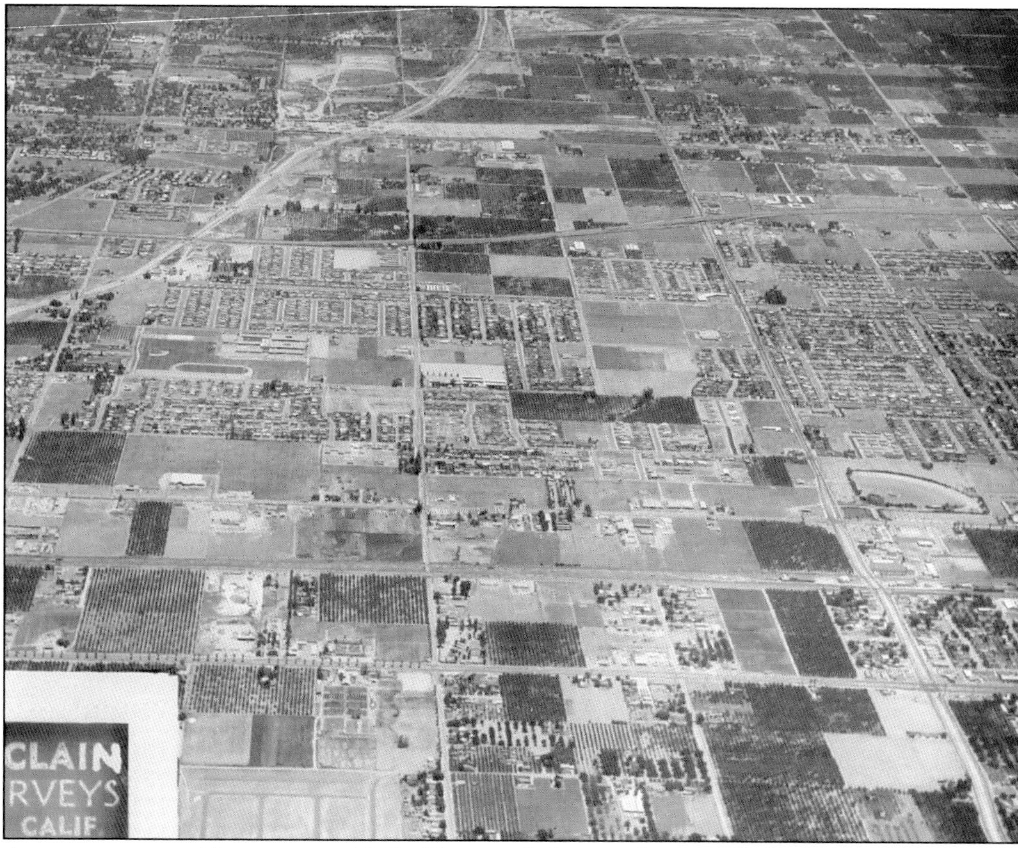

AERIAL VIEW OF MONTCLAIR, 1961. This north-facing photograph shows many of the city's original orange groves still in existence. The Mission Drive-In can be seen in the lower left corner, the Valley Drive-In can be seen on the right, and the I-10 Freeway can be seen toward the top. Orange groves fill the area where the Montclair Plaza would later be built.

Six

People, Places, and Things

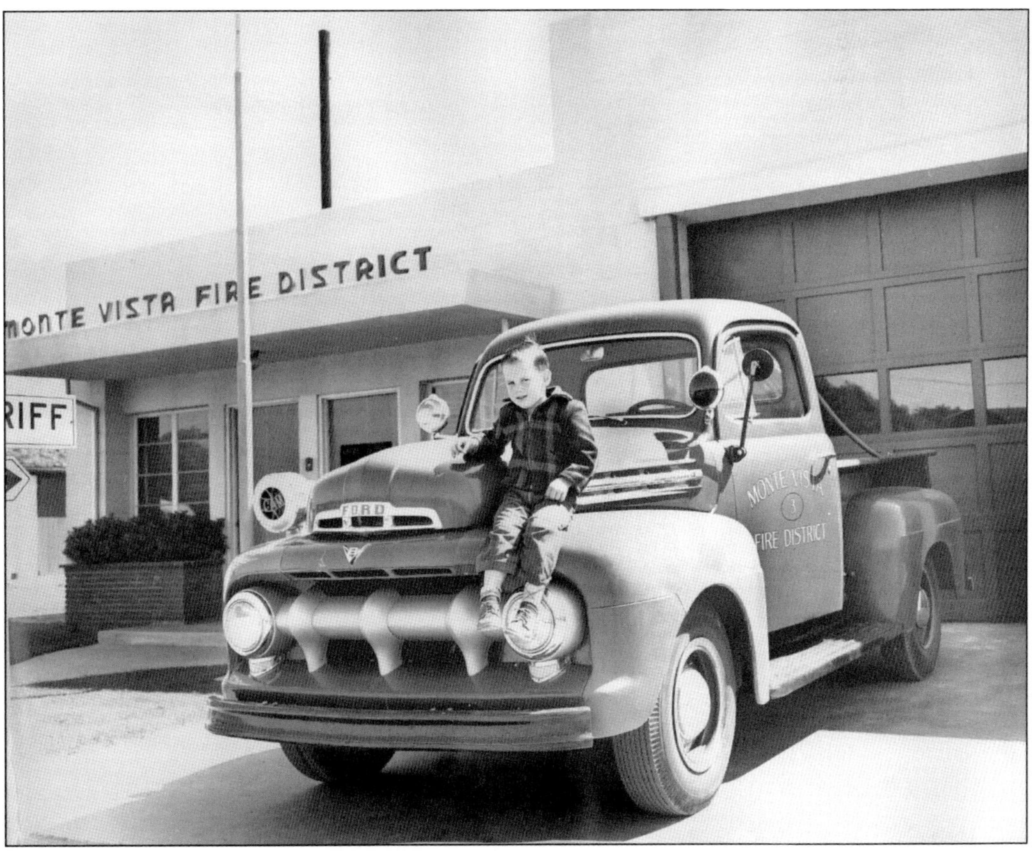

Volunteer Fireman, 1953. George Pantazin is the son of volunteer firefighter Art Pantazin. George is sitting on a 1951 Ford pickup truck with a pumper. This truck belonged to Unit No. 3 and the chief. (Courtesy of Doug Zoccoli.)

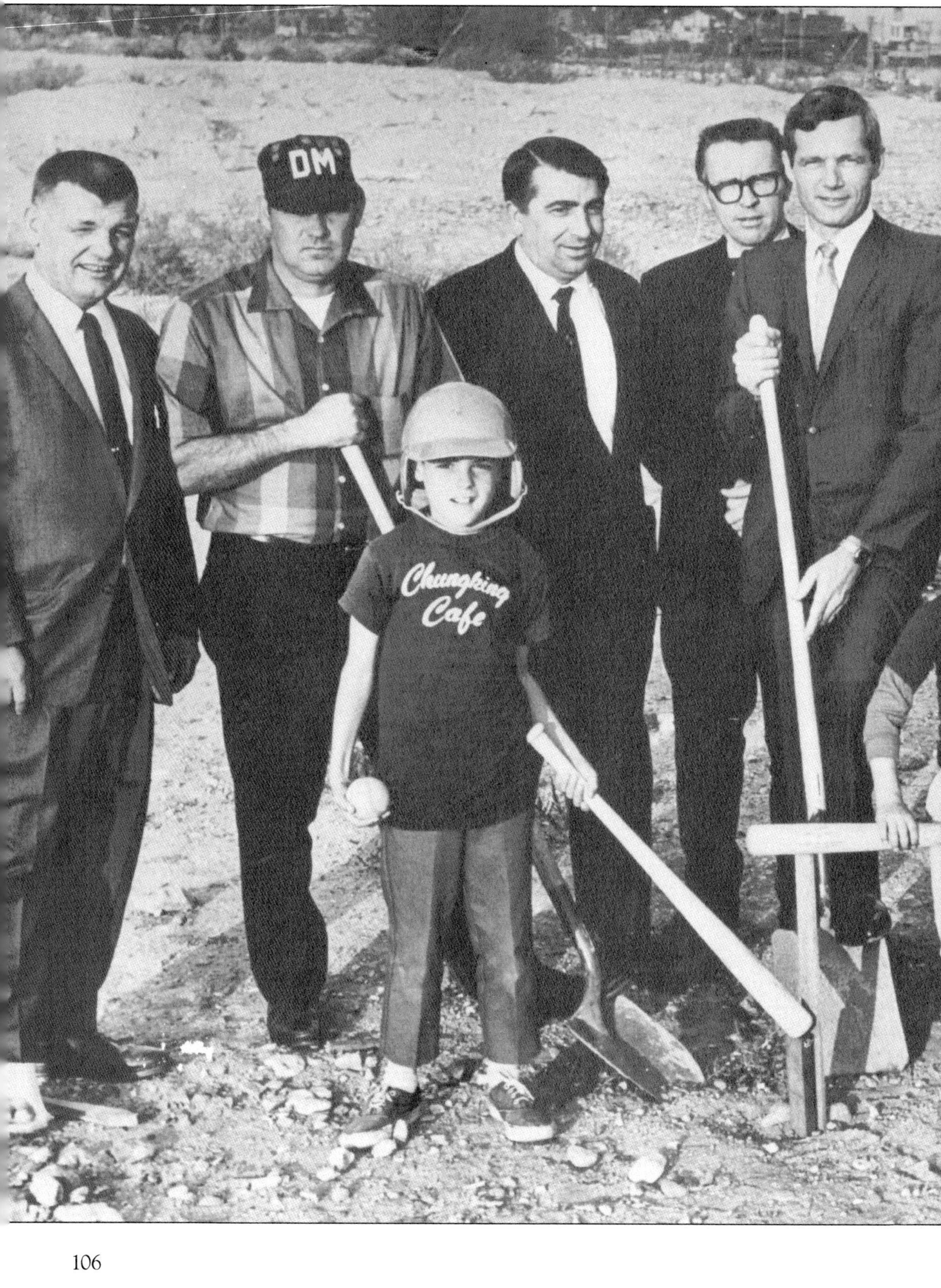
DM
Chungking
Cafe

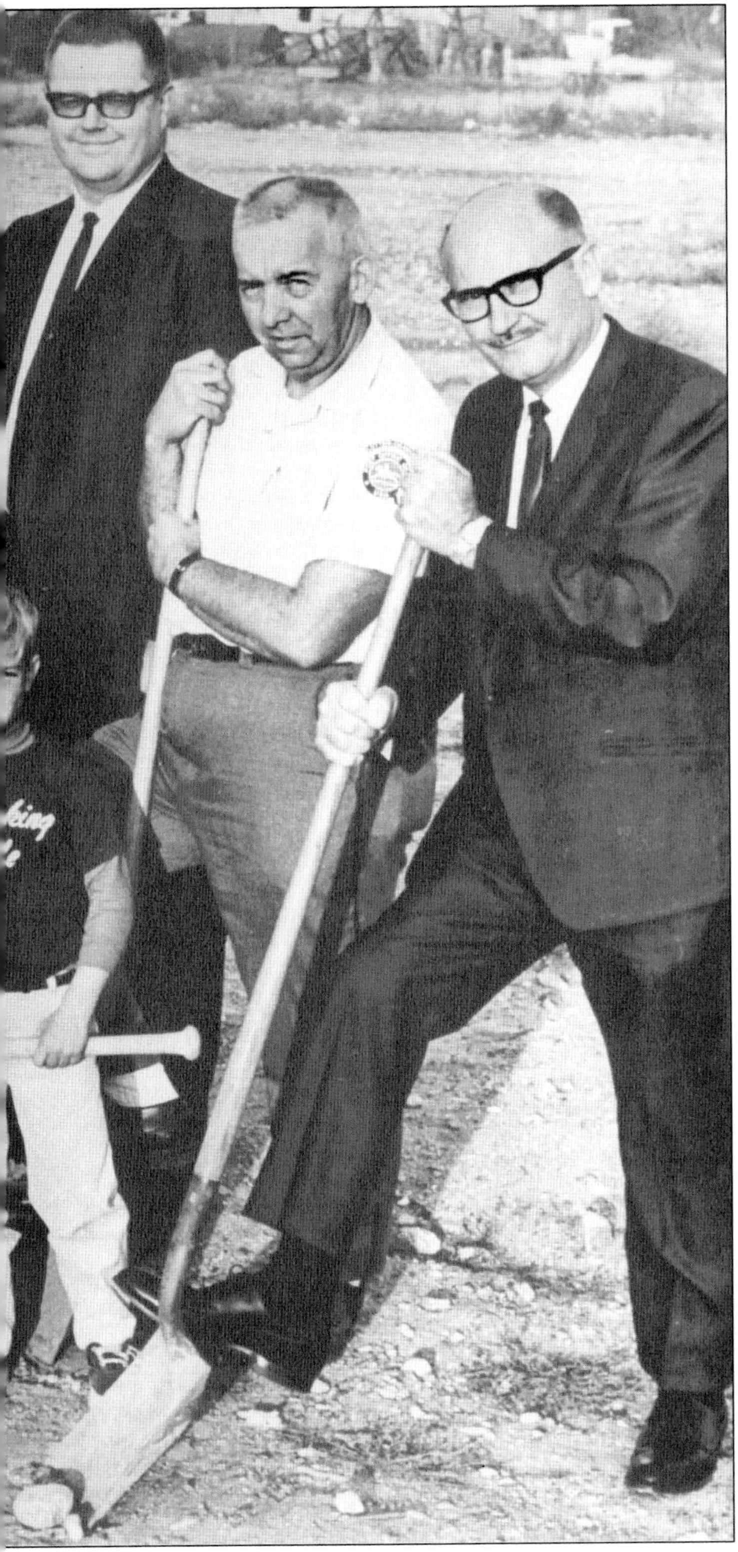

KENNEDY PARK GROUNDBREAKING, 1964. This was the first youth baseball park developed by the City of Montclair at Arrow Highway and Monte Vista Avenue. Fire Station No. 1 is now at this location.

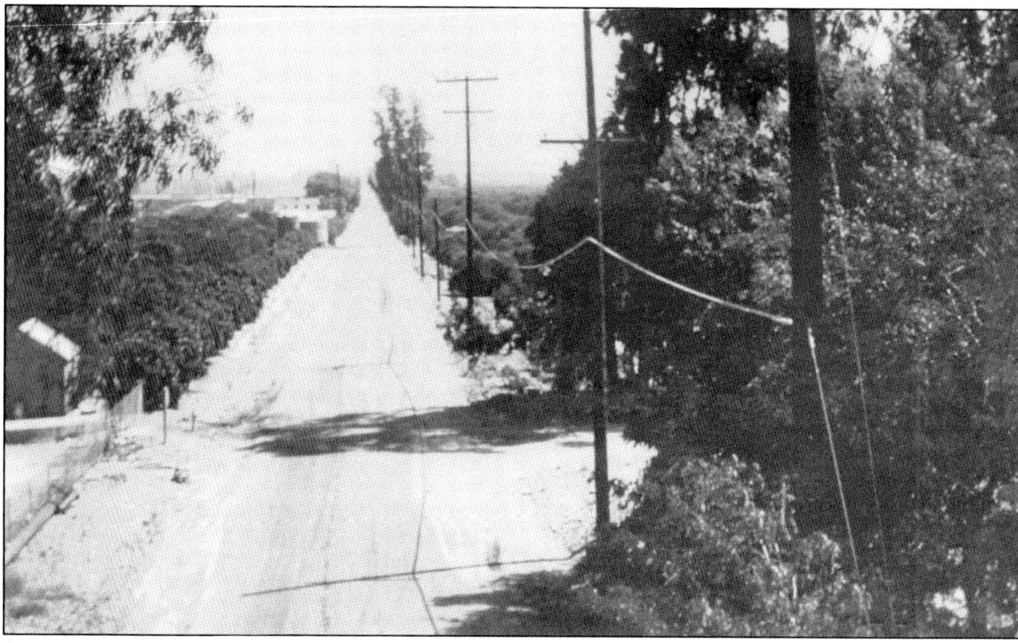

SAN BERNARDINO STREET. This photograph was taken of San Bernardino Street looking east towards Central Avenue.

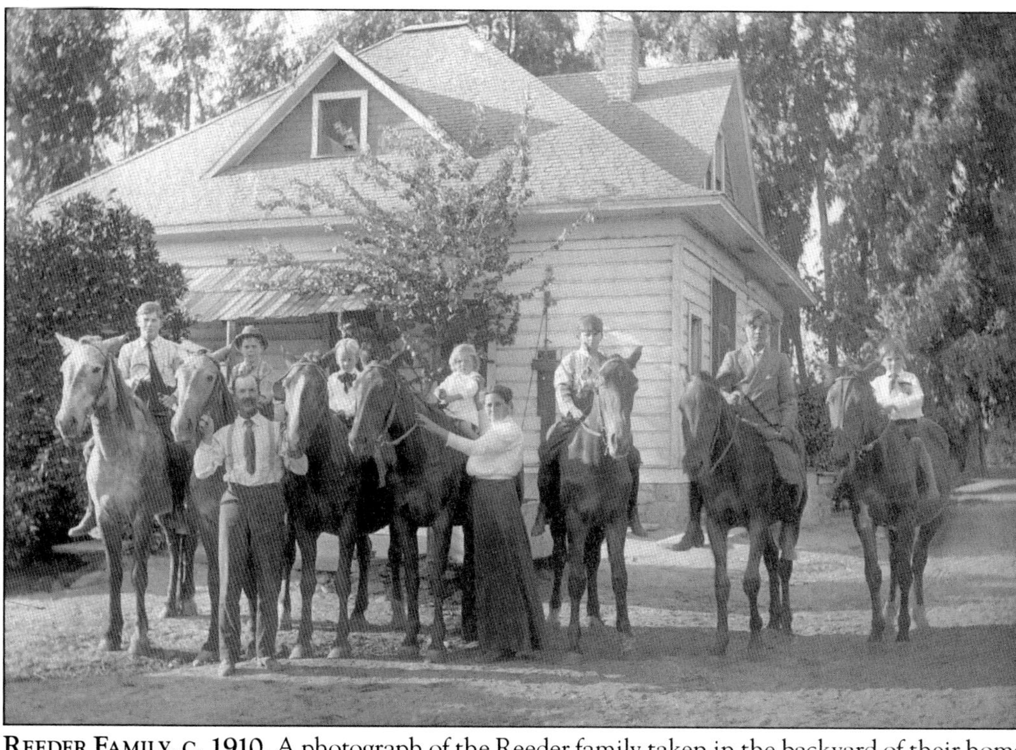

REEDER FAMILY, C. 1910. A photograph of the Reeder family taken in the backyard of their home located on Holt Boulevard, where the home still stands. Pictured in front of the horses are J. C. and Lulu B. Reeder. J. C. and Lulu had seven sons—Paul, Arthur, Donald, L. DeWitt, George, Teddy, and Stanley—who are pictured here on horseback. (Courtesy of Wes Reeder.)

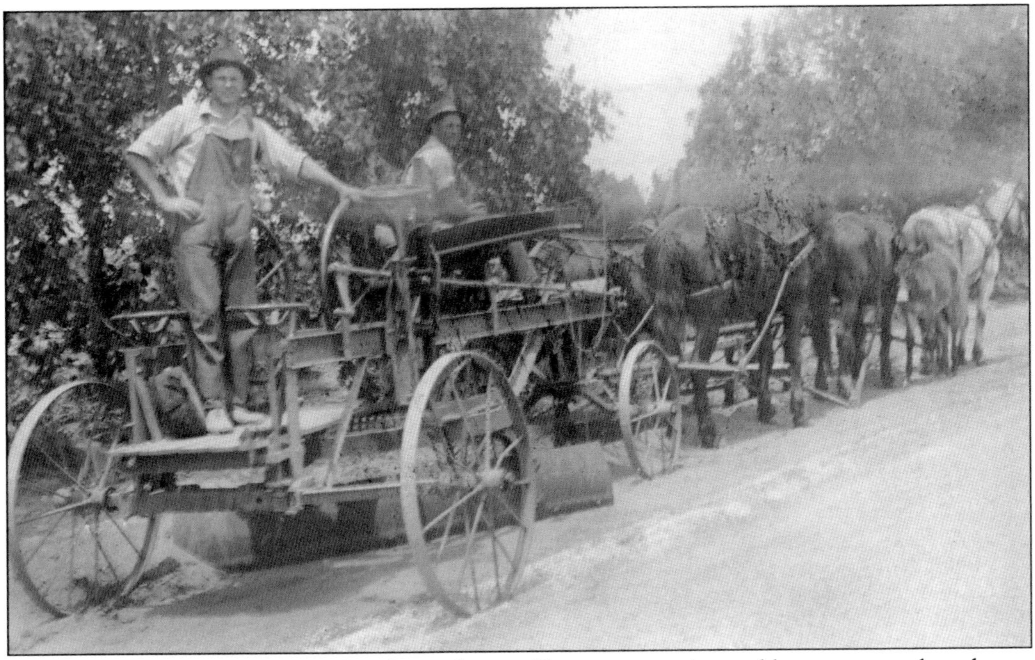

ROAD GRADER, C. 1912. J. C. Reeder and one of his sons are pictured here on a road grader on Holt Boulevard. (Courtesy of Wes Reeder.)

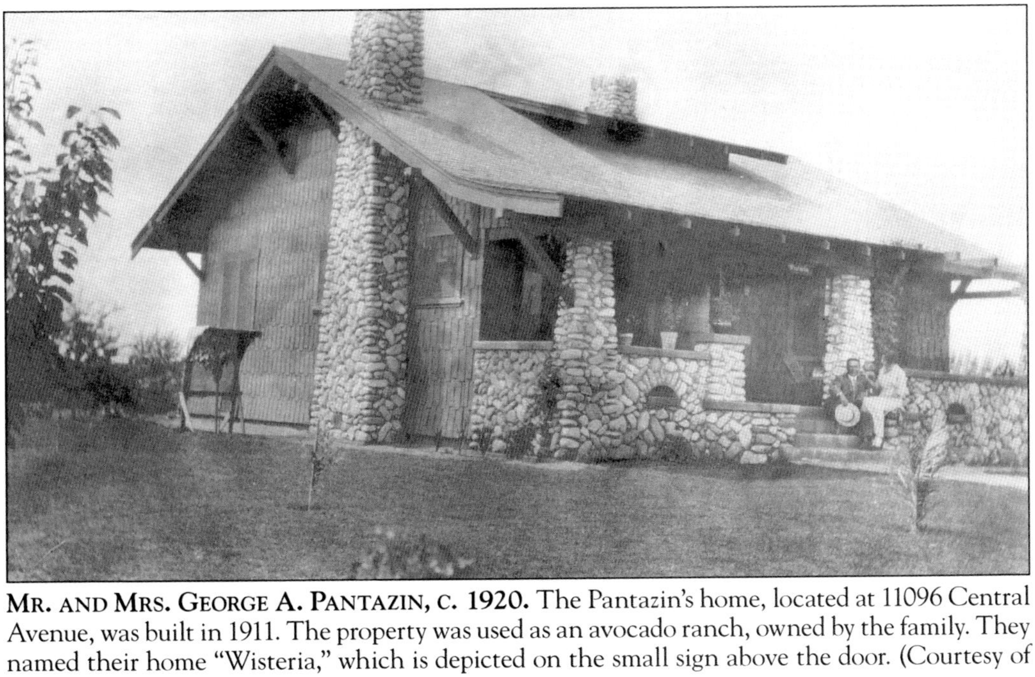

MR. AND MRS. GEORGE A. PANTAZIN, C. 1920. The Pantazin's home, located at 11096 Central Avenue, was built in 1911. The property was used as an avocado ranch, owned by the family. They named their home "Wisteria," which is depicted on the small sign above the door. (Courtesy of Doug Zoccoli.)

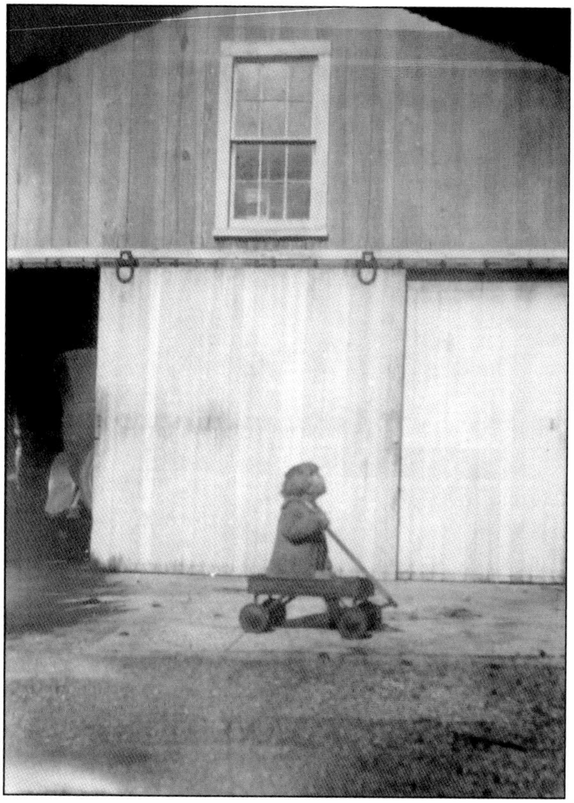

ARTHUR GEORGE PANTAZIN, AGE 4, 1928. This photograph was taken at the Pantazin home (by the barn) at 11096 Central Avenue. Art would later become a volunteer fireman for the Monte Vista Fire District. (Courtesy of Doug Zoccoli.)

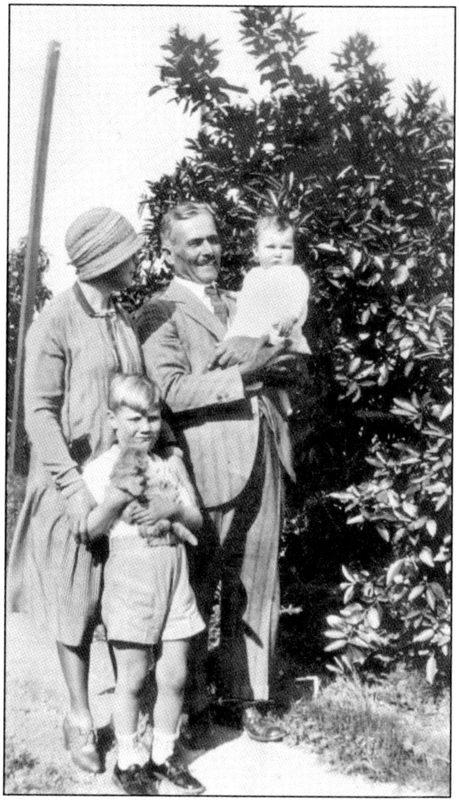

MR. AND MRS. GEORGE A. PANTAZIN WITH CHILDREN, C. 1935. The Pantazin family is seen at their Central Avenue home. (Courtesy of Doug Zoccoli.)

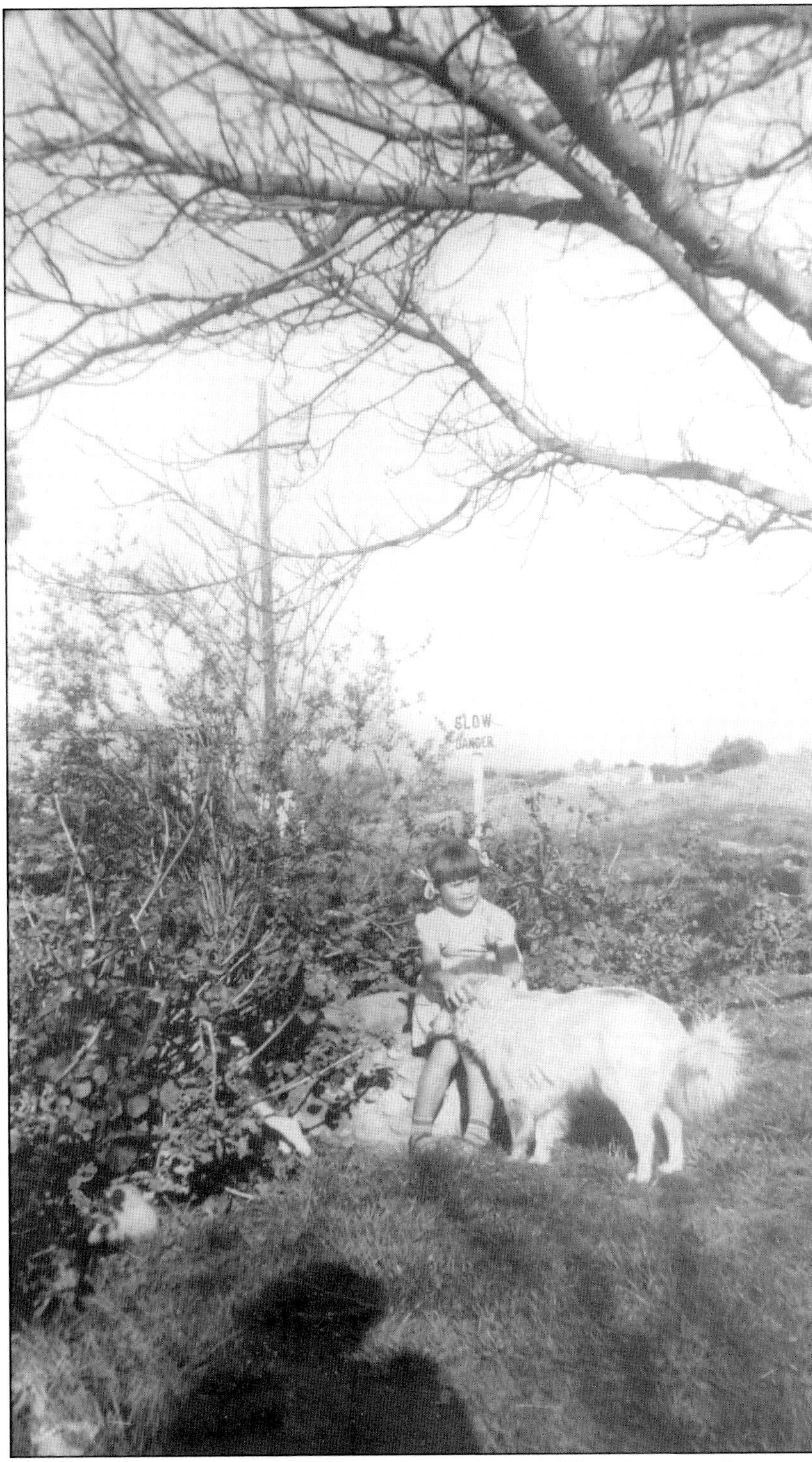

JANET MURRAY (TAYLOR) AND HER DOG SPOT, C. 1945. This photograph was taken on the Murray's property on Benito Street. Notice the "Slow Danger" sign in the background; this sign was located in the wash. (Courtesy of Janet Taylor.)

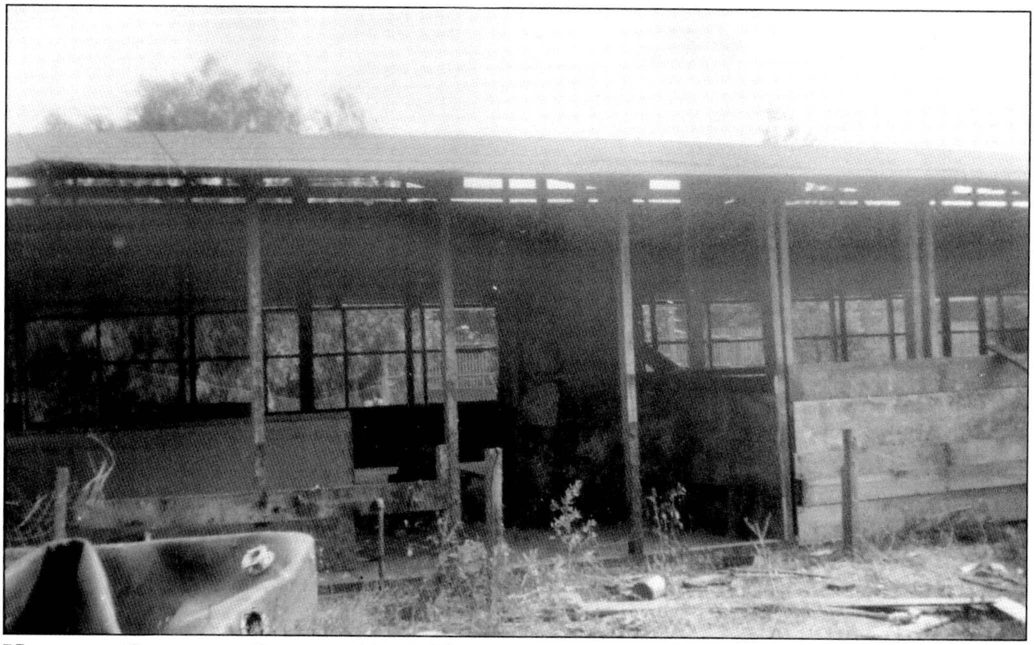

Home on Orchard Street, 1946. This structure, initially a chicken house until it was converted into a home, was located at 4530 Orchard Street, now 2848 Orchard Street. (Courtesy of Sylvia Martens.)

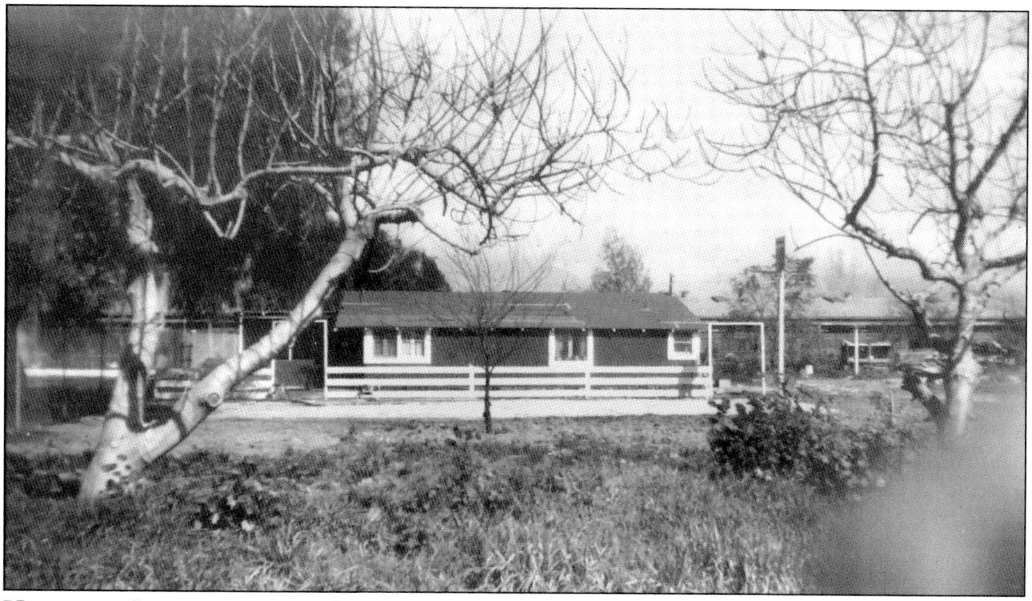

Home on Orchard after Completion, March 1947. This home was a chicken house until it was converted to a family residence in 1947. The family named the home "Casa Verde." (Courtesy of Sylvia Martens.)

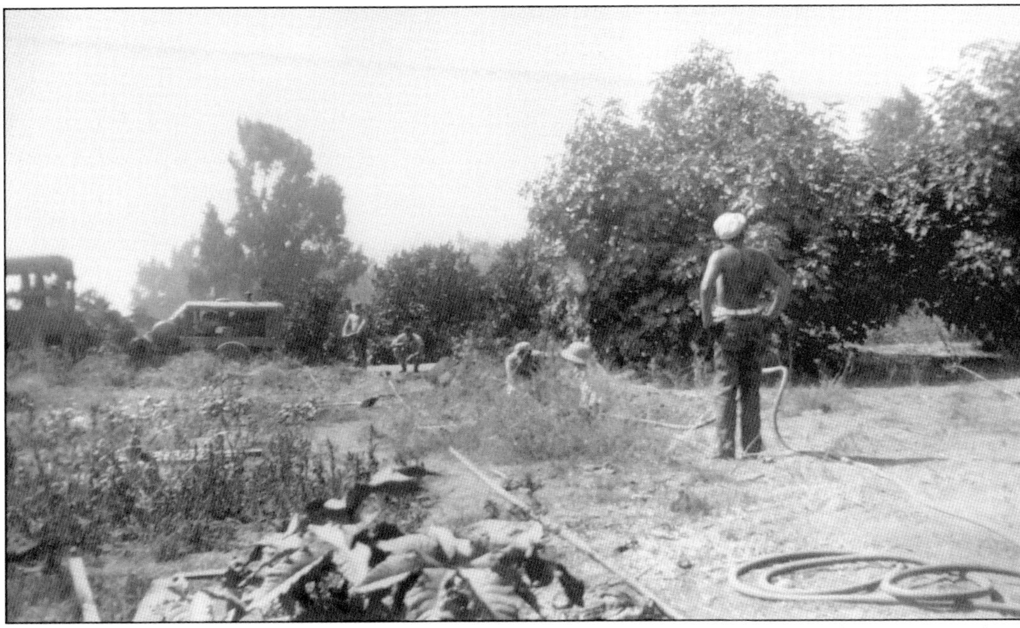

RUNNING THE LINES, 1946. Several men are running gas lines to the Jones home on Orchard Street. (Courtesy of Sylvia Martens.)

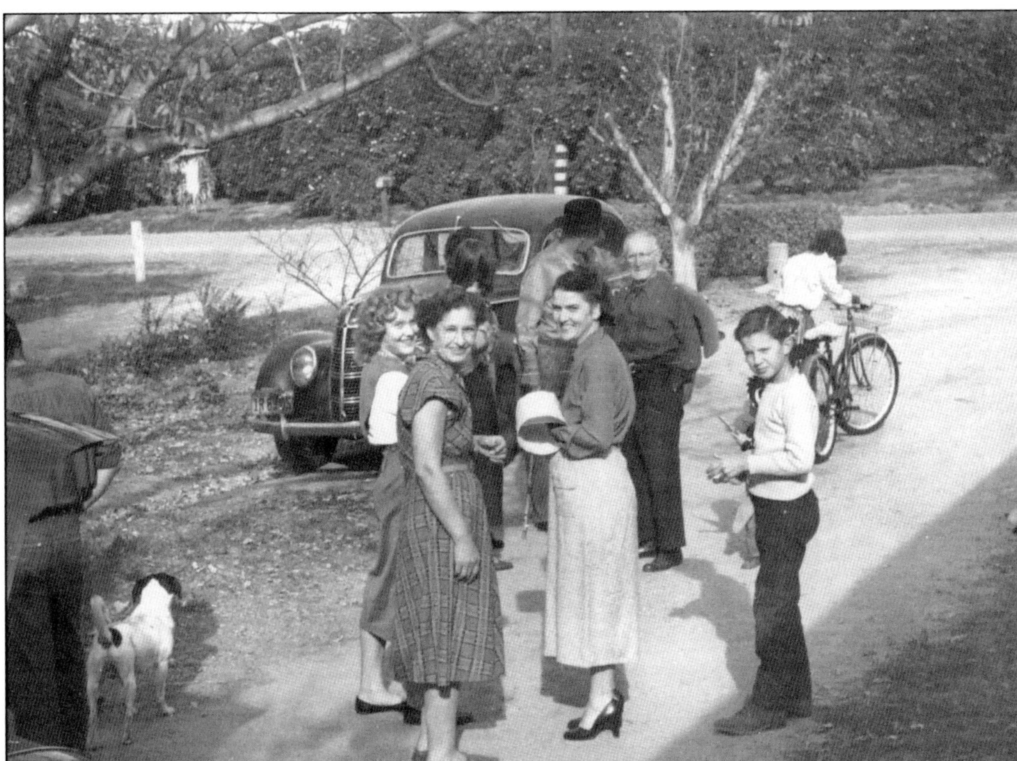

MURRAY HOME, C. 1950. Relatives of the Murrays gather at the Murray home located at 4357 Benito Street. (Courtesy of Janet Taylor.)

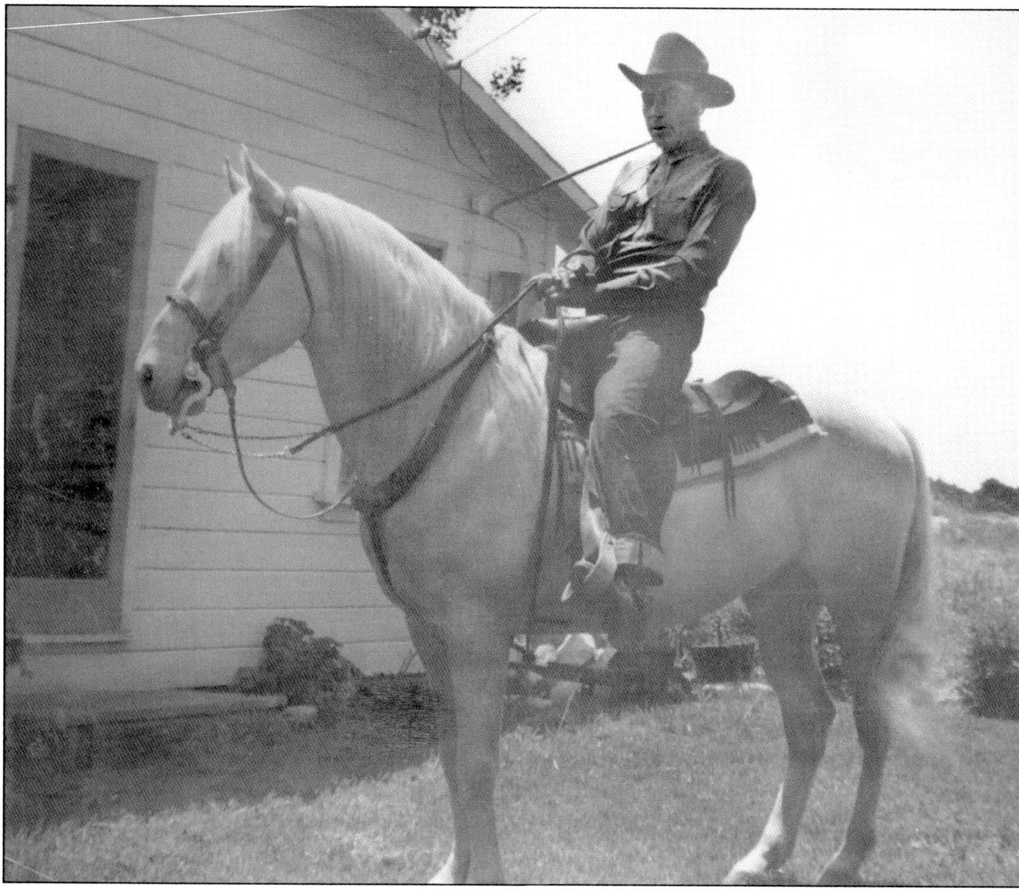

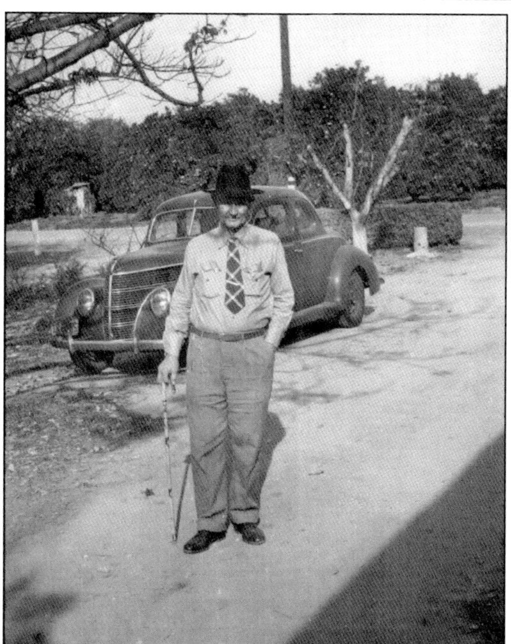

ART MURRAY AND HIS HORSE SILVER, C. 1950. Art rode Silver quite a bit—he led the All States Picnic in Ontario and always participated in the "Chino Ride." (Courtesy of Janet Taylor.)

GONG MURRAY, C. 1950. Gong Murray poses outside of his son's home at 4357 Benito Street. (Courtesy of Janet Taylor.)

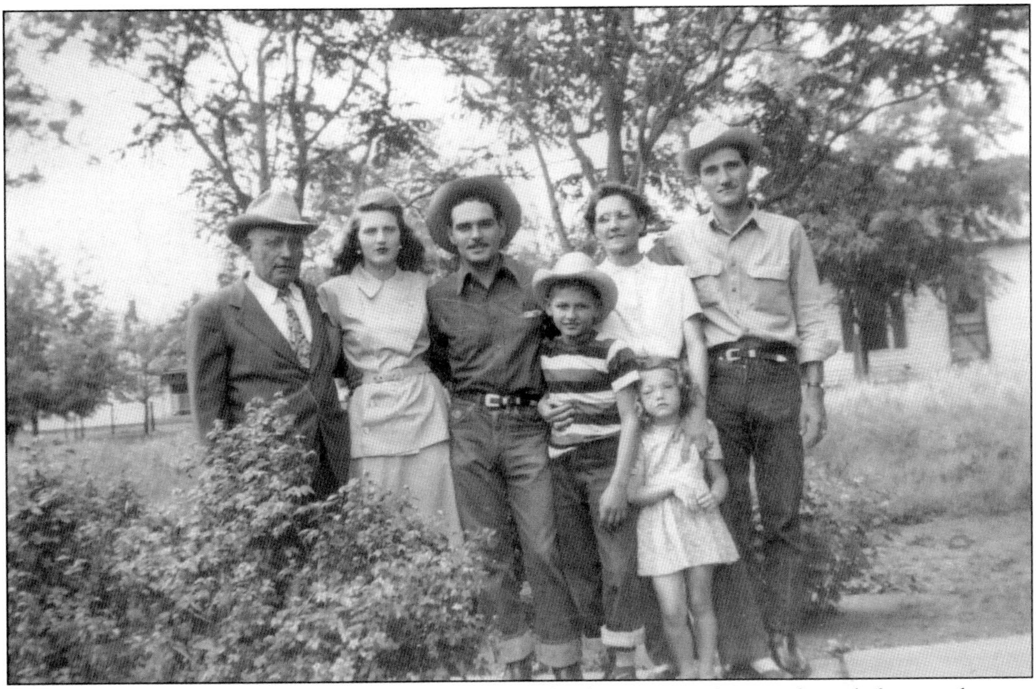

FAMILY AND FRIENDS, C. 1950. Pictured outside the Murray home, from left to right, are Ernie, Betty Dee Combs, Chalmer Combs, Fern, Janice, and Kenny. Dee and Chalmer were Montclair residents who lived on Helena Street. When Santa Claus Village in the San Bernardino Mountains first opened, Dee played the part of Santa Claus at Santa Claus Village in the San Bernardino Mountains.

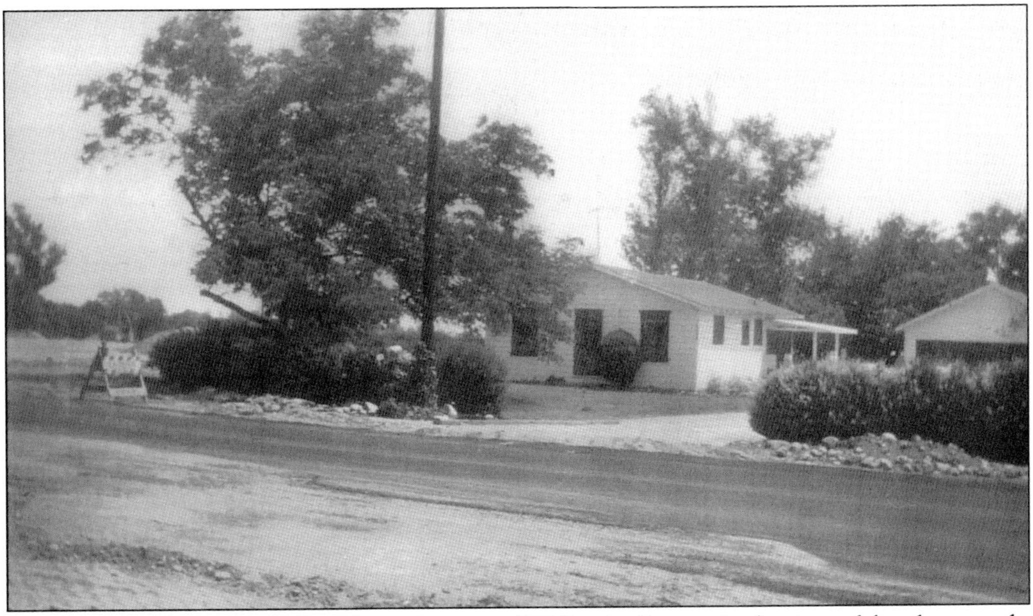

MURRAY HOME, C. 1950. The Murray home at 4357 Benito Street. At the time of the photograph, there were only a few homes on Benito Street. (Courtesy of Janet Taylor.)

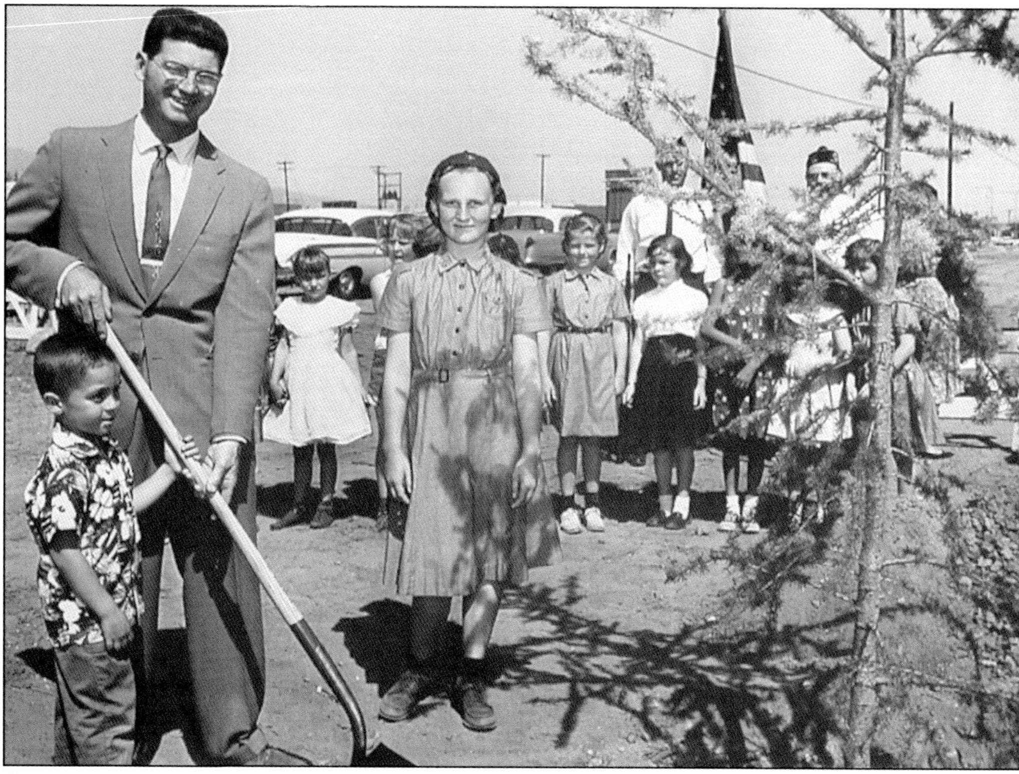

GROUNDBREAKING FOR CIVIC CENTER, APRIL 1960. Helping Mayor Paul Frame shovel dirt on a newly planted tree at the Montclair Civic Center groundbreaking are Paul's son Larry and Betty Lou Patterson, representing the Brownie Scouts troop seen in the background.

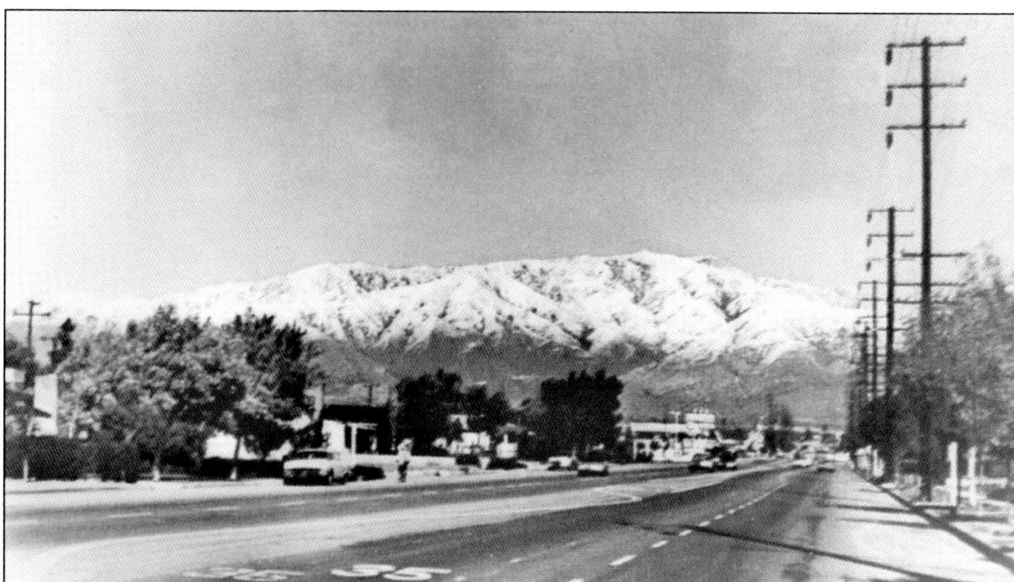

CENTRAL AVENUE AT BENITO STREET, C. 1955. This photograph was taken looking north on Central Avenue at Benito Street. (Courtesy of the San Bernardino County Museum.)

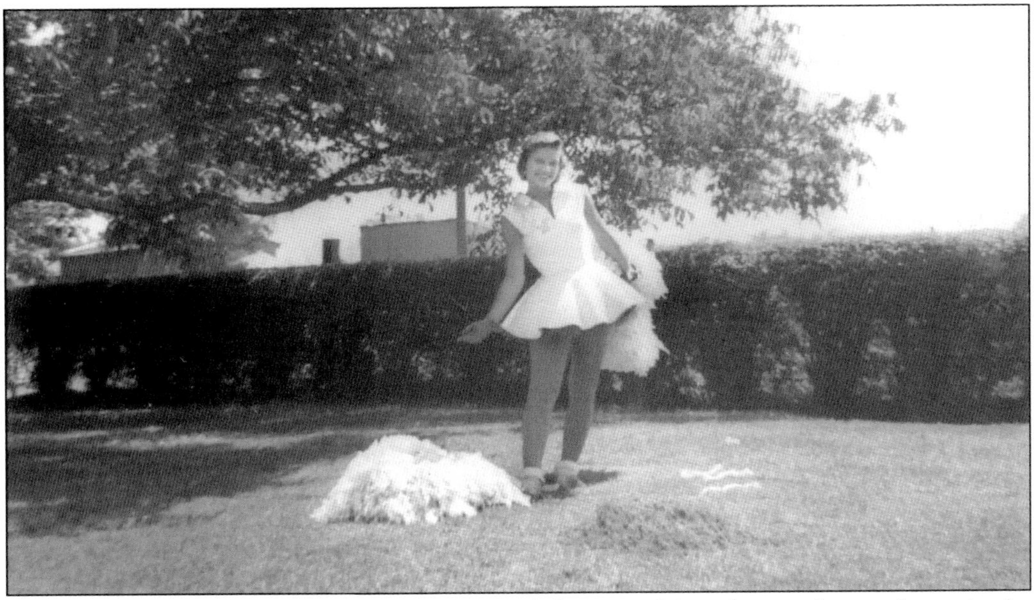

CHAFFEY HIGH SCHOOL SONG LEADER, 1957. A longtime Montclair resident and song leader for Chaffey High School, Janey Murray (Taylor) is pictured here. (Courtesy of Janet Taylor.)

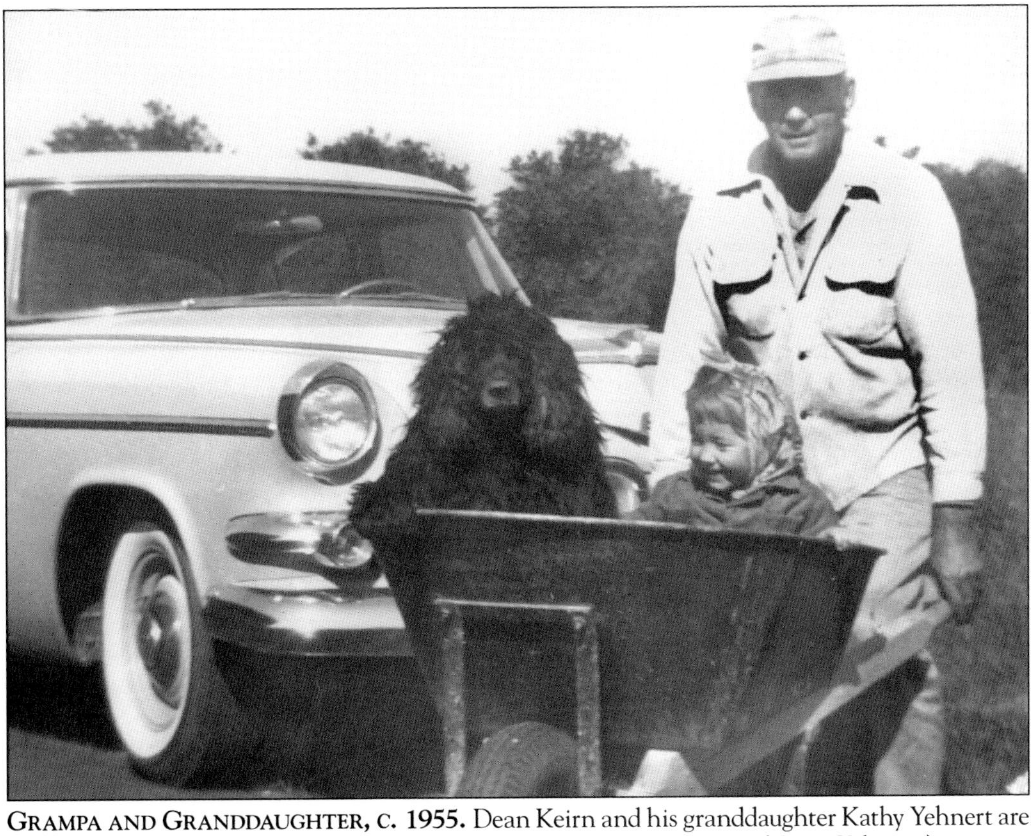

GRAMPA AND GRANDDAUGHTER, C. 1955. Dean Keirn and his granddaughter Kathy Yehnert are in front of Kathy's home located at 10047 Carrillo Avenue. (Courtesy of Doris Yehnert.)

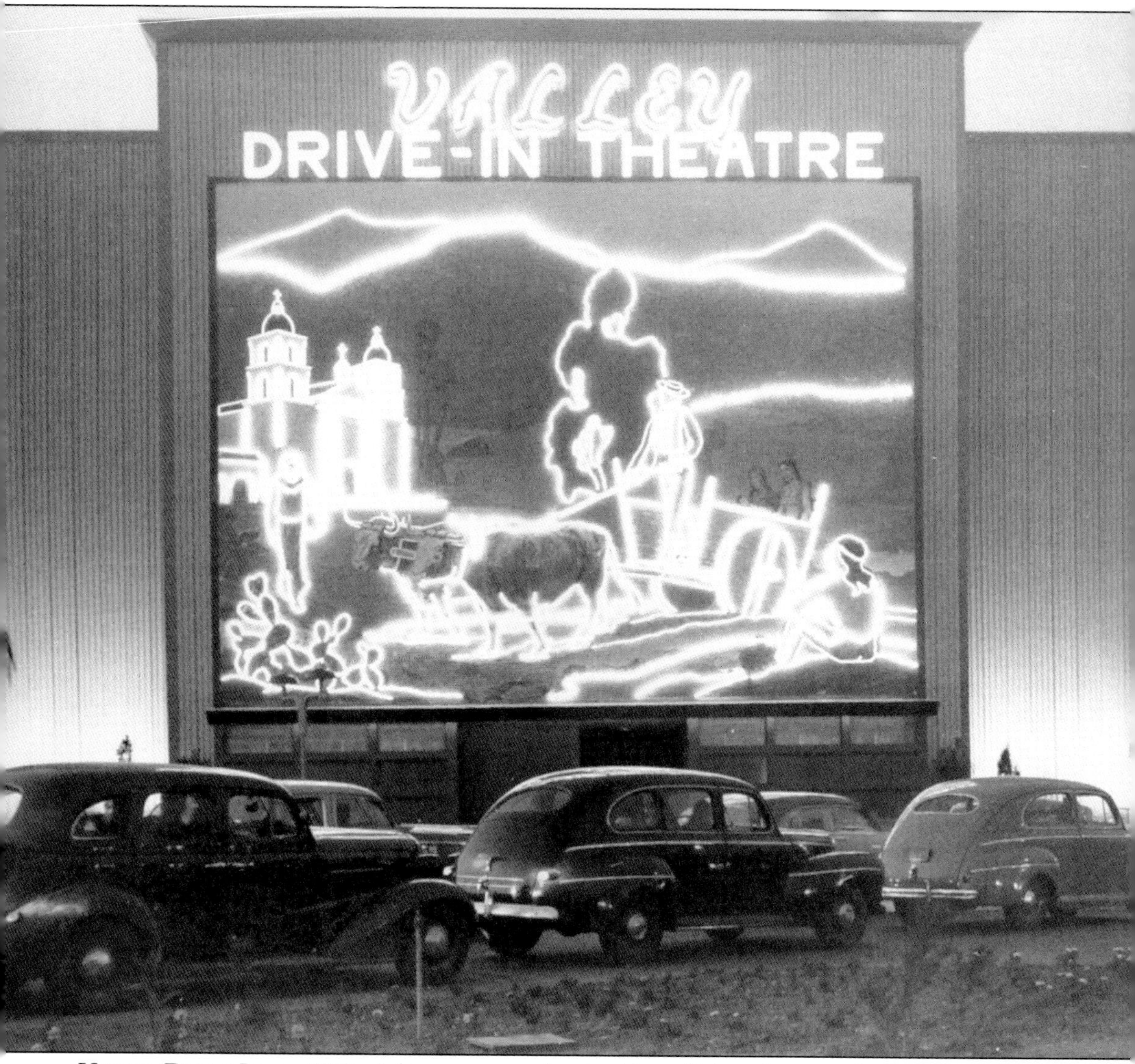

VALLEY DRIVE-IN, C. 1952. A big attraction for the City of Montclair was the Valley Drive-In, located on the northeast corner of Holt Boulevard and Central Avenue. This theatre, built in 1948, remained in operation until it was demolished in 1977.

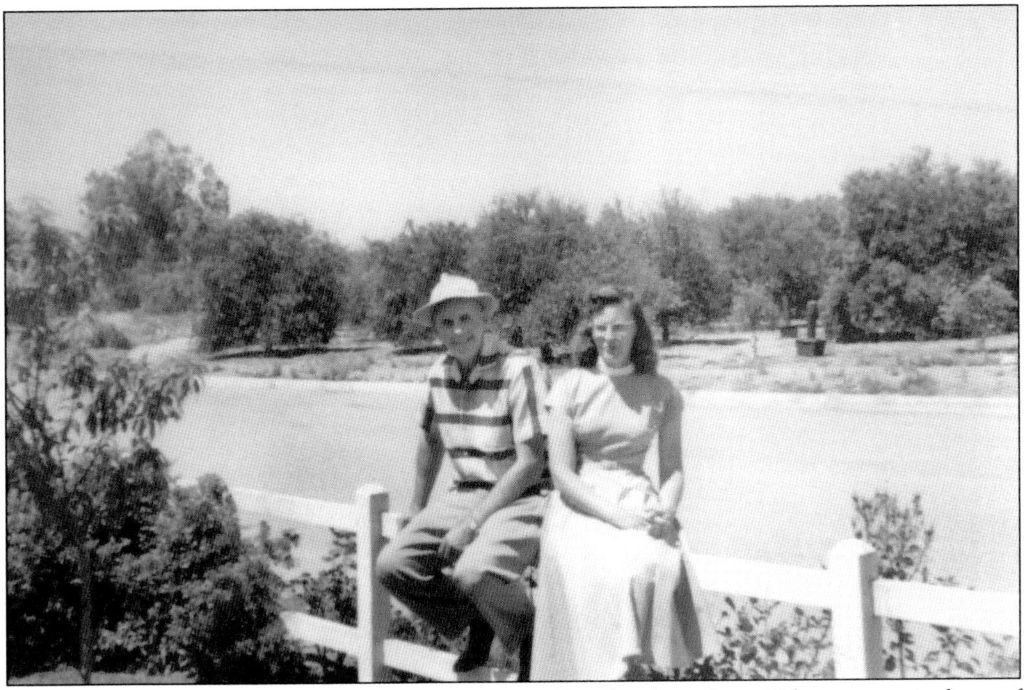

FATHER AND DAUGHTER, c. 1957. Dean Keirn and his daughter Doris Yehnert pose in front of Doris's home on Carrillo Avenue. Notice the orange groves and smudge pots across the street. (Courtesy of Doris Yehnert.)

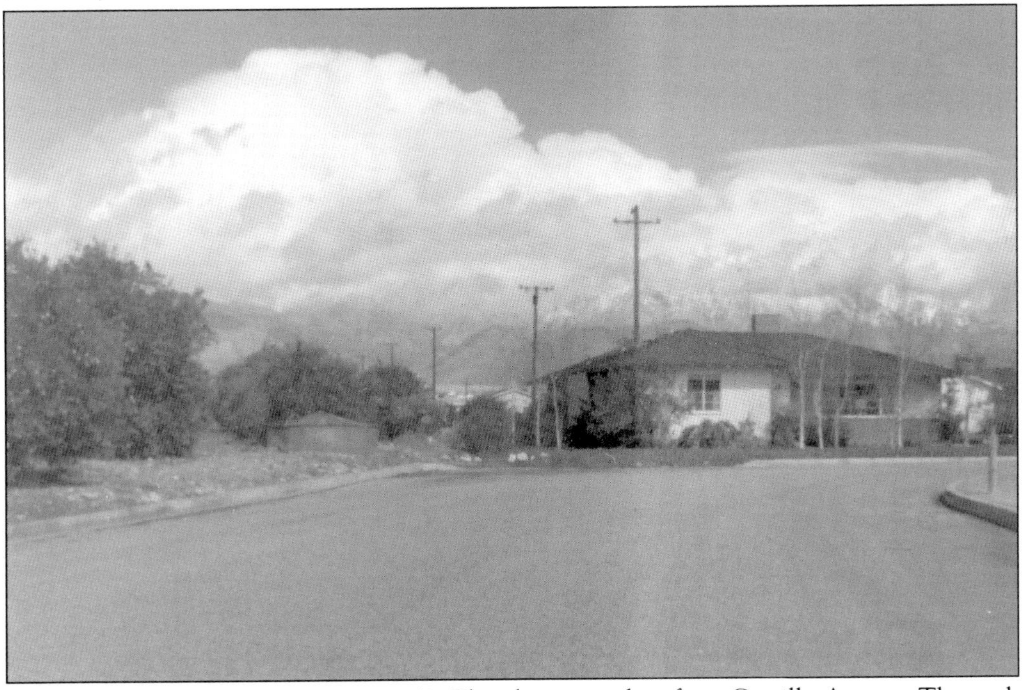

CLOUDS OVER MOUNT BALDY, c. 1959. This shot was taken from Carrillo Avenue. The tank on the left held oil for the smudge pots. Alma Hoffman Park is now located just beyond these orange groves. (Courtesy of Doris Yehnert.)

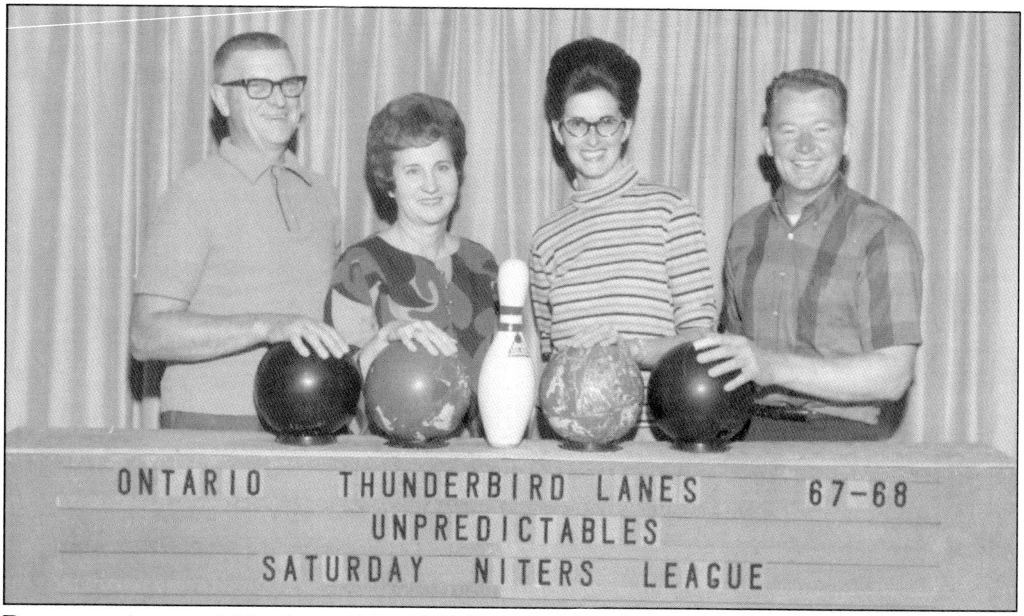

BOWLING, ANYONE? Members of the 1968 Ontario Thunderbird Lanes Unpredictables bowling team, from left to right, are Ernest Rowley, Rosalie Rowley, June Froese, and Neal Froese. Ernest Rowley was a former councilman and mayor for Montclair, and Neal Froese currently serves as the chaplain for the Montclair Police Department and pastor of Rock of Life Community Church. (Courtesy of Neal Froese.)

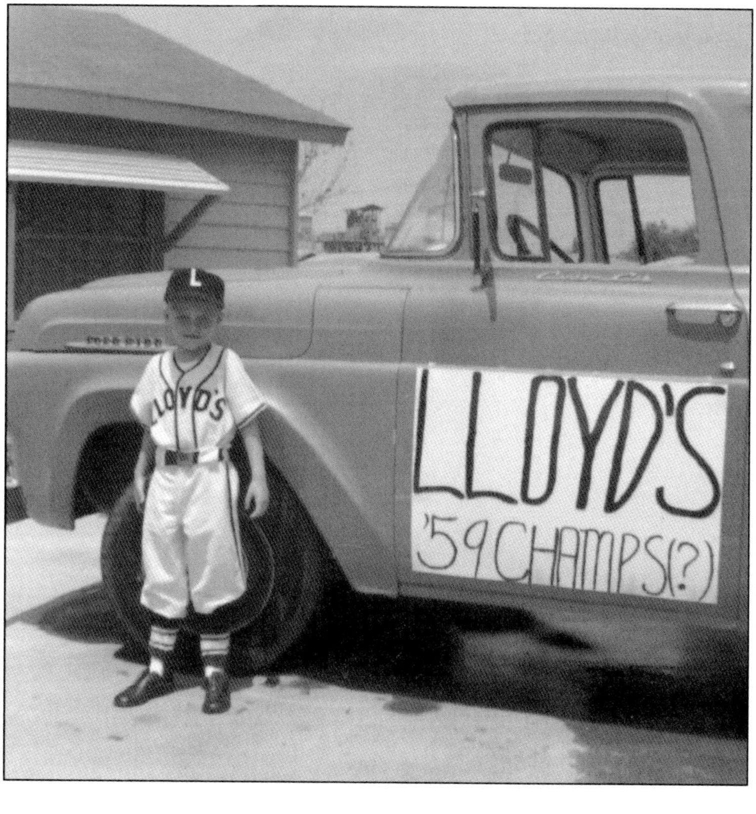

BATBOY MICHAEL MURPHY, 1959. Michael was a batboy for the little league team sponsored by Lloyd's Furniture. (Courtesy of Marcia Richter.)

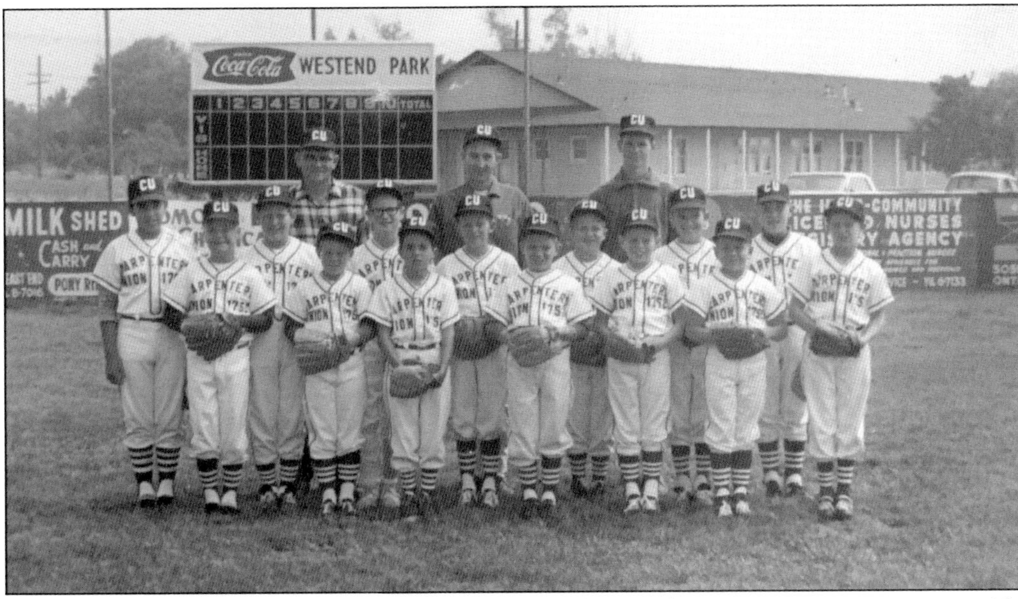

MONTCLAIR LITTLE LEAGUE, C. 1966. This Montclair Little League team was sponsored by Carpenters Union. (Courtesy of Doug Zoccoli.)

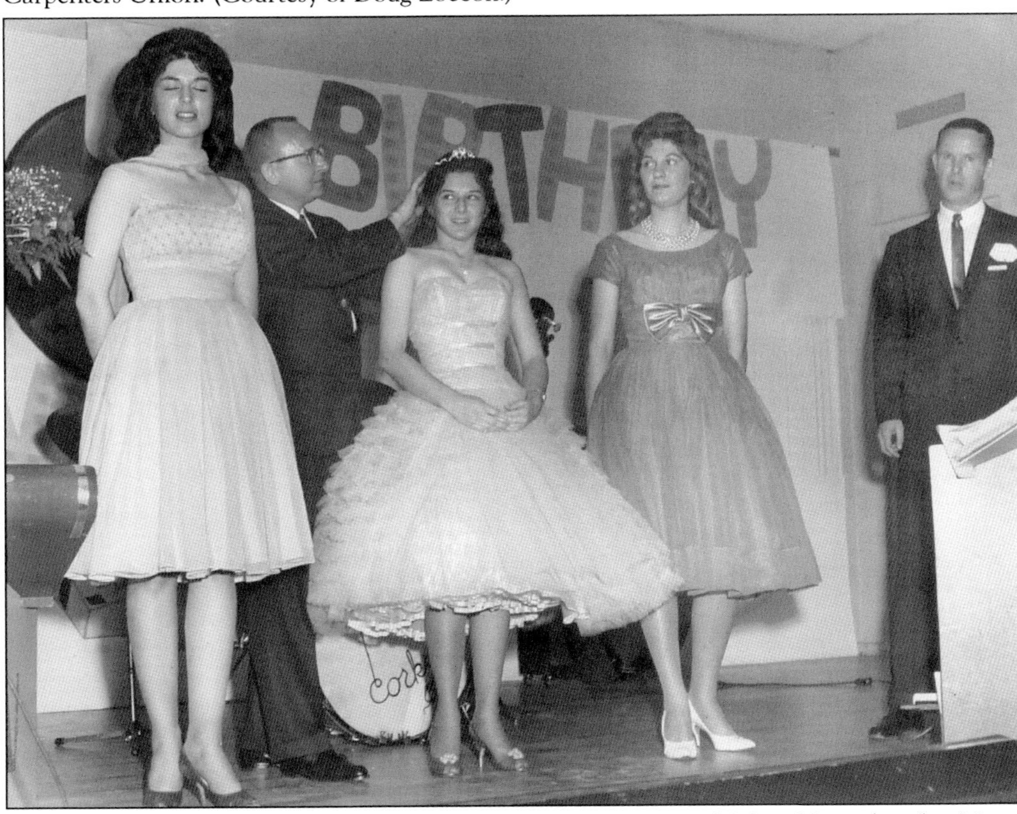

MISS MONTCLAIR, 1962. Barbara Jean Warren is crowned Miss Montclair by Mayor Robert Lock at the sixth-birthday celebration of the City of Montclair. (Courtesy of Vivian Warren.)

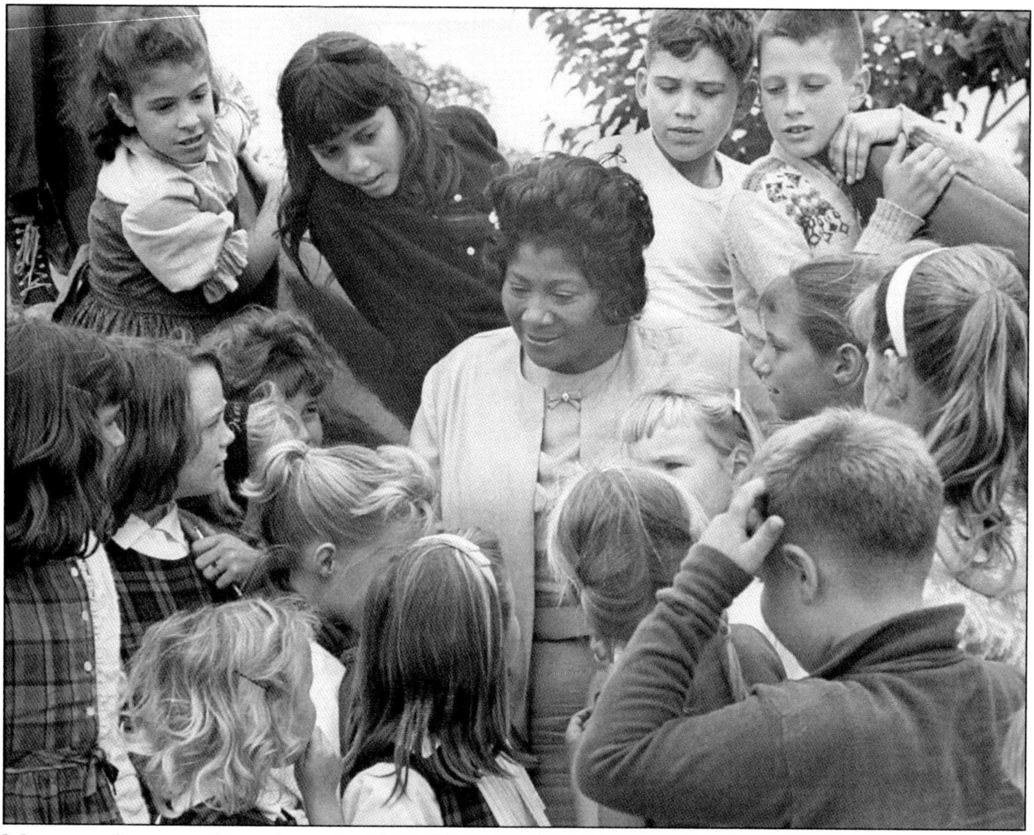

MAHALIA JACKSON DAY, JUNE 3, 1963. The gospel singer talks with the children and leads them in "God Bless America" at the shark in Alma Hoffman Park (below). (Courtesy of Montclair Chamber of Commerce.)

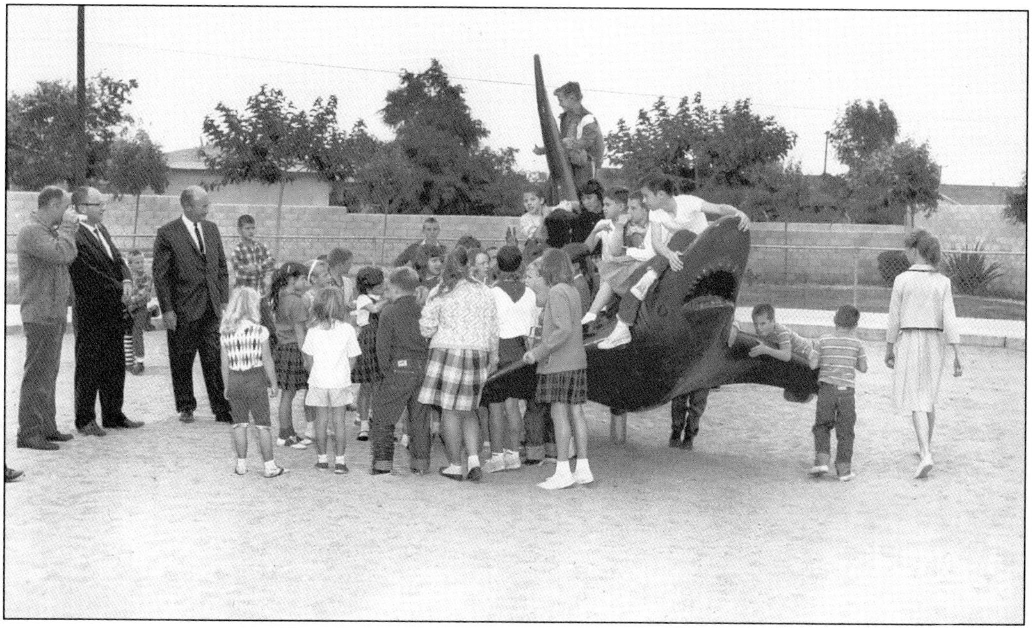

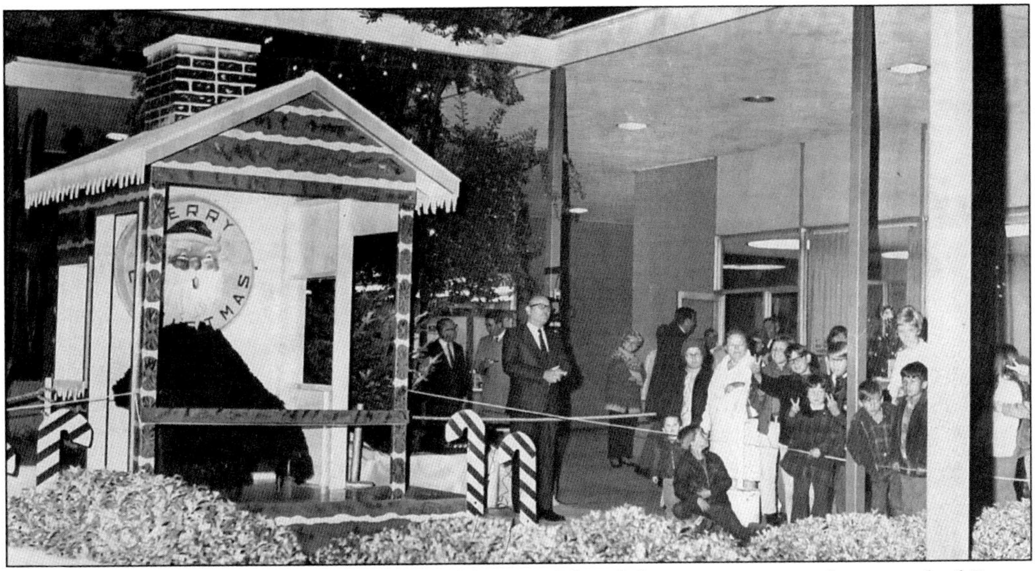

WAITING FOR SANTA CLAUS, 1970. Children and local dignitaries await the arrival of Santa Claus during the city's annual tree-lighting ceremony.

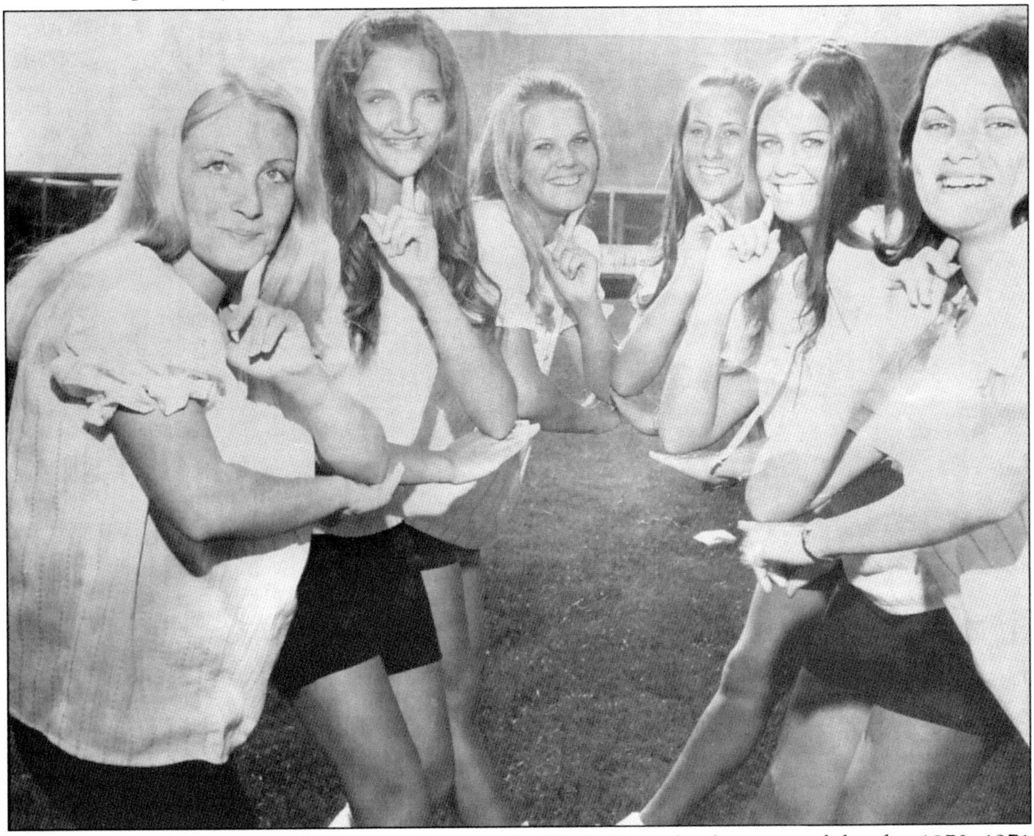

MONTCLAIR HIGH SONG LEADERS, APRIL 16, 1970. Song leaders named for the 1970–1971 school year, from left to right, are Eileen Walliser, Janet Schmitt, Jennifer Foss, Barbara Overgaard, Vona Hornbaker, and Janet Clark.

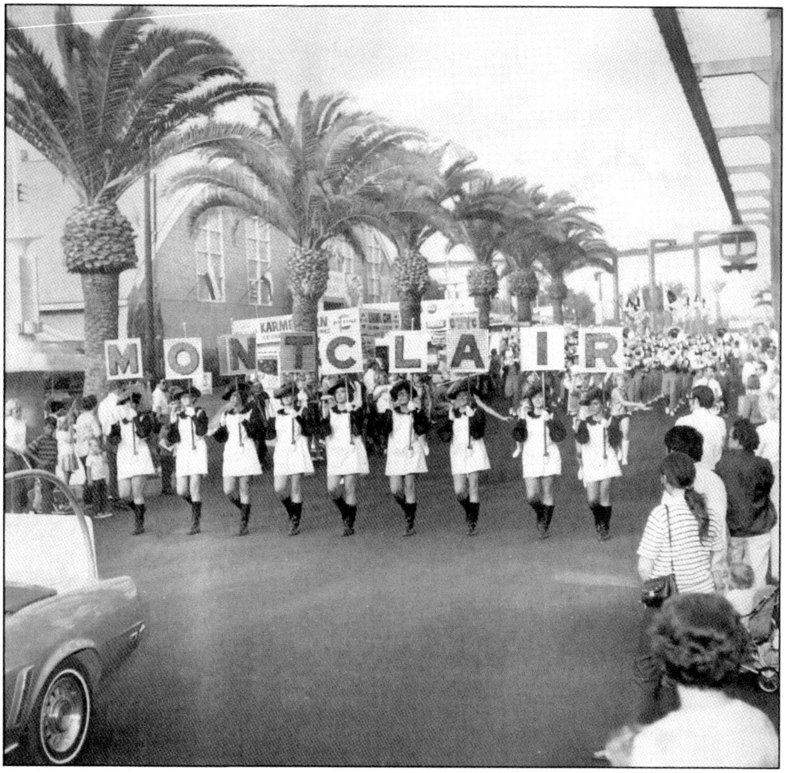

LOS ANGELES COUNTY FAIR, 1970. The Montclair High School Marching Band performs at "Montclair Day" at the fair.

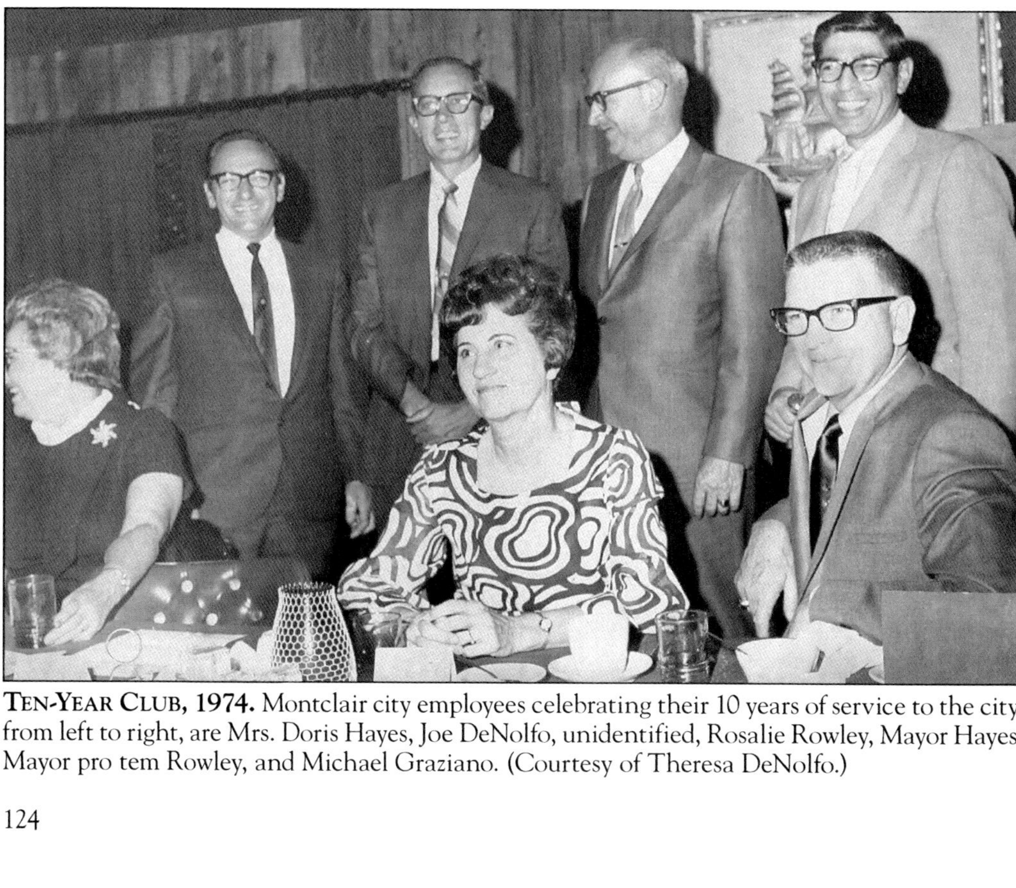

TEN-YEAR CLUB, 1974. Montclair city employees celebrating their 10 years of service to the city, from left to right, are Mrs. Doris Hayes, Joe DeNolfo, unidentified, Rosalie Rowley, Mayor Hayes, Mayor pro tem Rowley, and Michael Graziano. (Courtesy of Theresa DeNolfo.)

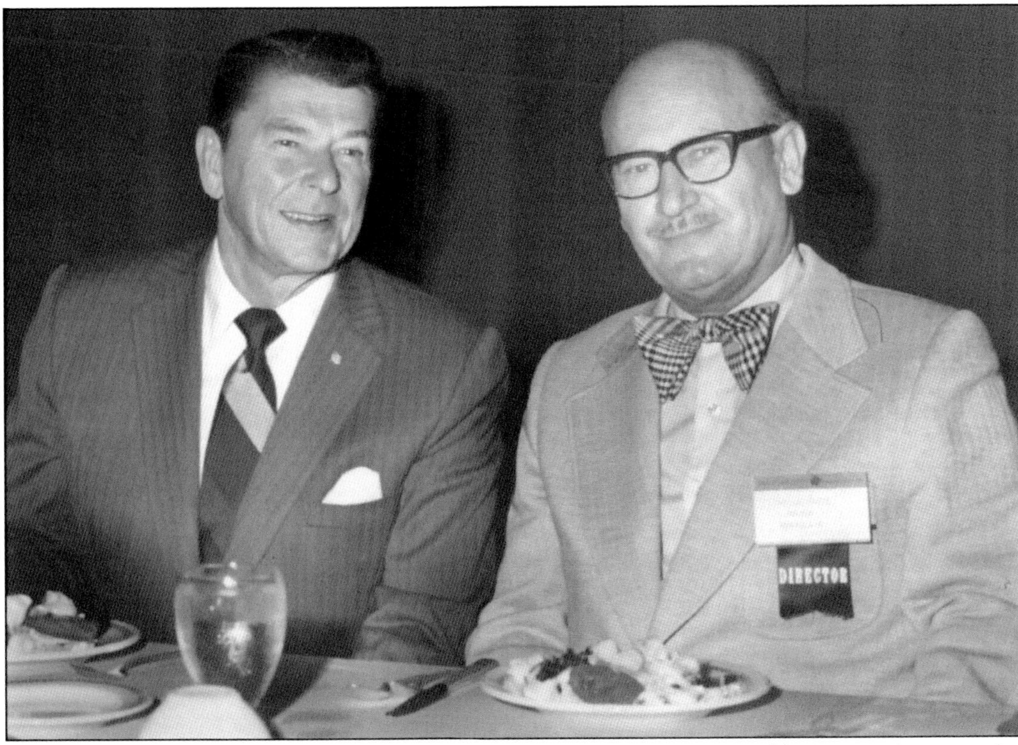

GOV. RONALD REAGAN AND MAYOR HAYES, C. 1970. Mayor Harold Hayes, who served as director of the League of California Cities, sits with Gov. Ronald Reagan during a league event. (Courtesy of Charlotte Hayes.)

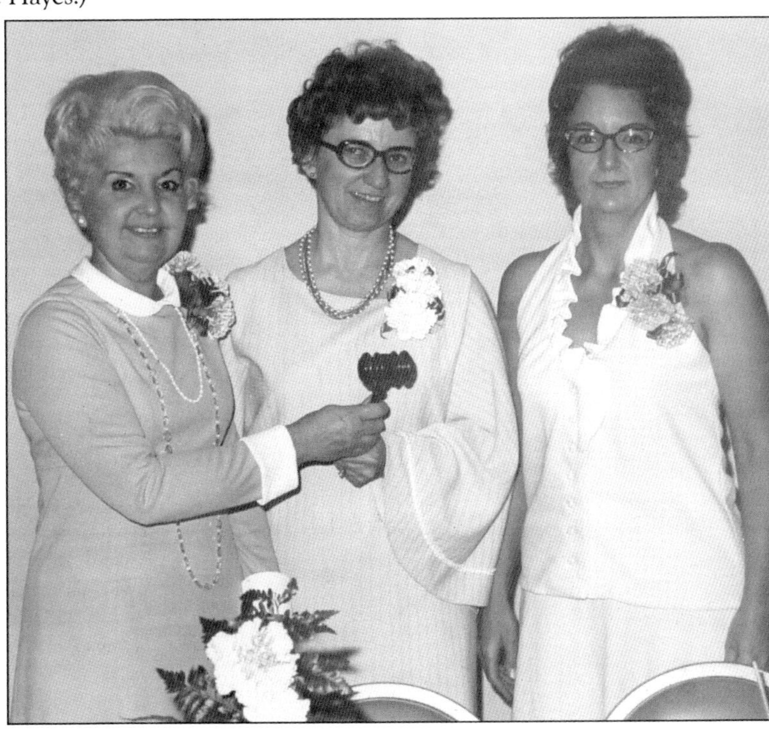

WOMAN'S CLUB INSTALLATION, C. 1972. Pictured here, from left to right, at the Montclair Vista Woman's Club installation, are Mrs. William Ashton, installing officer; Mrs. Russell Dietz, outgoing president; and Mrs. Carl Sawtell, incoming president.

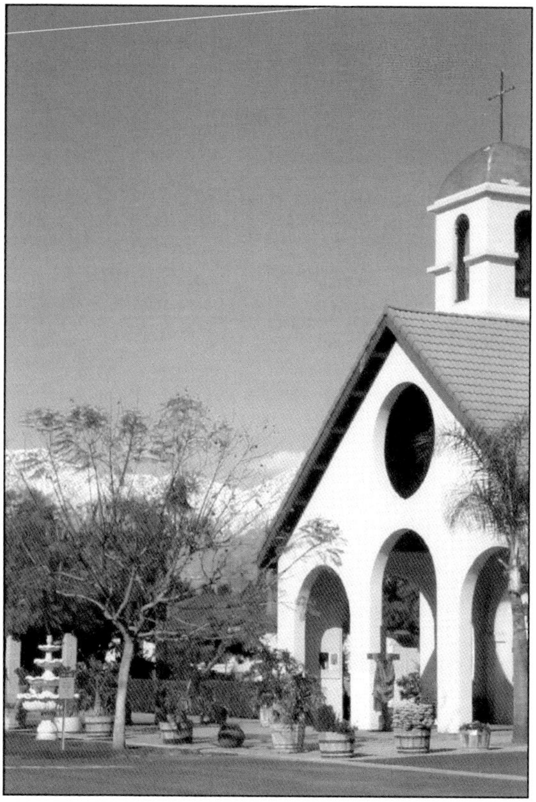

Our Lady of Lourdes Catholic Church, 2004. Our Lady of Lourdes Catholic Church was established in 1955 and celebrated its 50th anniversary in 2004.

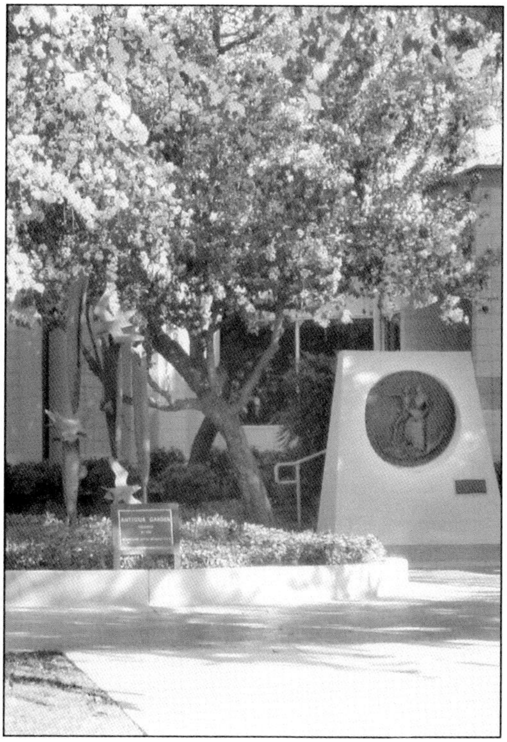

Antigua Garden, 2005. This garden was presented by the Montclair Vista Women's Club in 1965, marking the nine-year anniversary of the city. The garden features a bronze statue by sculptor John Svenson.

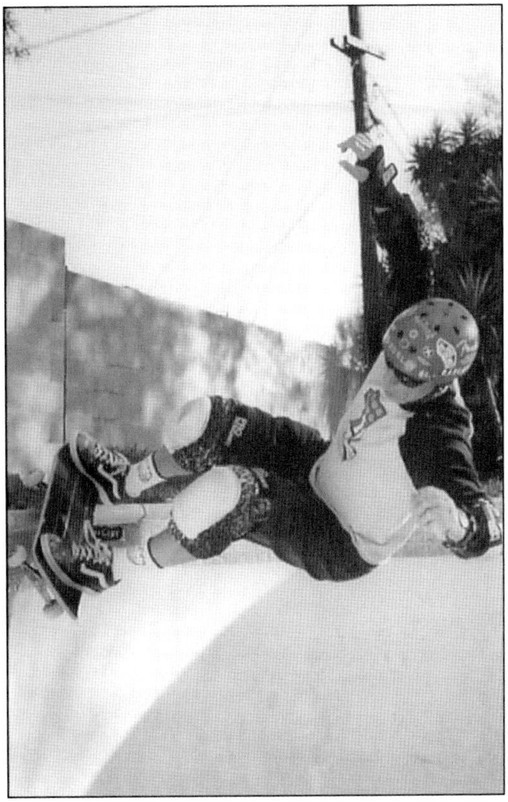

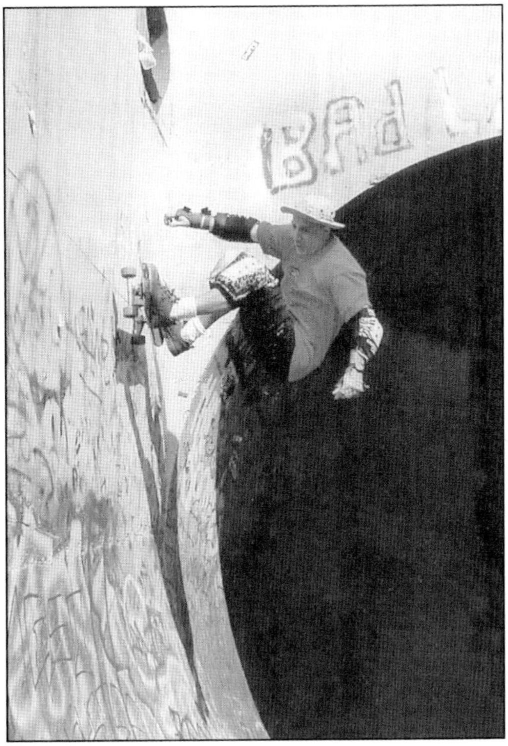

STEVE ALBA, 2005. An icon in the skateboarding world, Steve Alba grew up in Montclair and picked up a board for the first time in the third grade. He quickly became one of the most talented Badlands skaters to emerge during skateboarding's vertical period. Winning the first pool contest ever held at Spring Valley in 1978, Steve went on to win many other contests. He is seen here skating in an emptied pool (above) and at Baldy pipe (below). (Courtesy of Steve Alba.)

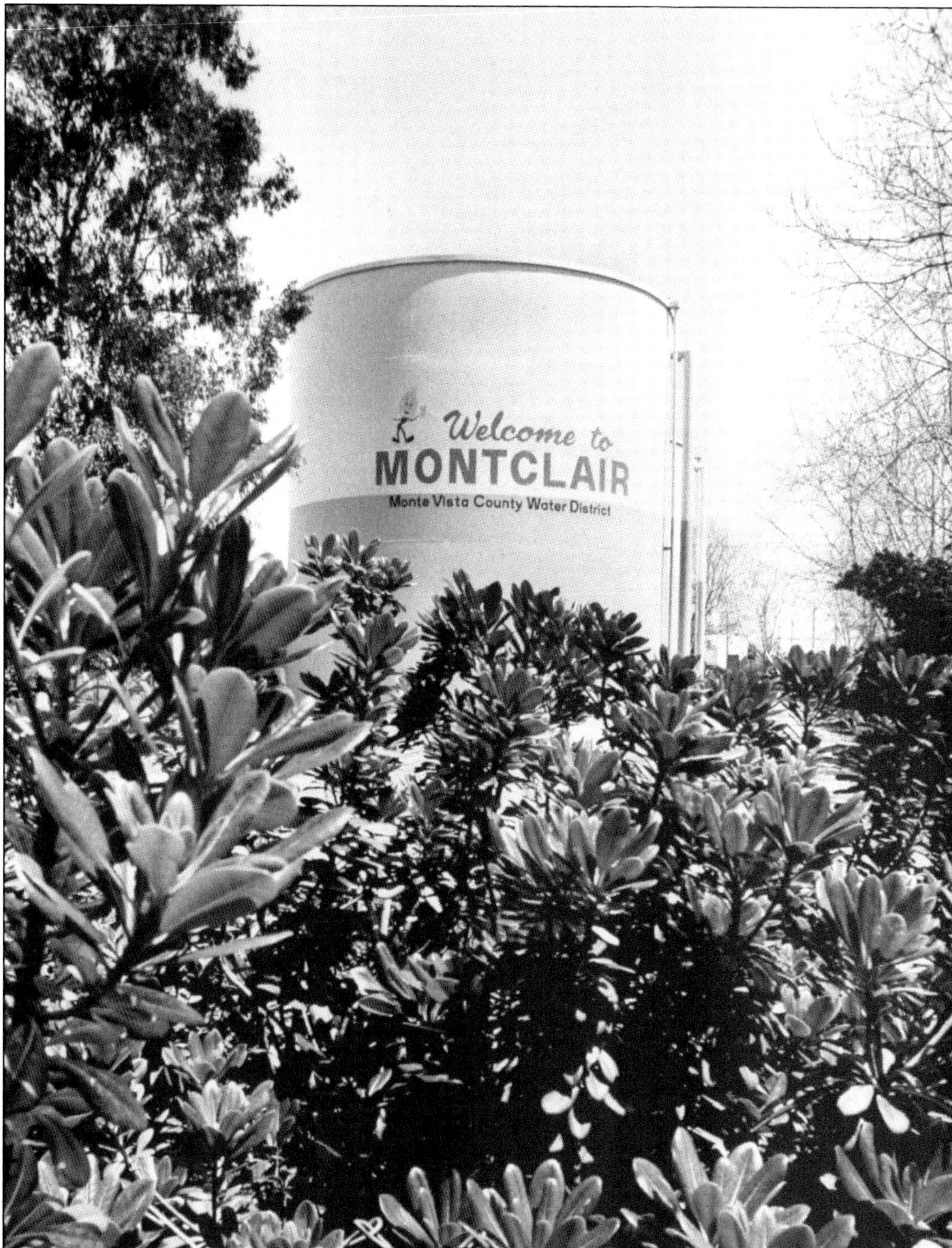

WELCOME TO MONTCLAIR. This water tank was located at Monte Vista Avenue and the eastbound I-10 Freeway, welcoming visitors to this great city.